Living Reality

My Extraordinary Summer
with "Sailor" Bob Adamson

ALSO BY JAMES BRAHA

Ancient Hindu Astrology for the Modern Western Astrologer

Astro-Logos: Revelations of a Hindu Astrologer

How to Be a Great Astrologer:
The Planetary Aspects Explained

How to Predict Your Future:
Secrets of Eastern And Western Astrology

The Art and Practice of Ancient Hindu Astrology:
Nine Intimate Sessions from Teacher to Student

Living Reality

My Extraordinary Summer
with "Sailor" Bob Adamson

JAMES BRAHA

HERMETICIAN PRESS
LONGBOAT KEY, FLORIDA

Hermetician Press
P.O. Box 195
Longboat Key, Fl. 34228

Cover Design by Susi Kilgore

ISBN 0935895-10-8
Library of Congress Control Number: 2005931964

Printed in Hong Kong by Liang Yu Printing Factory Limited
9-11 Sai Wan Ho St.
Shaukiwan, Hong Kong
Mr. Eric Hui   (852) 2560-4453

First Printing   1 2 3 4 5 6 7 8 9 10 15 20 25

To Sailor Bob Adamson,

the teacher I prayed for and nearly gave up hope of finding.

Words cannot express . . .

To understand the mystery of this One-essence is to be released from all entanglements.

—Seng T'san, *Hsin Hsin Ming*

Acknowledgments

*

I would like to thank the following individuals. First and foremost, Sailor Bob for all the marvelous knowledge and wisdom he has so generously shared. And for what he has done for myself, my wife, and my closest friends, as well as seekers all around the globe over the past thirty-plus years. Bob is the strictest non-dual proponent I know and the humblest, most patient teacher a person could hope for. As I have stated already, words cannot express my sense of appreciation.

I am also grateful to Bob's wife, Barbara, for her non-duality insights as well as her warmth and friendship. And for convincing Bob to make the long journey from Australia, after his traveling days had long since passed. Both Barb and Bob occupy a special place in my heart I could never have predicted.

I am deeply indebted to my editor, Cynthia Gordon, for her invaluable assistance. Aside from making my words readable, Cynthia fought tooth and nail to convince me to address questions and doubts she knew readers would want clarified. She also made me aware of important passages within the text which could easily have been wrongly interpreted. Cynthia's expertise and creativity have had a major impact on this text, which would certainly not have been the same without her. Most of all, I am grateful for Cynthia's intense desire to make this the best book possible. What more could an author ask?

For the last two or three years, I have logged more hours per week than I can count discussing non-duality with my dear friend Kerry Breitbart. Aside from the impact he has had on my thinking, only he, besides my wife Vashti, has been with me every step of the way throughout this book-making process. Kerry helped with innumerable suggestions, details, and nuances, as well as with the critical process of deciding which dialogues to include from the many hours we had taped. He also introduced me to many valued non-dualists, sent me wonderful articles to read, and has been an all-around great friend to boot. On top of all this, Kerry paid half the expenses of bringing Bob and Barb to the United States. His non-dual understanding is stellar, and his perceptions within the dialogues of this book are some of the wittiest, funniest, and most insightful of all. I am extremely grateful to Kerry, both for his company and his input on this text.

I would like to thank my friends Dell Dellarmo, Emmett Walz, Meryl Baratz, and Judy Seeger. Dell took a huge weight off my shoulders by organizing the public talks held in our home. He also gave Bob and Barb Trager sessions (a particular massage method) throughout their visit. Emmett, in his usual selfless way, managed all kinds of tasks and errands which freed Vashti and me up to care for Bob and Barb, as well as the many visitors who came to hear Bob's talks. Meryl Baratz introduced me to *What's Wrong With Right Now Unless You Think About It?* which started this whole Sailor-Bob-in-America affair in motion. My neighbor Judy Seeger read the text and made valuable suggestions that had an important impact on the text. She also spread the word of Bob's talks locally and hosted a memorable dinner for Bob, Barb, Vashti and myself one fine summer evening.

I also appreciate the comments and suggestions made by non-dualists Gregg Goode, Shannon Dixon, and John Wheeler. This text has benefitted from their input.

I heartily thank Marty Wolf for helping to rekindle my spiritual aspirations by introducing me to non-duality through the book *Meeting Papaji* in 1999. After thirty years of seeking and watching so many thousands of other seekers fail to reach the goal, I had essentially given up on becoming a finder.

Finally, the light of my life, Vashti. All too often I have witnessed married couples where one spouse is consumed by spiritual knowledge while the other is lukewarm or worse. In Vashti, I have been supremely blessed. We have traveled non-duality together from start to finish, and she has done everything possible to support this book. She is my most trusted critic and has reviewed the writings and dialogues of this book on a daily, indeed sometimes hourly, basis. Her opinions are my most treasured, and I would be lost without her. She is my North, my South, my East, and West.

Contents

*

Introduction

*

What you are about to read is the fulfillment of my thirty-year search for liberation. What I mean by liberation is an end to the nagging feeling of separateness from Source, or Essence, that had been present for as long as I can remember. Gone also is the previously inescapable sense of "becoming," as well as the relentless concerns over past and future that had plagued me, including the fear of death. After eluding me for some thirty years of spiritual work, fulfillment finally came through the Hindu teachings of *Advaita*, also known as non-duality.

The literal definition of Advaita (pronounced "ad-*vie*-ta") is "not two," a technically preferable way of describing oneness because the term "oneness" implies the possibility of more than one. Nonetheless, the word "oneness" is commonly used to refer to the underlying or essential indivisibility, sameness, or unity of all manifestation that Advaita reveals. Scientifically, this oneness is seen in quantum mechanical physics, which shows that all matter can be broken down into smaller and smaller subatomic particles, which eventually can be seen to be composed of nothing more than light, or emptiness, or space. Truly, everything in manifestation is made up of one, and only one, essence.

Thus, there is actually objective proof that within our experience of life, which is tremendously varied and full of differences, there is an integrating element that is almost entirely being ignored. And that element is the sameness, or oneness, that is constantly present and makes all experience possible. It is called presence awareness (among many other names), and it is essentially the present moment—right here, right now. It is the "right here, right now" that has always been and will always be. It is the "right here, right now" that you experienced at age five and experience even as you read this page. And this sameness is what makes a sixty- or seventy-year-old feel no different *inside* than he or she did as a child. Presence awareness. It was present at birth; it is present at death. Right here, right now. Our one constant.

In early 2004, I had the great good fortune to pick up a book called *What's Wrong With Right Now Unless You Think About It?* by an Australian teacher named Sailor Bob Adamson. Bob's search ended in the mid-1970s when he studied with the great Hindu sage Nisargadatta Maharaj. He has been teaching non-duality ever since. As fate would have it, Bob and his wife came to America and stayed at our home for five weeks. During that time, he gave many wonderful talks and teachings, most of which are transcribed in this book.

For most seekers of enlightenment or liberation, the search is long and arduous with many twists and turns along the way. Finding truth is all the more challenging because there are so many varying viewpoints. People are different genetically, culturally, emotionally, and so on. There are paths for devotional types, intellectual types, mystical types, and so forth. What most paths and religions have in common is that they allow the disciple to seek without ever actually finding. This does not mean such paths are fruitless. It simply means that there is always more to chase and more to seek. There is always a bigger and better experience to be had. There is always a promise of a better future (even though life can only be lived in the present). And there is almost never a point where one stops to say, "Aha! The goal is reached. I have found. I am complete." There is, of course, the rare case where that occurs, but it is sure to be the exception, not the rule. The few who claim to have found are nearly always the leaders, never the participants. This fact alone should give one pause.

In this regard, the teachings of non-duality are entirely unique. They are unique because they leave room only for finding and none for seeking! In Advaita, seeking is patently absurd because it implies a future time of finding. If all that exists is oneness, how can there be a past or future? Past and future are concepts in the mind, while the present moment—right here, right now—is all that truly is. If there is an opposite to Advaita, it is the act of seeking!

Advaita is based on understanding reality and existence from the broadest possible viewpoint. It is entirely unconcerned with practices, disciplines, rituals, and experiences. Seekers looking for self-development or for promises of a better future will not find them here. Non-duality rejects preferences and considers no experience, positive or negative, one iota better or worse than another.

For seekers who are *ripe*, non-duality brings ending upon ending, until only freedom remains. Once it is recognized that the reference point we live from, the "me," is based on nothing more than a collection of thoughts and images, any sense of self-importance and individuality ends. Once the definition of reality is seen to be "that which never changes," the illusory nature of our "apparent" creation is exposed. As soon as the essential oneness of existence is understood, the pervasive sense of separation gained in early childhood—when a so-called "individual" identity was created—cannot continue to exist. It simply disappears. Once it is realized that the present moment, right here, right now, is all that ever has been and all that ever will be, the senseless behavior of thinking about the past and worrying about the future utterly ceases. When we see clearly that who we are is actually "no thing"—non-conceptual, ever present, self-shining, just this and nothing else, as Sailor Bob puts it—any trying to change, fix, modify, or correct ourselves becomes pointless. One's sense of "becoming" immediately drops away. When it is understood that everything in creation is, in essence, actually one (because everything in creation is comprised of the same underlying consciousness), it becomes obvious that all reference points are false. When it is seen that all reference points are false, judging any experience or any person as good or bad, or right or wrong becomes ludicrous. Everything that occurs is seen simply as "what is." Once all experience is seen as "what is," the perpetual habit of craving pleasure and resisting pain is over. Thus, for the *ripe* seeker, Advaita is the endgame of a search that previously appeared to have no resolution. Let me repeat that: for the *ripe* seeker, non-duality is the endgame of a search that previously appeared to have no resolution.

What is meant by a "ripe" seeker? One who is willing to die to his or her apparent individuality. While many seekers have heard of the notion of being willing to have their individuality die and are actually ready to do so, most have no idea how. This is not for any lack of intelligence. It is because there is actually nothing one can *do* to die to the "small self"! What is needed is an *understanding* of reality from the most all-inclusive viewpoint. Then, one's apparent individuality becomes enveloped by universality in the same way a seemingly isolated wave merges back into the ocean.

While understanding may seem a far cry from liberation, it is not. In fact, it is positively essential to it. The key to ultimate freedom lies in one's *perception* of reality. Liberation, or awakening, is not a function of any particular experience or mode of behavior. It is a function of understanding reality. This is why there is no standard behavior among so-called enlightened souls. This is why each person must awaken on his or her own. There have been many yogis and mystics over the centuries who have granted spiritual experiences to others (which are sometimes powerful *catalysts* to understanding), but none has ever been able to grant the understanding itself, which gives rise to eternal freedom. Liberation occurs only by perception or understanding, and this is not something one can transfer to another. A person seeing a rope in the dark may first perceive the rope to be a dangerous snake and react with panic. Upon closer investigation, when the person sees the rope for what it is, all fear disappears. So it is that when a person understands his or her true, unbounded nature, liberation from previously perceived bondage is the inevitable result.

After some thirty years of engaging in an eclectic variety of evolutionary paths, I now have the impression that most seekers are actually content to remain on the path their entire lives. Some love the seeking process and some are enamored of blissful meditations, while others are just not ready to find. Seekers reading this book who have never rigorously investigated their willingness to become finders are about to be tested. Those who claim to agree with non-dual teachings while continuing their search demonstrate that they have not actually understood Advaita.

No one can say why one disciple is ready to end his or her search, while another is not. Advaita, which considers manifest existence an illusion, or appearance, comprised of the same oneness, or consciousness, from which it sprang, offers no reasons or causes for anything within the appearance. It is worth noting, however, that many, though not all, of the rare individuals who claim to have found awakening, or liberation, have said the same thing: there was a point, they declare, where they became extraordinarily intent on finding truth—finding freedom. Many, just like Sailor Bob Adamson, whose life you are about to become familiar with, have even said they left home vowing not to return until their apparent bondage had been lifted.

I mention this not as a hint or a method of how to pursue self-realization. I mention it because many seekers who approach Advaita find the teachings mental and cerebral, and wonder what use mere intellectual understanding can possibly be. For those who do not resonate with the teachings of non-duality, such a reaction is not false or wrong. In these cases, nothing is gained and there are no benefits. For the seeker who is serious about becoming a finder, however, for one who can no longer bear the perpetual sense of separation that began as far back as one can remember, understanding what one is—eternal and un-bounded—and what one is not—material, physical, transient, and limited—makes all the difference. Once this occurs, life is never the same.

Remarkably, understanding is all that is needed. Remarkably, what is not needed is lots of doing—as in meditating, chanting, breathing, purifying the nervous system, engaging in therapy, studying sacred texts, and so on. Self-realization is all in the *being* and not at all in the doing. There is a saying applicable to spiritual aspirants who have practiced powerful techniques and enjoyed blissful peak experiences from time to time: "You can never get enough of what will not make you happy." In a philosophy whose core and essence is oneness, what can be gained by doing? Of what value are bigger and better experiences?

This is, of course, not to say that the doings mentioned above are not wonderful and valuable. It is to say, however, that the finding of one's true nature occurs in a "moment of understanding." And that moment of understanding exists strictly in the present—right here, right now. And while that understanding may appear to result from some action, it does not. In a world of appearance, there are no actual causes—only apparent ones. There are no causes because the world of illusion, our world, has no independent nature. Everything within manifest creation has a beginning and an end. Everything that appears eventually disappears. There are only apparent causes, no actual ones.

As I hope is becoming clear, non-duality is a viewpoint beyond personal ego. It is a viewpoint that is counterintuitive and cares nothing of appearance. Nearly half the world accepts the concept of *maya*—the concept that the world is an illusion. But almost no one lives as if they believe the fact! This is because people live life from their own point of view—their own ego, or reference point. True understanding of non-duality takes place only when one realizes, and *actually sees clearly*, that his or her reference point is both limited and false. If this has not happened, understanding has not occurred.

The purpose of this book is to expose the personal reference point—the "me"—for what it is: a phantom created by the mind. My hope is to do for readers what Nisargadatta Maharaj, the great Indian sage, did for my teacher, Sailor Bob Adamson, and what Sailor Bob did for me. And that is "to take the seeker beyond the need for help." If, after reading this text, you are able to see clearly that the "me" you have lived with your entire life is a false creation of the mind, you will never need help again. You will know your true nature and the real meaning of understanding.

What I teach is the ancient and simple way of liberation through understanding. Understand your own mind and its hold on you will snap. The mind misunderstands — misunderstanding its own nature! Right understanding is the only remedy, whatever name you give it.

—Nisargadatta Maharaj
From *The Wisdom of Sri Nisargadatta Maharaj*
by Robert Powell

How to Use This Book

*

According to ancient seers and sages from nearly every path and religion, we are all free, eternal, infinite, and unbounded. The so-called bondage of our human condition is false. It appears solely because of societal conditioning, which has told us that we are separate individuals —separate from others and separate from our source. The purpose of non-dual teachings is to investigate our true nature to such an extent that we deeply understand who we are, even when unboundedness is seemingly hidden. Common sense suggests that if repetition of false concepts can bind us, repetition of the truth can set us free. Therefore, please be patient with the repetition within some of the dialogues in this book. While it may occasionally seem excessive, it is nonetheless purposeful.

It is also important to understand a certain distinction between truth and experience. Many people have enjoyed brief, or occasionally longer, revelatory moments of their true nature. This occurs when, for some reason, thoughts, feelings, and ordinary distractions fade dramatically into the background, and unboundedness—our underlying condition— suddenly becomes obvious. Within spiritual circles, these are called "peak experiences," and they are known to come and go. Because they are transitory, peak experiences are not valued within non-duality. Whatever comes and goes is not what we are looking for. This can be difficult for some longtime seekers to grasp, but it is essential to do so. Why? Because individuals most likely to find the freedom they seek are those who seek truth above experience. Nothing gives more meaning to the Biblical phrase "Know the truth and the truth shall set you free" than non-duality. Frankly, if your attention is constantly on the prize of bliss and rapture and good feelings, you are less likely to awaken to your true nature than if you long for truth. When truth is realized, experience follows.

The biggest obstacle for most non-duality students is the huge disparity between "reality"—which is defined as the unchanging, eternal oneness pervading creation—and the unreal world of ever-changing appearance in which we live. Reality, as understood within non-dualism, blatantly contradicts most of one's experience within the world of appearance. To try to help, most teachers use simple illustrations. For example, even though ocean water looks blue, no mature person would try to fetch blue water from the sea. Even though rainbows and mirages look tangible, we would never try to touch them. We *know* better. It is the same with non-duality. After some serious contemplation, experienced students of non-duality have no trouble grasping that who we *truly* are is neither the body nor the mind, because both depend on consciousness to exist. Neither do experienced students have too much difficulty understanding that the present moment is all that actually exists, because all experience occurs in the present while past and future are mental concepts (Beginners need not struggle with these ideas now. They are explained thoroughly in this book.). But the ability to see through illusory appearances and live one's life in accordance with reality is quite another matter. Briefly, the solution lies in deciding to what extent one wishes to live reality or to live appearance. Most seekers say they want to live reality, but their behavior demonstrates that they want to bring the world of illusion with them. This cannot be done. Of course we enjoy the world of appearance. But to the extent we consider it real, we lose awareness of our actual state of freedom. This point cannot be overemphasized.

This book is presented in the spirit of love. There may be times, however, when it appears otherwise. It may sometimes seem that I, along with non-dualists in general, am casually rejecting or criticizing the world's great religions and spiritual traditions. Please keep in mind that non-duality is, essentially, a viewpoint. And, as a viewpoint, it appears to clash with other viewpoints, particularly those related to spiritual truths. Because the core of non-duality is presence awareness, the key to our true nature lies in the present moment—the right here, right now that has always been and will always be. From this vantage point, the moment a person embraces any method which promises liberation in the future, all is lost. Consequently, all religions, methods, and philosophies, no matter how great and/or longstanding their histories, may seem to be callously discarded by non-dualists.

Throughout the text, I several times mention the folly of considering non-duality to be better than any other philosophy or path. I also mention that what is medicine to one may be poison to another. But the text contradicts this point whenever it mentions that anything other than attention to right here, right now is futile. Non-duality is full of paradox and contradiction, and this is one more instance. Absolutely no disrespect to other methods or philosophies is intended.

Finally, the question everyone wants to ask: Why the name Sailor Bob? It is because forty-some years ago, near the age of thirty, Bob entered Alcoholics Anonymous. There, only first names were used. Because there were quite a number of Bobs, each needed a nickname. Having been in the Navy, Bob became Sailor Bob. Later on, after returning from India, Bob began sharing the knowledge with people he knew from AA. Those who enjoyed the teachings told their friends about the wonderful man teaching non-duality—Sailor Bob Adamson.

CHAPTER ONE

The Natural State

*

During the first year or two of life, before language is grasped, life is lived as oneness. Nothing is experienced as outside the self because a self has not yet been conceptualized. There is only direct, pure experience—what ancient mystics describe as non-dual, one without a second, or "the natural state."

Sometime around the second year, language is slowly grasped, and the child learns he or she has a name and an individual identity. From this point on, life is lived from a reference point known as "me," and everything outside "me" is considered "other." Life as we know it begins, and a sense of separation from our own essence is born. This sense of separation creates a seemingly never-ending craving for completeness. It also breeds selfishness, desire, a pervasive sense of fear, and a host of other problems.

The teachings in this book, comprised largely of conversations between Sailor Bob Adamson and spiritual seekers, shed light on the lack of authenticity of this mind-based sense of personal identity known as "me." Once seen as illusory, this false "self center," or human-made reference point, begins to recede and fade, while the natural state, a state of wholeness and oneness with all that is, remains. Regaining the seemingly lost natural state has been the goal of spiritual seekers for thousands of years.

The natural state, also called presence awareness, is so constant, so ever present, that it is as overlooked as water is by fish, or air by people. One of the most common statements of individuals who say they have attained enlightenment, or self-realization, is that the moment they "awakened" they realized they had always been enlightened! This is because the natural state is always with us. Indeed, presence awareness is the *only* reality, the *only* constant in our lives. It is the very basis of our existence. The natural state is our underlying condition, or "ground of being," and it is what allows us to experience everything. But it has largely been ignored in favor of our conditioned behavior of living nearly every moment of every day from the perspective of the completely automatic, yet utterly false, reference point of "me."

What you are about to read is an examination and investigation, actually an exposé, of the "me" we all unconsciously live with. Beyond this point, for earnest seekers, lies ultimate freedom, the natural state. I do not mean to imply non-stop ecstasy or the ability to walk on water. I do mean nothing less than the end of psychological suffering.

*

A Parable

Once upon a time there was a spiritual seeker who traveled the globe in search of enlightenment. After some time, he heard about a genuine self-realized teacher, and he went to see him. He spoke his desire to the sage, who was eager to help. The sage said only three words: "You are That" ("That" meaning presence awareness, pure consciousness, one without a second, God, the ultimate, and so forth). The seeker, unmoved and unchanged by the statement, was completely disappointed and went on his way to continue his search.

Not far from that *ashram* (home of the guru), he found another highly revered teacher and again put forth his desire to know the Truth that would set him free. The new guru inquired into the seeker's previous search, at which point the seeker related his disappointing story. The current guru, who was quite familiar with the first teacher, proclaimed, "I can certainly help you, but you will have to make yourself ready for Truth. If you are willing to serve me for twelve years, I will help you. Go see the ashram manager, and he will give you a service to perform."

The seeker was elated and went to the manager, who immediately gave him the task of cleaning toilets.

Twelve long years and many clean toilets later, the seeker went to his beloved guru and told him he was ready to hear the Truth—the Truth that would set him eternally free.

The guru said, "You are That."

End of parable.

In my case, the twelve years of cleaning toilets equate to my thirty-some years of daily meditation, nine or ten several-month-long meditation courses, hatha yoga, *kundalini* breathing techniques, Rebirthing sessions, macrobiotics and other purifying diets, Rolfing, Bioenergetic analysis, EST seminars, Actualizations, Lifespring, Reichian Therapy, Hindu/Vedic astrology, spiritual books, and on and on.

Like the seeker in the story, I encountered the statement "You are That" (the complete statement being "I am That, thou art That, all of this is That") many times during my search. And, like the seeker, I took them to be mere words with little or no relevance to me or my current situation. From all my previous teachings, I believed enlightenment to be a miraculous, ecstatic state of consciousness, characterized by continual bliss, which, once gained, could positively never disappear. No sadness, no problems, no bad feelings, and so on—a state only one in a million could gain, despite scores of spiritual movements with millions of followers around the globe. A state reserved for Christs, Buddhas, Lao-tzus, and the like.

After my version of twelve years of cleaning toilets came *Advaita*, a Hindu spiritual paradigm also known as non-dualism, and the teachings of Nisargadatta Maharaj and his Australian student Sailor Bob Adamson. The literal meaning of Advaita is "not two," a term preferable to "one" because "one" implies a possibility of more than one. Advaita presents awakening as an understanding, or a knowingness; a clear, unshakable grasp of truth that corresponds to the Biblical statement "Know the truth and the truth will set you free." Nisargadatta Maharaj, the great Hindu sage who brought freedom to so many seekers during his fifty-odd years of teaching and who died in 1981, stated, "Liberation is not a matter of acquisition, but a matter of faith and conviction that you have always been free, and a matter of courage to act on this conviction. There is nothing to change; it is only when the very idea of changing is seen as false that the changeless can come into its own."

Radical words to a seeker who had heard over and over that awakening occurs strictly as a result of purifying the nervous system by doing yoga, chanting mantras, performing austerities, and doing this or that spiritual technique. Radical words to a seeker who believed that enlightenment could be gotten only by changing, by doing, by anything but simply *being*!

Nisaragadatta, describing his own awakening process, said, "My teacher told me to hold onto the sense "I AM" tenaciously and not to swerve from it even for a moment." Note that he does not say the *thought* "I am," but "the *sense* "I am." He means presence awareness, or the natural state—the stillness of our ground of being without mental labeling. He continues, "I did my best to follow his advice and in a comparatively short time I realized within myself the truth of his teaching. All I did was remember his teaching, his face, his words constantly. This brought an end to the mind; in the stillness of the mind I saw myself as I am—unbound."

As much as I have gained from Nisargadatta's books, particularly his masterpiece *I Am That,* I am much more indebted to his memory for instructing Sailor Bob Adamson, who for thirty years has carried on the teaching and who, quite fortunately, appeared in my life long after I had given up on finding an authentic teacher. A teacher unsullied by ego, money, power, fame, sex, scandal, and the rest. A simple teacher, ordinary in the best sense, yet also compassionate, humorous, loving, and *awake.*

*

My Luck in Meeting Sailor Bob:
Another Parable

Once upon a time, there was a farmer who had a horse. His neighbor, who had no horse, said to him, "You own a horse; you are very lucky."

"Maybe I am, maybe I'm not," said the farmer. The next day, his horse ran away. His neighbor proclaimed, "Your horse ran away; what bad luck."

"Maybe so, maybe not," said the farmer. Soon after, the horse came back home, bringing five wild horses with him. Now the neighbor said,

"You have six horses now; you are so lucky!"

"Maybe I am, maybe I'm not," said the farmer. The next day, the farmer's son rode one of the wild horses and was thrown off violently, breaking his leg in the process. His neighbor exclaimed, "Your son has broken his leg. How unfortunate."

"Maybe so, maybe not," said the farmer. Soon after, government officials declared war and went to every house looking for all the eligible young men they could find to fight the war. . . . And so the story goes.

One evening, in 1999, I boarded a plane to England where I was scheduled to give the keynote address at the British Association of Vedic Astrology. Exhausted as I was for a myriad of reasons, I suddenly experienced a short-lived but frightening panic attack, coupled with claustrophobia. Having never experienced such an occurrence before, I was both stunned and confused. Further, there appeared no obvious, favorable option. Leaving the plane, which meant dropping out of the conference at this late moment, would cause great trouble to conference organizers, as well as disappointment to attendees, not to mention a possible stain on my reputation. But remaining on the plane left open the distinct possibility of another fearful attack in the air, over the Atlantic Ocean. That scenario was positively unbearable, so my decision was clear. Painful as hell, but at least clear. I left the plane, collected my luggage, and found a hotel room for the night.

I was upset, confused, embarrassed, and frightened in a way I had never felt before. I had been a spiritual seeker, practicing meditation and other self-development techniques my entire adult life, and had never lost mental control in this way. This awful experience of claustrophobia on a plane felt like one of the most unlucky experiences of my life.

Shortly after the incident, I entered Bioenergetic Analysis, a physical/psychological therapy system, to try to understand and heal my newfound problem. After three or four months of work and an eventual psychological understanding of what had possibly caused my panic, I braved another plane flight (armed with tranquilizers) to fulfill a previously made speaking commitment. All went fairly smoothly. As the years passed, my fear of flying became somewhat, but not fully, manageable. By 2004, I had flown seven or eight times with only another one or two fearful moments. But these moments were still quite frightening. Therefore, five years after my "unlucky" panic attack, I had decided that long flights—particularly flights to other continents—were positively out of the question.

A few months after starting Bioenergetic Therapy, I learned of Advaita through a friend who, to my astonishment, told me that enlightenment was not just for superhumans and that many seekers were now becoming finders. This was amazing because no one in any of the spiritual movements I joined ever seemed to reach the goal! The goal was, again, reserved for Christs, Buddhas, Lao-tzus, and the like.

The more I read of non-dualism, the more I liked. After I had read fifteen or twenty books on the subject, my friend Meryl told me that one of her all-time favorites was one by Sailor Bob Adamson, called *What's Wrong With Right Now Unless You Think About It?* She noted that any time she became confused about enlightenment or her current experiences, she would read Sailor Bob's book, and he would bring her "right back to reality."

I got the book and, upon reading it, I felt such a kinship, such a powerful sense of resonance with the author that I dearly wanted to meet him. But Sailor Bob lived in Australia, and I knew instantly I could not fly that far. My next thought, crazy though it seemed, was to try to bring Sailor Bob over here—an ass-backwards version of the saying "If the mountain won't go to Mohammed, then Mohammed will go to the mountain."

So it was that I decided to invite Sailor Bob to visit my home in Florida. At the time, I did not fully realize the absurdity of it all. I knew the plane flight from Melbourne to Florida was long, but not that it was a full twenty-five hours of flying, plus plenty of extra hours in airports, boarding and deplaning. I knew that Sailor Bob was older, but not that he was 75 years old and had long since stopped traveling to teach, or that he had told students that he had "no desire whatsoever" to visit America. Well—maybe so, maybe not.

In the end, like the farmer's loss of his horse in the parable, my 1999 panic attack on the plane and the resulting fear of flying proved to be one of the luckiest experiences of my life. Sailor Bob agreed to visit. He came in July 2004 with his remarkable wife, Barbara, and stayed for a glorious five weeks, giving talks, spreading knowledge, making merry with the wonderful parables above, and ending psychological suffering and the lifelong struggle for completeness for some very lucky seekers.

When I first called Bob, it was not to make the invitation, but to try to clarify my biggest confusion regarding self-realization. As mentioned earlier, I had learned from many different teachings that enlightenment occurred strictly as a result of purification, which could take many forms, including meditation, yoga, prayer, austerities, therapies, and so on. Now, through non-dualism, came the notion "Understanding is all." I had asked other teachers what, exactly, was the role of the intellect in awakening and had never gotten a satisfactory reply. It seemed to me that if understanding is all, then the intellect actually plays an important role.

So I made the call, introduced myself as a reader of his book and was immediately, and quite warmly, welcomed to ask whatever questions or doubts I had. What follows below is an edited dialogue of our conversation, coming not from memory but from a tape recording I made of our talk. I offer this dialogue with the following caveats. Be aware that I had already been reading books on non-dualism for about three or four years, so Bob did not have to explain all the concepts we spoke about. I mention this in order to emphasize that readers should not strain to understand anything within the conversation, as all the concepts will be analyzed in detail further on.

Also, be aware that within the talk are terms or concepts which are no longer relevant to my understanding. For example, I no longer entertain such notions as "gaining enlightenment" or "attaining realization" since there is really nothing to get, nowhere to go, and nothing to do. These actions imply some future time in which to do them, and this is impossible because it has become clear that there is no future—or past. Time is a mental concept. All that can ever be experienced are present moments—present moment, present moment, present moment, and so forth—which *appear* to make up a future.

In the thirty-five days I spent with Sailor Bob he rarely, and I mean very rarely, spoke about some growth experience happening in our future. The last thing he wanted was to hold out for us some future spiritual reward for actions taken in the present. He continually reiterated that the act of *seeking* enlightenment or liberation was a huge distraction and actually a mistake, guaranteeing failure because it puts one's focus on the future, outside of presence awareness and the Self (the "I am"), which is all that exists. And Bob immediately chastised, in a teasing way, those of us who did speak of future growth or future experiences.

Nevertheless, there were some few times when he felt it appropriate and useful to speak of the future. This seemed to happen when he would talk with a seeker for the first or second time, after which he became a taskmaster, insisting that the future is nothing more than a phantom. In the conversation below, my first ever with Sailor Bob, he speaks at one point about the false identity, or false reference point, falling away "in time." This is highly uncharacteristic of his teachings, though it was appropriate for me to hear then. It was a concept for the moment, not for permanence. If there is any long-term concept to remember, it is to focus always on presence awareness and hold onto the sense, but not the thought, "I am."

*

Our First Conversation

James: I am trying to understand the role of the intellect. Does one gain realization through the intellect?

Bob: No. The intellect has nothing to do with enlightenment. It's that spontaneous presence awareness that is with you right now—and with you all the time. If you look at the intellect or the mind, all the mind does is translate.

You're seeing right now, aren't you?

James: Yes.

Bob: Well, if you look around the room and try to label what you see, you can only label or distinguish a small number of things. In fact, you are seeing *everything* in the room. You're seeing much more than what you can label through the mind. You may label four or five items, yet you've seen everything.

James: Right.

Bob: Well, that's the difference between the pure intelligence, or pure functioning awareness [other terms for presence awareness, or the natural state], and the thinking mind. The mind translates; that's all it does. It says, "I think this," or "I feel that." That's all it's doing.

But the seeing and the hearing, the *actual* functioning, is prior to the labeling. It's always happening in its entirety, in the present moment.

James: I've been reading lots of Advaita and recently realized that I have been chasing enlightenment like it's a thing, an attainment. That's ridiculous.

Bob: Of course it is.

James: I know, but thoughts keep coming up that "I don't want to waste my life. I want to realize whatever is possible to realize. . . ." I know one cannot make enlightenment happen. . . .

Bob: You see, enlightenment, or liberation, and all the rest of it, is something fabricated by the mind. These are labels, concepts.

James: Exactly, but what do I do now?

Bob: *You* don't do anything. You never have done anything as a separate entity! But the doing happens.

It's the same as when the sperm and ovum that created you came together. Where were you then?

James: I understand that. But what do I *do*?

Bob: Just let life unfold, just the same as your life has been lived so far. You must realize that the mind, which is the "I" that you take yourself to be, has never done a thing. It hasn't got any power to do anything. All it's doing is translating what is actually going on.

So the going on still happens the same way it did before, but you no longer attribute to it a separate entity, or an individual that gets itself into trouble. It's the separate identity, the idea of separation, that causes all psychological problems. There is no separation. Everything is equal.

If you look in nature, you'll see the equality of everything. Day follows night, silence follows sound, the tides go in and out, seasons come and go.

We put these labels on everything, this differentiation on everything. . . . But really, all is one. All is consciousness. It's like a wave on water. The wave is still only water. The wave that arises on the ocean is still only ocean. There is no differentiation, except in the mind, in the labels. All is one. All is consciousness.

James: Well, for example, tonight I had the thought, "I'll call Sailor Bob. . . ."

Bob: Yes, well, that thought simply came up at that particular time. When the actual experience happened, you picked up the phone and dialed. There is no *entity* who did that. The thought to call did not do the calling; that was simply a translation of what might or might not happen.

James: Okay. Well, I know that chasing liberation like it's a thing is absurd, but every day thoughts keep coming up that "I want to get rid of this 'me' identity."

Bob: If you look closely, you'll see that this "me" identity has no power or independent nature. Could you have that idea of a "me" if you weren't conscious or aware?

James: So, you're saying it's fine to have the "me" identity?

Bob: Yes. It's going to appear, but now you know the falseness of it. Look, you go down to the ocean, and you see that the water is blue. But you and I know that you can't get a bucket of blue water from the sea.

James: Right.

Bob: You're not going to stop seeing the blue sea or the blue sky, but you know the truth about it. And the same with the water in a mirage. You're never going to try to drink the water in a mirage.

Knowing the truth about it, you're not bound by it. Remember the old scriptural saying "Know the truth and the truth will set you free"? So in knowing the truth that you are not a separate entity and never have been and never will be, you are no longer bound.

It's the same with the idea of a "James" as an independent entity. It's still going to be there, but you know the truth about it. You're not bound by it. It loses its hold.

James: So it gradually loses its hold.

Bob: Yes.

James: Or it doesn't. But it doesn't really matter, either way.

Bob: That's right. It's equal. In essence, it's equal. It's got no independent nature. You couldn't have that thought of an identity, or that concept of a "me," if you weren't conscious and aware. When the life essence goes out of your body, the body still has eyes and ears and a nose and a heart, but none of it is functioning. It's like having all the information in the world on your computer, but if the power isn't on, it's worthless to you.

So you are that functioning intelligence energy, that presence awareness, that has never had any beginning and will never have any end. It always was and always will be. The energy vibrates into different patterns, into different shapes and forms, just like the ocean appears to be blue, but it never was blue.

So the self identity is still going to be there. First, you've got to look through it and see the falseness of it. When you take a stance in the concept of being a separate identity, that's resistance to "what is," and that's stopping the flow of energy. That's where all our problems arise from.

James: So the thing to do is to simply be with "what is"?

Bob: Yes. You can't be anything else, if you examine it closely. Look, you're aware of presence right now, aren't you? You know that you "are."

James: Yes.

Bob: What do you have to do to cause that to be?

James: Nothing.

Bob: It's spontaneous; it's self-shining presence awareness. It's functioning by itself. And on that presence awareness appear all sorts of different patterns.

James: The problem is that I get everything you're saying right now, and tomorrow I'll probably feel great and peaceful, and I won't be seeking like an addict. But in two or three days, I'll remember some spiritual book where the author talks about his or her fantastic bliss experiences and all the miracles constantly occurring. And then I'll want my individual identity to go away *completely*, so I can have all that great stuff. And I'll start wondering what I can do to make that happen.

Bob: You see, your individual identity started around the age of two, when you learned language. That's when your sense of separation started, and the seeking of wholeness began. But now, you've seen clearly through that false identity. That's it.

But the old habit patterns, which have been constantly reinforced, day in and day out for so many years, will come up again. Now, as you immediately recognize an old habit pattern, then no energy goes into it. Nothing can live without energy.

Now that you've seen through it, how can you believe it again?

James: So, what you're describing is *understanding*?

Bob: Yes. By realizing falseness, you can't believe in it again. Even though you're seemingly caught in it, the energy drops out of it immediately, and the "head of it" will fall off. The self identity, or false reference point, may come up for a while, but the more and more that you catch yourself just going back into a habit pattern, eventually the habit is broken. Haven't you had habits that you have broken before?

James: Of course.

Bob: Well, this habit can be broken also. Just by seeing through it.

James: The times that I feel separate mostly occur when I am dealing with other people. You know, some upset or hurt feelings come up. Then, later on I realize that what happened previously was absurd because there is no James to get hurt or upset. James is a false identity, a false reference point.

Bob: That's right. Interactions happen. That's the functioning of the universe. Things will happen. But you know that there are no people. If you see clearly that there is no self center in you, with any independent nature, then you must know for certain that there is no self center in anyone else, with any independent nature. That puts you in the box seat, doesn't it?

So you know where everybody comes from. Ninety-nine percent of the world don't see this, or grasp it. So they're coming from that false self center; even many who preach enlightenment—which implies some future time, and there is no future time—are coming from a false self center.

So others will have a concept about you. And you will have a concept about yourself. Now, which concept is right?

James: Neither one.

Bob: That's right. So you can't believe the concept you have about yourself. That's garbage. And you can't believe someone else's concept about you. That's also garbage. So there's no one superior to you and no one inferior from that point. It's all equal.

So you go along, and you have an argument with someone if necessary, but you don't take it to heart because there's no self center, or reference point, where it can take hold. They might, but that's their perception. That might be the thing that turns them around. It's generally suffering that turns people to this teaching, you see?

So it all goes along the way it should. But the actuality is always this moment. You can never live this moment again. If we're worrying about yesterday or anticipating tomorrow, we're not living fully. Half our senses are taken up in that past and future, and we're not totally with the present, where everything is happening.

James: So, when I live my life . . .

Bob: *You* don't live your life. Your life is being lived.

James: Okay. As my life is being lived, it's just as well if I have no thoughts about gaining enlightenment?

Bob: Well, have a look at this, James: enlightenment implies something that you haven't already got. And that's taking you away from presence, taking you away from omnipresence, *which is all there is*, into an anticipated and imagined future that doesn't exist. So, you've put yourself in a trap!

James: That's a habit pattern developed over the last thirty years.

Bob: Yes, but if you see it as a habit pattern, are you going to believe it anymore? Now that you see it as a habit pattern and see its falseness, it will drop off on its own.

James: Okay.

Bob: Now, you can't force it away because the idea of a "you" trying to stop it again has got you subtly. It's got you into duality, into a false reference point again.

James: It's really a strong habit. Often, when I find myself not chasing enlightenment or feeling I'm thinking about it enough, I actually feel guilty.

Bob: James, you always have *been* and you always will *be*. *What you're seeking, you already are.* Start from that.

You don't have to try to do anything; you only have to scrape away the rubbish that is stopping you from seeing that. Recognize the garbage that is stopping you from seeing it. It's as simple as that. It's so simple that we miss it.

James: What about all these teachers who say you must do meditation and yoga and all the techniques? What's that all about? Is it useful?

Bob: For some people, it might help to slow down the mind a bit; it might thin the cloud out a little bit, so they can see the sun shining in its fullness. For some people, meditation and other techniques just happen. But if you can see the directness of this teaching, all these things aren't necessary. There is no need to go anywhere or do anything. *Presence awareness is what you are. Just relax into presence awareness.*

James: I see. Well, I really appreciate your speaking with me. It was a bit hard for me to call. It took some guts.

Bob: Well, if you see that you have no self center, you know that no one else does either. Then the fear of dealing with other people fades away. No one is superior and no one is inferior.

James: My friend Kerry is going to see Ramesh Balsekar [a famous Indian teacher who was a disciple of Nisargadatta]; that will be exciting for him. I often think about going to see awakened teachers, but then I wonder what exactly will they do for me. They aren't going to give me enlightenment. I may feel good for a few days, and then in time I'll feel the same as before. The good feeling comes and goes. It's just some peak experience.

Bob: That's the trouble. Many seekers get stuck in experiences. All experiences are in the mind; they are mind stuff. I was with Muktananda in the 1970s when I met Nisargadatta. I was in Muktananda's ashram at the time. Well, some people have been going to Muktananda's ashram for thirty years, and they are stuck in the experiences. They don't move away from that.

James: You mean blissful experiences?

Bob: Yes, people have all kinds of experiences, but they are transitory. People have kundalini experiences [energy rushing up the spine], bliss experiences, all kinds of things. But these come and go. They are not what you're looking for. Presence awareness is beyond experience, prior to experience. It's what allows all experiences to occur.

Many people want to go into silence and stillness. For me, it doesn't matter whether there's chatter or silence happening. They are both experiences. Presence awareness is beyond experience, prior to experience. I have long periods of silence, and I have periods of mental chatter. It's all the same to me.

James: You don't prefer the silence?

Bob: No, because these things are experiences. I am beyond experience. What I am is that in which all experience happens—the experiencING, not the experiencER or the experience. Just like seeing, in which the seer and the seen appear, the seer becomes the pseudo-subject, and the seen is the object. But they're both contained in seeing. If there weren't seeing, there couldn't be a seer. If there weren't seeing, there couldn't be a seen.

James: So, there's really no need to do all those purification techniques, meditation and yoga and all?

Bob: No, no need whatsoever. Of course, if it happens, there's nothing wrong with it. But all they will produce are experiences. They come and they go.

James: Right.

Bob: You see, since you've been talking to me has the presence awareness changed?

James: No.

Bob: Thoughts have come; thoughts have gone. Feelings have come and gone. You've heard sounds and seen things. But the presence awareness here is uncontaminated, spontaneously ever present, isn't it?

James: Yes.

Bob: Well, that is what you *are*. To the mind, that's "no thing." That's where the fear of that, or confusion, comes in because the mind is used to grasping at some thing. The mind can't understand no thing because the mind is a thing itself.

You are *That*.

James: Your teacher, Nisargadatta, used to say [in dialogues in his book *I Am That*], "Be with the 'I am.'"

Bob: Yes. But be careful. He didn't mean the thought or the words "I am"; he meant the sense of presence, the knowingness that you *are*. You can't get away from presence awareness.

James: Yes, I understand. But there seems to be some paradox going on in the Advaita teaching because non-dualism implies oneness, literally "not two." And that means there is nothing to do, nowhere to go, and so on. But Nisargadatta was teaching that we should focus constantly on the sense of presence, the "I am." That sounds like a prescription.

Bob: It's true. But remember that Nisargadatta was teaching all kinds of people, from all walks of life, from all sorts of different levels, not that there are ultimately any levels. And some people had no clue what he was trying to convey. So he spoke differently to different people. He was unable to teach many of his fellow Indians because they were consumed with their religion. For them, he performed prayers and chants and sent them on their way.

James: So, it's just a matter of being, and of being aware.

Bob: Yes, and that's spontaneously and effortlessly with you now. When you realize that there is actually no self center, or reference point, in you, then what must be there?

James: Everything?

Bob: Emptiness. And what's happening in life is what the ancients call "cognizing emptiness." It's the emptiness that's cognizing. Cognizing is the intelligence factor, the knowing—the knowing that you are. So, "intelligence energy" is not two things. It's emptiness cognizing emptiness, which everything appears and disappears on.

Something can't come from nothing. Everything is appearing in emptiness, so essentially the appearances must be emptiness also. In other words, all the manifestation is an appearance only.

James: Yes, I've read about that and I get it.

I don't mean to beat a dead horse, but I want to make sure I'm hearing properly. This whole enlightenment, liberation, self-realization business is really about understanding?

Bob: Yes. As Nisargadatta put it, "Understanding is all." Understanding is all that is necessary. Look at what the ancient sage Patanjali spoke about. He spoke about *right understanding*; that's what he emphasized. [Note: Some non-dualists prefer the term "knowingness" because they feel the word "understanding" unwittingly conveys the idea that there is a person to *do* the understanding.]

Just remember that the mind is not you. The mind is just a translator. As an infant, before reasoning, you were functioning effortlessly, from the natural state. There was no labeling going on. You were in the natural state. You were seeing, hearing, and you didn't know there was an "I" there. That came along after reasoning started. From that point on, everything is acquired mind. Everything is learned from then on. But the natural state is still functioning, still beating your heart, growing your fingernails, digesting your food, causing your thinking to happen, and so on.

So, the natural state is still functioning, but it's seemingly clouded over by that acquired stuff. The acquired stuff is like a cloud. It seemingly blocks out the natural state. Our focus goes into that mind stuff, and we keep repeating it and believing it, so that habit patterns form. And we go on like this until we pause and question what has happened.

But you must realize that the natural state is still there and has always been there.

James: Is it us questioning? The thoughts are just coming into our minds, right?

Bob: That's right; it's not us doing anything. Get that out of your mind. It's one without a second. That's the simplicity of this. The ancients have told us all the way through the ages that it's non-dual, one without a second. In *Dzogchen* [pronounced "zog-shen"] Buddhism, it's described as "non-conceptual, ever-fresh, self-shining presence awareness, just this and nothing else." The Israelis say, "Hear, oh Israel, the Lord our God, the Lord is One."

James: Well, where are my thoughts coming from?

Bob: They're coming from that cognizing emptiness. They're nothing more than vibrating patterns of energy appearing on the emptiness.

James: And we have nothing to do with this?

Bob: No, the idea of "we" is just another vibrating pattern that is appearing on the emptiness. In *essence*, the thought is the same as the emptiness. It's still that oneness.

So, nothing has ever happened! To no none!

*

After Our Conversation

I got off the phone in a state of gratitude. I was thrilled to have had such a warm and fruitful conversation with Sailor Bob and was happy I had taped our talk. I knew I would be listening to the tape several times in the days to come. Although I had encountered the concept "Understanding is all" in Advaita books, I was pleased to hear this straight from the horse's mouth—from a teacher who had been living the teaching for nearly thirty years.

More than anything however, I was moved—stunned actually—by Bob's profound words: "James, you always have been and you always will be. *What you're seeking, you already are.* Start from that. You don't have to try to do anything; you only have to scrape away the rubbish that is stopping you from seeing that. Recognize the garbage that is stopping you from seeing it. It's as simple as that. It's so simple that we miss it."

I had spent my entire adult life seeking liberation, enlightenment, nirvana, or whatever name one calls it, as something outside myself. I had been chasing a condition that already is, as if it were not. How odd! And I saw that the more I held awakening as something outside myself, the more certain it was that it could not be found. I had always thought enlightenment was some kind of experience to be enjoyed, when in fact it is simply a natural state that is constant and therefore can only be acknowledged, not experienced—not attained or grasped.

In times subsequent to Sailor Bob's visit when I am completely "relaxed into presence awareness," that is to say when I have blissfully found "the rubbish scraped away," it is clear that unboundedness is simply present. I am not experiencing unboundedness, because unboundedness contains no qualities or boundaries to be experienced. There is no subject-object type of experience occurring because unboundedness is precisely who I am; it is who we all are—saints, sinners, yogis, drug addicts, and so on. The unboundedness, or pure consciousness, is forever present, but is sometimes seemingly obstructed by thoughts, feelings, concepts, desires, mental chatter, and the like, in the same way the sun is obstructed by clouds.

And so, after speaking with Bob I felt like Dorothy from *The Wizard of Oz,* who traveled through forests and mountains, encountering lions, tigers, and bears, as well as munchkins, wizards, and wicked witches, only to find that all she ever needed to do to return home was to click her heels three times and say, "There's no place like home; there's no place like home; there's no place like home!"

I slept well that night. Just before bed, I put a large reminder on the wall that was to stay there for several months. It said in large, bold letters:

WHAT YOU ARE SEEKING, YOU ALREADY ARE.

I wanted this understanding seared into my brain. If I were going to find out what the ancient, so-called enlightened seers were raving about, I needed to be reminded as often as possible that it was actually who I already was. That first conversation with Sailor Bob closed the door on thirty years of seeking awakening outside myself. Mind you, when I say I had been seeking awakening outside myself, I do not mean I had been trying to find the Self through externals such as money, fame, power, and the rest. My most constant spiritual path had always been meditation, an introspective process with the mind directed within. It's just that, as long as I believed that the Self was anywhere other than right here, right now—eyes open or eyes closed, with the mind running or the mind at peace, in the midst of good feelings or bad feelings then I was essentially focused 180 degrees away from where I needed to be. I was searching for something outside my Self. And that was true even if I just felt that the Self was something to be gained (as if the unbounded Self were not who I already am!).

And when I say that pure consciousness is to be acknowledged rather than experienced, do not think that I am not extraordinarily content and thrilled beyond words in the periods when "the rubbish has been scraped away" and I am seeing clearly. Of course I am. The feeling is wonderful, and afterwards I even find myself labeling the occurrence an experience. But it is not an experience. The definition of "experience" is "the apprehension of an object, a thought, or an emotion through the senses or mind." Pure consciousness, or presence awareness, is not that; it is more like the *absence* of that. As I see it, it only appears to be an experience because of how dramatically the clarity contrasts with my normal activity where thoughts and feelings obstruct my true nature.

To call the clarity an experience is similar to referring to a "blue" ocean and a "blue" sky. Of course, they both appear blue and we experience them as such. But in reality they are not. If we want to know the truth, we must remember that they are not blue. Likewise, if we want to know the truth of our existence, we must see that unboundedness, or presence awareness, is not an experience. It is who we are. During periods when thoughts and feelings have so receded that I know my unbounded Self, the feeling is as good or better than anything I have ever felt. But under close scrutiny, it is clear there is no experience occurring. The unboundedness that I am is beyond experience. I am constant, with no beginning and no end.

And when I say that unboundedness, or pure consciousness, is forever present but is sometimes seemingly obstructed by "clouds" (thoughts and feelings, and so on), I say "seemingly" because, again, this is our experience, but it is not reality. It may be our experience that a mirage appears to be water, or a rope appears to be a snake, but that does not make it real. The clouds of thoughts and feelings can obstruct our view, but they cannot obstruct our true Selves any more than the rope can bite us or the mirage can quench our thirst. This is why the ancients said, "I am That, thou art That, all of this is That." They understood. They understood that *everything* is an expression of consciousness, even thoughts, feelings, and desires. In other words, even the "clouds" are consciousness. And they understood this whether they felt unbounded and peaceful, or agitated and restless, whether they felt good, bad, or indifferent. Hence the teaching *Understanding is all.*

*

But I Want the Clouds to Disappear

Like most spiritual seekers, I was for a long time under the illusion that enlightened sages are absolutely never distracted by the clouds of thoughts, desires, and overwhelming feelings. I thought they were so steeped in pure consciousness that they could never be bothered by worries, concerns, distractions, and so on. After studying non-dualism for a few years, I heard a revealing story from a friend of Ramesh Balsekar. Ramesh was one of Nisargadatta Maharaj's translators and a very close disciple during Nisargadatta's final years. It seems that every day after Nisargadatta's rather intense daily talks and interactions with seekers, Ramesh would take him for a drive to "cool out," something I did not realize such a highly revered, self-realized soul could possibly need. During one of the rides, Nisargadatta explained that he was worried about how his daughter would get along (mainly with the running of the household) after he was gone. Then, after a few seconds, he turned to Ramesh and said, "How many of my students would understand my saying that?"

Many seekers, if not most, cannot grasp that clouds are simply part of our experience. Clouds—thoughts, feelings, desires, and so on—are, in essence, only an expression of presence awareness. They too are consciousness, the same as a wave on the ocean is still only ocean. And clouds can take our attention away from presence awareness temporarily, no matter how evolved, pure, or spiritual we may be.

In reality, clouds are just another form of energy. Energy vibrates into patterns, which appear for a while and then dissipate. These appearances, which feel quite real and solid and important, simply appear on the screen of presence awareness, just like images on a movie screen. The screen remains constant; the images keep changing. But we forget that these patterns are transitory and have no independent nature or power of their own. We believe that the patterns themselves are real and take them far too seriously. Indeed, we actually believe the thoughts are us.

One day in my living room, some weeks into Sailor Bob's visit, he said rather casually, "People think that Ramana Maharshi had no thoughts going on. What rubbish." (Ramana Maharshi was one of India's greatest twentieth-century sages.) Even for a great saint, thoughts, feelings, and desires never completely disappear, other than for temporary periods. But they may be "seen through" very quickly, indeed often instantly. It is for this that seekers want what sages have—the tendency to breeze through life with ease and grace, rarely, if ever, "taking delivery," as Sailor Bob aptly puts it, of conflicts, problems, and psychological and/or emotional complexes.

But there is always the possibility, for the most enlightened as well as the most ignorant, of clouds *appearing* to cover up the presence awareness. They appear to cover up presence awareness only because our attention goes to them. Why does our attention go toward these distractions, even after years of meditation and perhaps some rare experiences of God-like visions or mystical bliss?

Let me offer a few salient reasons: Money, power, fame, gold, silver, diamonds, a beautiful woman, raging hormones, a beautiful man, sublime love, sex, drugs, rock and roll, going to prison, an overwhelming meditation, writing a great book, health problems, bankruptcy, money problems, politics, reading a great book, being a celebrity, killing a celebrity, being adored, a beautiful sunset, booze, fine wine, a beautiful infant, the thought "I am not good enough," getting cancer, wanting to be Madonna, the thought or experience of rape, a fantastic career, torture, an ocean-front mansion, a Corvette, getting blown up in war, the thought of someone else getting blown up in war, becoming a hermit so "I will never have any more thoughts," baseball, football, a great dinner, the Internet, hitting the game-winning home run, watching Al Pacino in a thrilling Mafia film, being Al Pacino, a car accident, hearing a Frank Sinatra record, meeting a Beatle, killing in the name of religion, mountain climbing, visiting Tibet, winning the lottery, meeting President Kennedy, being a racist, hating a racist, movies, acting, dancing, singing, being great, hating child molesters, painting the world's greatest work of art, a robbery, a Van Gogh painting, riding a horse, never having a good love relationship, feeling ugly, being born blind, worshiping God, trying to stop the land mines, being humble, being arrogant, loving a five-year-old child, trying to free Tibet, an earthquake, thinking about suicide, cheating, becoming a rock star, failing at becoming a rock star. Do you get the picture? Life—the *appearance* that happens on the screen of presence awareness—distracts us from our unboundedness, our ground of being.

All of this, of course, is not to mention the unconscious clouds still apparently affecting our vision, such as the emotional scar of losing a parent at the age of four, never forgiving a loved one, guilt about sex or sexual preferences, the wound caused when our first date stood us up, guilt over treating someone badly, unconscious fear of terrorism, repressed fear of dying, unconscious fear of being left by a spouse, and on and on and on.

Think these could be hindrances to seeing your unbounded Self clearly? Think these things could create some apparent clouds? You bet they could. But, remember, the clouds are nothing more than consciousness, or energy—the same consciousness, or energy, that we are.

Why do we need to remember this? Because, when we appreciate the unity of everything, we are set free—free to stop resisting our experiences, free to stop trying to fix what appear to be outside hostile forces, free to stop investing such importance and energy in transitory experiences, free to stop devoting our life to chasing pleasure and avoiding pain. Most importantly, we become free to stop approaching life from the perspective of "me" and "other," and to see the phenomenal world and our own existence for the ultimate illusion that they are.

Can this be true? Does life deserve to be seen as an illusion? Consider this. Science tells us that all physical matter is actually made up of infinitesimal subatomic particles. It says that the only reason we cannot put our hands through walls or tables, for example, is because the particles are moving too fast! This phenomenon is somewhat similar to an operating fan, which has spaces between its blades, but you can't put your hand through them.

Science also tells us that if a person is sent into outer space at the speed of light for 100 earth years, she returns to earth only a few days later, according to her calendar. It is also a fact that the earth, which looks and feels stationary, is actually spinning in space at 1000 miles per hour. These examples are clues that various Eastern societies that use the term *maya,* or illusion, to describe the material world are on to something.

So, why does consciousness vibrate into patterns and create all these attention-grabbing phenomena that cover up our unbounded presence awareness? Who is to say? But if it didn't, there would be no life. There would only be presence awareness, what the Dzogchen Buddhists describe as "non-conceptual, ever present, self-shining, one without a second. Just this and nothing else." There would only be emptiness, or nothing—literally, no thing.

Regarding the list of distractions listed above that are continually drawing our attention away from presence awareness, many spiritual seekers feel they have lost interest in the material items listed, as well as many of the psychological or unconscious distractions. So, what is the biggest cloud? What is the distraction that turns everybody's head? It is of course the "me," the all-special, all-wonderful, all-important "me" that is our false identity—the one we acquired when our reasoning began. It is the false identity we acquired when we learned our name, the particulars of our personality, our looks, our likes and dislikes, and so on. It is the false reference point, which allows us to feel that we are the center of the universe, despite the fact that, from the vantage point of far-off galaxies, we are as insignificant as tiny grains of sand. It is also the false "me" that allows us to crave enlightenment, or awakening—as if this made-up "me" could ever be enlightened! Enlightenment, or liberation, is awakening to the reality that there is no individual being. There is only oneness, consciousness, unboundedness, and that unboundedness is who we are.

How are we conditioned to believe in an individual self? What is the essence of this false self center? It is the mind, of course, more specifically our thoughts, since there is actually no such thing as mind. Mind is a term used to denote the sum total of all our thoughts, which seemingly are created by us, but which in fact involuntarily appear on our radar screen. Because we have been conditioned to believe we are individuals, we assume that the thoughts appearing to us are part of us. We believe we have created the thoughts and are responsible for them. We take pride in creative thoughts and feel bad about negative or destructive ones. If others disagree with our thoughts and beliefs or deride them, we become defensive and upset, as if who we are is being ridiculed or shamed. In fact, our thoughts are not us, they are not created by us, and they have no independent nature. They are like clouds that appear and disappear in the sky.

Can anyone control which types of thoughts will appear, or when? If we had control of our thoughts, would we ever allow sad ones, depressing ones, or angry, jealous, or bitter ones? If a person with low self-confidence and continual self-negating thoughts is told to stop thinking such thoughts, can he or she do it? Can a person with bi-polar disorder stop thinking depressing thoughts, just because he or she decides to? Can a person who has just been dumped by a lover decide to have joyous, pleasant thoughts? Of course not, because we do not think thoughts—thoughts think us.

While it certainly appears that people create their own thoughts, the truth is that when instructed to create one, all we can do is sit and wait for one to arise. If asked to think about a particular subject—any subject—we have no control or say over the exact nature of what will come up. Five people instructed to think of a football field will conjure up five different fields of various sizes, shapes, and colors. When told to think of a happy or pleasant scene, one person sees an ocean, one sees a sunset, another sees a romantic love embrace, and so on. There is simply no way to control who will see what or why.

Yet, due to our conditioning, which has taught us that we are individuals, we believe our thoughts belong to us, and worse, actually *are* us. Nothing could be further from the truth. As Sailor Bob reiterates, thoughts have no independent nature. They are simply patterns of energy that arise and dissipate. They come, they hang around for a while (sometimes for years), they change and modify, and then they disappear because they ultimately have no independent nature. They depend for their existence upon our aliveness, our essence—presence awareness—as does all manifest creation.

All material existence consists of vibrations, or energy patterns, that appear and (eventually) disappear. It is only presence awareness, or pure intelligence energy, as Sailor Bob also calls it, that has an independent nature, because it is continual, non-ending, ever present, and cannot be destroyed. It is this underlying, ever-present pure intelligence energy that is who and what we are. And it is actually this ever-present pure intelligence energy that is perceiving the vibrations, or energy patterns, that make up life as we know it.

Of course, these vibrations, or energy patterns, that make up material creation and appear to be so physical are actually made up of nothing more than the same underlying pure intelligence energy from which they are created. In the same way that seemingly independent waves are made up of ocean, the physical universe is mysteriously and miraculously made up of pure intelligence energy in an apparent process that many sages and seers term "cognizing emptiness." Ultimately, what is happening is that presence awareness, or pure intelligence energy, is enjoying itself. Said another way, we—as infinite, unbounded pure intelligence energy—are enjoying ourselves in the apparent form of human beings in an apparent physical world. Therefore, when spiritual seekers try to discover their own immortal, unbounded nature, what is really happening is a game of hide and seek in which the one hiding and the one seeking are in fact one and the same. Those who are unaware of the concept of enlightenment and have no knowledge of non-duality are also playing hide and seek, but in a less obvious form. Every time one attempts to fulfill a desire, any desire, one is essentially looking (consciously or not) for the wholeness and completeness that were lost when the false personal identity was born.

Another feature helping to keep the illusion of an individual "me" alive is the body. In the same way thoughts depend on presence awareness for their existence, so do our bodies. Although we have been conditioned to believe that it is our nerve endings that allow us to feel sensations and pain, that is only apparently so. A dead body has plenty of nerve endings, yet feels nothing. It is the underlying aliveness, or presence awareness, that allows feeling to occur. A dead body, as Sailor Bob teaches, is like a computer without power. Such a computer is useless.

The body, like everything else in creation, has no independent nature. It is fleeting and is certainly not who we are. Who we are is presence awareness, or pure intelligence energy, which is infinite, eternal, immortal, and never ending. We are literally "no thing." As it says in the *Bhagavad Gita,* what we are cannot be cut by the sword, burned by fire, drowned by water, or dried by wind. Who we are was never born and will never die. This is why, when the great sage Ramana Maharshi was asked by his disciples not to leave them (that is, not to die), he responded, "Where would I go?"

Although we cannot experience pure intelligence energy in the *normal* sense, because there is no way to grasp or feel that which is infinite, it is sufficient and profoundly life altering merely to understand who and what we are. Why? Because once we see manifest creation (including our thoughts and our bodies) for the illusion and transient experience that it is, we can relax into our immortal being and stop resisting. And instead of constantly reacting to the boundaries and restrictions around us, and relegating all power and reality to the outer world, we find that all power reverts back to us.

Because we cannot experience our infinite nature using our usual modes of perception, it is by understanding what we are *not* that we come to know who and what we actually are. What we are not, if it is not already clear, is everything material and physical. What we are not is everything that is born and dies. How do we know this? We start from the only thing we truly know for certain: We cannot say that we are not; we cannot say that we do not exist. And the same presence aware-ness—the same "now" that is with us presently—is the exact same presence awareness, or now, that has been with us since memory allows.

With this insight into what we are not, we are left knowing who we truly are—completeness and wholeness, as is. We are left knowing that we are the source, and we see all material life to be as transient and fleeting as a puff of smoke.

It is important, critical really, not to forget for a moment that thoughts have no independent nature. Nothing creates suffering and discontent more instantly than the persistent thought that we are individuals, separated from our source. Why is the mind so good at perpetuating this profound misunderstanding, long-term societal conditioning aside? For two reasons: First, the mind—which perceives itself to be a thing—cannot conceive of "no thing," which is what presence awareness is. The mind is frightened, horrified actually, by the concept of nothing-ness (no-thing-ness). More significantly, the mind believes it is inde-pendent and cannot comprehend that it is contained by something outside itself—particularly nothingness! To the mind, "no thing" can only be seen as death, pure and simple. Horrifying.

The second reason the mind is so good at perpetuating the sense of separation is that the sole purpose of the mind is to divide, to make distinctions. Everything in existence occurs solely by virtue of the pairs of opposites. Without darkness, there can be no light. Without cold, there is no heat. Without joy, there is no sadness, and so on. The mind's job is to make the distinctions, to perceive differences, so that life as we know it can occur. Without the mind labeling everything, there would only be oneness everywhere. Boring.

Awakening, enlightenment, liberation, or whatever name seekers give it, is simply the realization and the letting go of the false sense of personal identity, the false reference point we refer to as "me." Awaken-ing is not an experience, despite the fact that it is promoted as such by many gurus. It is the understanding that the wholeness you seek, you already are. It is the understanding that the separation you perceive is merely an erroneous thought that began in early childhood and was never seriously questioned or investigated. When that thought is investigated, found to be false, and removed, what do you find? There is nowhere to go, nothing to do, and no future or past. There are only apparent successive moments of now—right now, right now, right now, and so on. Moreover, there is no meaning, no purpose, and no significance to life. What is, is. Period. Everything else is an interpretation made by a mind whose job is to label everything it perceives in order to make differences. Why make differences? For fun. To create all the wonderful/terrible distractions mentioned earlier in this chapter. Awakening is the under-standing that the only thing we know for certain is that we cannot say we "are not." We cannot say we do not exist. And that leaves us with nothing but presence awareness, the eternal now that always was and always will be. It leaves us with reality—with "no thing."

But I have gotten ahead of my story. Way ahead. And for those who still believe, despite what I've said, that enlightenment is a state of non-ending bliss, special superhuman powers, never having negative thoughts or feelings, no anger, no sadness, and so on, the rest of the story is important.

During my first phone conversation, Sailor Bob asked me a bit about myself, and I told him I was an astrologer and had spent time in India in the early 1980s learning Hindu/Vedic astrology. I said I would send him a few of the books I had written, one of which was autobiographical about my studies in India. After our talk, I e-mailed him a thank-you note and mentioned that if he had any desire to come to America, I would pay his way, as well as his wife's. By this time, I was actually already aware that he had no desire to travel. I knew this because one of my closest friends, Kerry Breitbart, had already posed the question, and Bob had told him as much. A year or so earlier, I had shared my love of Advaita with Kerry, who soon became consumed with it. Kerry had been on the spiritual path since we were college students, and he was as thrilled with Bob's book as I was. In the weeks I was building up the nerve to call Bob, Kerry, being as gregarious and outgoing as he is, got tired of waiting and called Bob to have a chat. They spoke for nearly an hour, and during that time Kerry, who knew I was planning to invite Bob, asked whether he would enjoy coming to the United States. Bob said he had no desire whatsoever to visit.

But that was all very informal. I intended to make a concerted effort to see if he might change his mind. And so, in my thank-you note I told him that there were plenty of seekers here who would love to hear him speak and that if he had any desire to visit, I would pay for the plane tickets. Or, if he wanted a vacation without speaking, that was also fine. I also told him that Longboat Key, where we live, is one of the nicest spots in Florida—with world-famous beaches within walking distance of my house.

Expecting the same reply that Kerry heard, I was thus startled when Bob wrote a message containing a glimmer of hope. He said the offer was "very generous" but that they didn't travel much anymore. Then he said, "Well, who knows? Maybe in the winter." Not having a clue about Australian winters, I e-mailed my one and only Australian friend, Peter Jones, to inquire. He said that June through September was cold in Melbourne. And so, the wheels began to turn. I gathered from Bob's message that he didn't like the cold, and wondered whether he had any idea how hot Florida is during those months. In any case, I decided to take photos of our beautiful island and the brand new cottage in our back yard where they could stay, and sent them via airmail. Along with the photos and letter, I wrote, "We have read your book and heard your CDs, and it is clear that you have nothing to offer. We want this NOTHING!"

I didn't know it then, but as Bob has gotten older, he has had less and less tolerance for cold weather. As fate would have it, I learned months later, the very day after Bob said, "Well, who knows? Maybe in the winter," it started getting cold and never let up! And this was only April, the beginning of his winter. So, after sending the photos and a formal invitation, as well as some cash for spending so much time on the phone in our spiritual discussion (I didn't know this either at the time, but Bob does much of his counseling work by phone and makes his living that way), I waited with bated breath. After some weeks I phoned Bob, who replied that he and Barb were reading my autobiography as quickly as possible to find out more about me. He also said that my astrology books had piqued Barb's interest in a major way, and that it had been quite some years since they had had a nice vacation. Surprise of surprises, the invitation was accepted.

Our phone call occurred around 8:00 p.m. Eastern Standard Time, which was early the next morning in Australia. Afterwards, I was so excited I barely slept. The next morning I called Kerry, knowing he would be thrilled. Kerry immediately asked if he could share the plane expenses and invite Bob to come to his home in Connecticut as well. I agreed, and so did Bob and Barbara. The next time I spoke with Bob to work out details of the trip, he asked me how I was progressing.

*

My Second Phone Call with Sailor Bob

Bob: So, how are you doing?

James: Well, when I read books about non-duality, I find myself understanding quite well and feeling good. But then I start to question whether the false reference point—the "me"—will ever go away. That's the big problem.

Bob: Have you had a look and seen that it's not really there?

James: Yes.

Bob: It's just an idea or a concept.

James: Yes, it's absolutely a concept. And when I'm speaking about it, it's all very clear. But then, for example, one day I wake up tired and start having some fear. And I ask myself, "Why am I having fear?" And I see that the answer is that I'm having fear because I'm feeling separate—I'm feeling like an individual, and I have some particular problem.

Bob: When you see that you're not an individual, do you drop the thought? The dropping of the thought, once you see it, is a discipline or habit that comes up spontaneously through the mind. You're seeing that you're having a problem because you think you're an individual who is separate. That's the cause of the problem.

James: Yes, I get that.

Bob: Do you see clearly that there is really no separation?

James: Yes, but there's such a strong *feeling* of a problem. . . . I mean I can analyze it and see that the "me" is false, but there is such strong conditioning of being an individual.

Actually, if the pain or the psychological problem isn't too intense, then it's easy to see what's causing it and then it can go away.

Bob: Look, you're seeing right now, aren't you?

James: Yes.

Bob: You're aware of being present right now, aren't you?

James: Yes.

Bob: That presence awareness is there, isn't it? You can't negate it.

James: That's right.

Bob: You cannot negate the knowing that you *are*.

James: Right.

Bob: Well, what did you have to do to see that?

James: Nothing.

Bob: So, it's spontaneous?

James: Absolutely.

Bob: It's spontaneous awareness. You're looking out and seeing the things around you?

James: Yes.

Bob: You're hearing my voice on the phone?

James: Yes.

Bob: All that is spontaneous. You don't have to think about it. You're spontaneously hearing, seeing, thinking, and so on. It's all spontaneous.

James: Right.

Bob: So, is there any separation between the awareness and the appearances in it?

James: No.

Bob: So, though these things are appearing as something other than awareness, when you break them down to their essence, you see that the essence of everything is nothing other than spontaneous presence—that timeless, spontaneous nowness.

James: Yes.

Bob: So, even when the thoughts come out as this and that, see them in their essence. No matter how they're appearing, their essence is still only That.

Then, if you feel something is good or bad or painful or pleasant, look carefully and you'll see they are equal in their essence. They're pure equality.

James: Yes.

Bob: Now, if something is equal, where can you latch onto it?

James: You can't.

Bob: Right.

James: So, if pain or some emotional suffering is there, the best thing to do is just be with it and consider it just to be what is happening now.

Bob: Yes. That's what's going on now. Pure presence awareness. As long as you haven't fixated on it, and you're not relating the pain to some reference point, such that you start to judge it as this, that, or the other . . .

James: That's what makes it a problem?

Bob: Yes, and the reference point is essentially invalid because it's based on past events and circumstances. It's dead. You're trying to evaluate the actuality, the spontaneous presence, with a dead memory or image.

Where else would you get the word "pain" from? The sensation would be there, but where did you label it "pain" from? From some previous experience you called pain.

If you came into existence right now, would you know pleasure or pain or anything else? These sensations would be there, but you wouldn't have the labels for them. We've acquired these labels through the living process from around the age of two.

James: So, the labeling of negative or difficult sensations as pain is faulty?

Bob: Yes, concepts and ideas are all false because they are conceptual. But that doesn't mean to say they have to go away. You understand the concepts are just labels. But, in *essence*, everything is the same thing. Everything is, in essence, presence awareness. Therefore, everything becomes all-inclusive again. These very words are It. The feeling you have is It. The pain is It. Everything is It.

James: Like the statement "I am That, thou art That, all of this is That."

Bob: Yes. So, everything becomes all-inclusive because it's all happening spontaneously, presently. When you're feeling pain, the actuality of it is right now.

James: It's the psychological stuff that drives us crazy.

Bob: The psychological stuff can only happen to a reference point, a "me." "Me" is the cause of all psychological problems. And if you see that the "me" is false, then you realize, how can there be an effect without a cause? So what happens to the effects? You don't overcome them, suppress them, or force them out. If you see that the cause you are referring to is false, then the effects must drop away of themselves. The effects can't be there without a cause.

So, although issues and problems may come up, they are not going to lodge there and snowball and cause greater psychological dramas and traumas. They will come up and then quickly disappear. The pairs of opposites will always come up and play, like they're playing in nature. The tide comes in, the tide goes out. Winter comes now, soon comes spring.

The pairs of opposites are always manifesting in nature, *but they're not in opposition with one another*. With us, when we see something we don't like, we take a stand to modify it, alter it, and correct it, and that resistance to it is the pain. That's the conflict. That's the problem. That's where we differ with nature and that causes massive problems.

But, seeing everything as spontaneous presence awareness, there's nowhere to go, nothing to do. It happens by itself. And that is what you really are, that essence. Consciousness. No thing.

James: But I find that the reference point keeps re-surfacing.

Bob: Yes, but when that happens, the discipline or habit will also come up as a thought: "Hey, there's that same old false reference point." And then you immediately drop it. That innate intelligence within you will express through the mind as thought—as a kind of discipline, or habit, to do. It will happen naturally. You don't have to try.

You see, there's actually no entity that is a doer. The doing simply happens. There's no entity that is a seer. The seeing just happens. Life is going on in you all by itself, just as it is all over the universe. There's no difference in what's going on in the macrocosm or the microcosm. It's all the oneness. You are *That*. Full stop. ["Full stop" is the British and Australian term for the period at the end of a sentence.]

James: It's all so paradoxical. The mind is the source of all our problems because that's how we create the "me," the false reference point. But it's also the mind that lets us figure out that the "me" is false and tells us to drop it!

Bob: Yes, you have to look in the mind to find the answer to the mind. Like Ramana Maharshi said, "If you have a thorn stuck in your hand, you have to use another thorn to get it out. Then you throw them both away."

But, is there really such a thing as mind?

James: No.

Bob: There's nothing you can grasp with any substance or any independent nature that you can call mind. Thoughts are just energy, patterning into an appearance. Just the same as energy is patterning into an appearance of the entire material manifestation. It's all energy, vibrating into different patterns.

The body is made up of elements, which are broken down into space. Now, an extension of that body is a vibration of thought. Thought is just a pattern of energy also. Thought is just subtle sound. At the spoken level, sound is word. Word is a vibration. Vibration is a movement of energy.

So, everything can be broken down into pure intelligence energy. That emptiness, that empty energy is not a vacuum or void because it has that capacity of knowing. That knowing is intelligence. You see?

James: Yes.

Bob: And knowing is happening with you right now. I'm not talking about the knower or the known. That's false. The knowing is the actuality, and knowing implies what is happening right now. Knowing is intelligence—not your intellect, which is knowing or not knowing—but the knowing itself, the knowing that you are, which you can't negate. The subtle essence of being.

Because knowing is happening right now, it's an activity. And any activity is a movement of energy also. So it's that intelligence energy, that knowing.

If you take the "k" off of "knowing," you have "nowing"! That knowing is "nowing." So it's omnipresence whichever way you look at it. When are you going to move away from it? Can you ever move away from it?

James: You can't.

Bob: So, even if the seeming clouds of chatter and thought are with you, you know that the sun is still in the sky, don't you? And you know that the sun can never fall out of space.

Even if the mind has got you believing that you are away from the pure intelligence energy—the presence awareness—that innate knowing will now come up and tell you, "I'm not away from it."

James: So, no matter what the suffering is, if a person can simply be aware of being in the present, then the suffering soon subsides.

Bob: Yes, because suffering is only thought.

Pain is a different matter; that's the body telling you there is a problem that needs attention. But, for example, that psychological pain I went through earlier in my life doesn't happen anymore. It hasn't happened for years. It falls away. It's not necessary.

James: Ha! It's not necessary. That's nice!

Bob: It's all mind created. It's all about a "me," a seeming separate entity. A "me" that needs to do something, that needs to acquire or get something. But that me doesn't have any substance or independent nature.

James: When the "me" falls away . . .

Bob: What do you mean "when the 'me' falls away"? When has the "me" ever actually been there? You said that you've seen the "me" is false, so when was it ever there?

You've got an erroneous belief. Drop that.

James: When you realized, fully realized, that there is no "me," and you started living in the Now, moment by moment, the world became a concept. Correct?

Bob: Yes, it's all conceptual.

James: So, when you see the news, with all the wars and tragedies going on, does that have any meaning for you?

Bob: Yes, it has meaning. Look, when certain concepts come up, you might need to take an active part; you might have to do something about it. Whatever the functioning brings about is fine.

But, *ultimately,* it doesn't have any meaning whatsoever. There is no meaning anywhere. Meaning can only exist from a reference point. And reference points are false. They're made up.

James: Well, for example, in my astrology practice, for many years I thought I was doing something helpful. Then, when I encountered Advaita, this knowledge, it became clear that I am taking illusory actions to help illusory people in an illusory world!

Whatever worldly problems are occurring are just what's happening.

Of course, it would be nice if the world were a nicer place with happier people. But people are just "being lived," and this is how they're being lived. Nothing *ultimately* needs changing. [Note: If our thoughts are not us, then it only appears that we are making choices. Therefore, we are in actuality being lived. This will be discussed later.]

I guess what I am trying to ask is this: Once a person has the final understanding, is life essentially over? [Note: Non-dualists prefer terms such as "the understanding" or "the final understanding" or "the knowingness" rather than liberation or enlightenment. This is because bondage is simply a mind-created fiction and therefore enlightenment, or liberation, does not, as such, exist. One simply has or does not have the understanding, or the knowingness.]

Bob: Well, actually life never began! But, to answer your question . . .

James: Wait, you mean that? It never began?

Bob: Yes, it's all just an appearance. Nothing ever happened really.

But you don't take a deliberate stance: "I can do nothing." If you see people suffering, you might find yourself taking an active part to help. A natural compassion may be there. The living continues to go on.

Anyway, you've seen that there's no "me." If there's no "me" now, when was there ever one?

James: There never was.

Bob: All right, so you've lived your life up until now, doing the things that seemed necessary to do. But there was no "me" there doing it at all. That's just the way it happened. Life took you through astrology, through meditation and all, and it took you to Advaita. If necessary, people will be attracted to you to hear what you have to say. And you can alleviate their suffering and so on. And the natural compassion will be there to do it.

It's not a matter of just sitting around saying, "I can't do anything about this, and I'm not going to." That's a deliberate "not doing" from a reference point again.

Ultimately, everything becomes all-inclusive, and the functioning goes on. It takes you where it's going to take you.

James: But, for you there must be less and less of a hook to the entire appearance?

Bob: Yes, there's nowhere to dig your hooks in anymore.

But in the beginning, the old habit patterns will come up and trap you again. Then you see through it, and a thought comes up and says, "Hold on, this is the same old garbage again," and you drop it. And the energy doesn't go into those old erroneous beliefs like it used to. Nothing can live without energy, so it drops away.

And though there is no such thing as time, it may seemingly take some time before it completely drops away. Once you've seen all this, you can never be the same again. Once you've seen that you have no self center, you can never believe it again.

James: I've read so many books by enlightened people who say that their mind stops and they have all kinds of wonderful stillness. Do you have that? Do you ever have periods where the mind stops, I mean, completely stops?

Bob: Yes. And sometimes I have to kick start it to get it going. When I'm just seeing without labeling. Registering without labeling.

But I don't prefer silence to thoughts because they're both experiences. They're both conceptual. What you are is the experiencing in which the experience of silence or chatter, or good or bad, is happening. You are that experiencing essence, just like you are the seeing. You are the seeing before it's split up into a seer and the seen. You are thinking before it's split up into a thinker and the thought. You are the experiencing.

James: Do you *feel* that? Is there a feeling?

Bob: A feeling would be an experience.

James: So, it's an understanding?

Bob: An understanding, or an innate, deep—not that there's any depth to it—knowing. Knowing that you've always been That—actually, there's no "always," there's *only* That. You are That. You can't be anything else. And That is no thing. What you are is the no thing—the nothingness. It's no thing because it can't be grasped with the mind. You can never grasp it with the mind because the mind is contained within It.

That's why in the *Bhagavad Gita* it says the sword can't cut it, fire can't burn it, wind can't dry it, water can't drown it.

James: What a wonderful description!

Bob: A puny thought, a "me," certainly can't capture it. When you realize you won't find the answer in the mind, then the mind's there just for what it's meant to be. It just translates these energy patterns that come up.

James: You say in your book that the mind is a beautiful tool. So, you're telling the truth when you say that?

Bob: Yes, I am. It's just an instrument with a purpose. But, because it vibrates in the pairs of opposites, at one end of the scale it's a wonderfully creative instrument, and at the other end of the scale it becomes self-destructive. When it tells us we're not good enough, we can't do this or the other, it puts all kinds of boundaries and limitations on us.

James: The mind seems to be the source of all our problems, so it's hard sometimes for me to see the wonderfulness of the mind.

Bob: There's an old expression: *The mind is a wonderful servant, but a terrible master.* So, it's just a matter of using it properly.

James: Yes. Well, okay. I'm anxious to have more talks with you when you come here. And I'm thrilled that you will be visiting. There will be plenty of people here who want to hear you talk.

*

More Phone Calls

Over the next few months, there were more phone calls. Most were made in order to make arrangements and to determine what needs Bob and Barb would have in America. Bob laughingly said he had no intention whatsoever of driving in the States, where car makers place steering wheels on the wrong side of the car, and people drive on the wrong side of the road! He asked me if I was interested in taping his talks, what the weather would be like, and other such matters. Barb mentioned that she had heard there were hurricanes and tornadoes in Florida, and wanted to know if we would be having any. I laughed and said it was extremely unlikely, but privately hoped Barb wasn't psychically sensing weather problems. I had no clue that 2004 would turn out to be a record year with four hurricanes in one summer, one of which caused us to evacuate on Bob and Barb's last weekend here.

Determining how many talks Bob wanted to give was somewhat difficult. It seems he was leaving much up to me, while I wanted simply to fulfill his wishes. Many of my scheduling questions Bob answered by saying, "Well, let's see how it all unfolds." I had no idea how many people would be attracted to talks on non-duality and was frightened by my lack of promotional skills. Having lived a fairly secluded life since moving to the West Coast of Florida did not help one bit. Fortunately, I had the assistance of a neighborhood friend named Dell Dellarmo, a massage and Trager therapist with an outgoing personality, who knew many local seekers and spiritual groups. Whenever I became nervous about the prospect of organizing Bob's talks, Dell would quickly put me at ease.

Another puzzle was how long Bob and Barb should stay. In my original invitation, I said, "Stay a week, or stay a few months." I felt five or six weeks would be perfect. By the time we got down to actual planning, however, their "vacation" became a four-city speaking tour of the U.S. For one thing, Kerry was planning a few talks in Connecticut, where Bob and Barb would be staying for one week. Next, Barb had discussed with Bob the possibility of stopping in Chicago to see Joan Tollifson, a wonderful Advaitan author and teacher they knew. Finally, as long as their journey home took them through California, why not also go see John Wheeler in Santa Cruz? John had been a seeker for many years before traveling to Australia to meet with Bob, where his search finally ended once and for all.

As teachers, both John and Joan had their own networks of students and were able to gather more students for Bob than either Kerry or myself. The Connecticut talks drew around forty people each, while John and Joan attracted around sixty seekers each in their respective areas. Our talks in Florida were smaller, ten or fifteen attending each, but there were many more of them. As it turned out, Bob and Barb stayed in the other cities for only four to seven days, while they were with us for five wonderful weeks. The talks here were somewhat more informal and wonderfully intimate.

Having learned of Bob's desire to speak in three other cities, I drew up a potential itinerary for him and Barb to consider. Because they are elderly and would be doing so much traveling, I scheduled only three weeks in Florida. This would make their entire trip nearly a full six weeks. Barb, however, felt that would be unfair to me. She was as grateful to me for inviting them as I was to Bob for agreeing to visit. In fact, I was at this point more grateful to Barb for convincing Bob to come. I knew Bob had stopped traveling years ago and had no real desire to see the States. Barb, on the other hand, wanted a vacation and was also interested in learning some astrology with me. In any case, I told Barb they were welcome to stay longer, and five weeks would suit me just fine if she felt they could handle an eight-week stay in the States. Of course, I had no idea what five weeks in my home would be like, or how we could fill so much time discussing Advaita. But I suspected, actually fully believed, that what was about to occur was the chance of a lifetime. I was not wrong.

In the end, we were thrilled they stayed as long as they did. I thanked Barb heartily for suggesting that I could benefit from more than three weeks with Bob. There is simply no comparison between reading books or listening to CDs and being in the presence of a master. Up to the last minute of Bob's visit, never would he let me slip into images of a better future or regret over something past. He was constantly bringing my attention to presence awareness and living without labeling. On the last day of their visit, as Barb gave me a relaxing session of Bowen Therapy (a profound physical healing method developed in Australia which Barb has been practicing for many years), she explained why she had felt five weeks would be the right period of time. That was how long she had spent with Nisargadatta Maharaj more than twenty years ago. It had worked out fine for her. She wanted me to get from Bob what she had gotten from Nisargadatta, for which I am eternally grateful—moment by moment, of course.

Barb, at seventy-two years old, incidentally, is no timid flower. Aside from her striking beauty, she is powerful and remarkable in her own right. Through her practice of Bowen Therapy, she has healed innumerable people of serious ailments that would not respond to conventional treatments. Many of the accounts of healing she gave us were fascinating. She also has a fine grasp of non-duality, as is readily seen by her remarks in conversations throughout this book. For a long time Barb sat in on Bob's thrice-weekly talks until a few years ago when her Bowen Therapy practice became so large it demanded all her energy. Thus, she was thrilled to be able to attend the meetings in our home and help seekers grapple with the ins and outs and subtleties of non-duality. Barb told us she had thoroughly enjoyed her five weeks with Nisargadatta. She had gone to Bombay to take a tour of the country with two friends, who suddenly got sick and returned home. When Bob, who had already been visiting with Nisargadatta for some time, asked her if she would like to hear Nisargadatta talk, she jumped at the chance. Barb was very ripe for non-duality and got the understanding almost immediately. She then decided to attend the talks six days a week for her entire stay. Barb loves to tell how Sailor Bob and Nisargadatta used to fiercely "go at it," as Bob presented all his questions and doubts about non-duality. She also mentions how Nisargadatta put her smack in the middle of the room and kept commenting on the fact that her boyfriend (Sailor Bob) was the reason so many Westerners were now coming to see him.

Barb, incidentally, often comments on how men, much more than women, seem to make a big deal out of Advaita, while for her it is simply a very normal and natural understanding, or knowingness. At any rate, she was helpful to many seekers while she was with us. And Kerry told me that Barb had a profound influence on his wife, Laurie, and his mother during her visit in Connecticut. We were certainly glad Barb visited, and in the end she formed a very powerful bond with my family, which we continue to enjoy by telephone.

During each and every phone call I made to them before their arrival in Florida, Bob always asked in his charming Australian accent, "So, how are you going?" This, I came to realize, meant, "How are you doing with your understanding?" The following dialogues are from those conversations.

May 16, 2004

James: I find that sometimes when upsetting things come up, I get caught up in the reference point. Life becomes very personal. It seems to me that one of the most difficult issues is desire. Sometimes desires are very intense.

Bob: Desire is a fixation of the mind on an idea.

James: So the idea is to let it go?

Bob: Yes. Intelligence will recognize it, and the fixation drops away.

James: When a desire comes up and becomes frustrating, I remember that there is no James.

Bob: So you're remembering it. Realize that whatever you can remember or forget is not you. You are that which everything appears on—which is no thing.

As long as you know that something is not you, you treat it as the traffic going by. You're aware of what's happening, but you're not concerned with it.

James: The reason desire ever arises, or the reason I get stuck in desire, is because I think there is a "me."

Bob: Desire is a fixation of the mind on an idea. There's a belief going on in the mind. And that belief is another reference point. When you examine the reference point, you'll see it's insubstantial and has no independent nature. If there's no consciousness or awareness there, you can't have a desire, can you?

James: No.

Bob: So you see that you are what underlies it. Even though the desire is happening, you are the underlying essence that has never been touched. So the sting goes out of it. If there's no energy or belief going into it, it must fall away. You don't have to do anything. It all happens in the seeing of it.

James: I've been thinking lately about the world of appearance and how incredible it is.

Bob: Yes, they call it the dynamic display of the energy of awareness.

Displaying in all its diversity, all appearances and possibilities. The magical show.

James: Non-duality is so counterintuitive. The idea that everything is happening and we're not doing anything. The illusion that we are the doers is so conditioned and so ingrained. Why did I become an actor and an astrologer, and not something else? It's so odd that it never was actually my choice.

Bob: There was never any entity within you that was capable of doing or choosing anything. That's the key to it all. That was our first and only erroneous belief that we took on.

James: Because we have no self center?

Bob: That's right. There's no entity there with an independent nature that can stand on its own—that can stand outside of consciousness, or awareness. If you're not conscious, or aware, your body is just a corpse.

James: I remember, as a child, beginning to conceptualize my identity. It's a very early memory. We're not born with an identity. We somehow make it up.

Bob: Yes. When we start to reason, the knowing that you are expresses as the thought "I am." Thought is just a vibration.

The opposite of "I am" is "not I" or "other than I." As a child, everything started out as "I." Everything was just that functioning intelligence energy. When the reasoning started, that's when our separation began. That reasoning is what we call "acquired mind." And that becomes the cloud over your natural state. The natural state is still functioning in its fullness, but it's *seemingly* obliterated by all this acquired stuff, this learned stuff.

James: But the learned stuff has to occur for the child to become a human being.

Bob: Of course it does. But, in certain cases, in certain people, it turns itself around and comes back to its true nature that it never left. In other instances, in other people, it doesn't. Whether it does or doesn't is of no consequence. You were always that functioning intelligence energy displaying as someone who doesn't know or somebody who does know, or whatever. Whatever way you display doesn't matter because you've never been anything other than that one essence. That essence has been everything. It has been every manifestation that's ever appeared or is likely to appear. It's all appearances and possibilities.

That's why in the manifestation, even way back in 1962 when I went to see the Maharishi, and his guru appeared to me . . . all that functioning was there then. [Note: Sailor Bob learned Transcendental Meditation from Maharishi Mahesh Yogi very early on in his search. And he had some sort of mystical vision of Maharishi's teacher, Guru Dev, who had long since passed away.] Every saint, sage, or savior that's ever been—their *essence* is what you are. You take on their words or their understanding and it continues to express. So, you sit back and enjoy it all.

But that's only a story in the manifestation.

May 18

James: In order to get the understanding of non-duality, to really get it and never forget it, there must be some responsibility that goes into it. For instance, you were going to see Nisargadatta day after day, day after day, and then suddenly you got it. You got that there is no doer—no individual "me."

I mention this because non-duality is so counter to our experience, and the conditioning of the reasoning mind is so strong. . . . Is there something that needs to be done to really fully get the understanding?

If I set my mind to something, I can succeed. I can say, "Look, damn it, I'm going to remember this understanding and not forget it. . . ." In other words, I can bring something "to the table," so the understanding stays with me all the time, without the reference point intermittently popping up. Does that make sense, or is that just more doing?

Bob: What is necessary to see is that there couldn't possibly be any doer. Do you understand what the so-called self center is?

James: Yes. There is nothing I can point to that is actually a "me." At the same time, though, my conditioning has me thinking that there is a "me."

Bob: Never mind your conditioning for now. Just see that the so-called "me" is only an "I" thought which is *translating* that sense of presence—the knowing that you are. You don't have to go around saying, "I am, I am, I am" all day in order to confirm that you are. Knowing that you are is there. That's the pure intelligence energy.

James: Right.

Bob: And then the "I am" comes up and translates it. But then we add to that "I am" all the events and conditioning and experiences, and we form a mental image. And that's all the self center is—that mental image. Everything is related to that. Everything is considered relative to that.

And that "I " thought, being a thought—being a vibration—vibrates into its opposite, which is "not I" or "other than I." That's the seeming sense of separation. That's where seeming personal doership arises—from that belief that there is an entity there that has some power and independent nature.

But you see clearly that you can't have a thought if awareness or consciousness is not present. So the "I" thought and everything that goes with it—the image that you have about yourself—has no independent nature. It can't stand on it own, and it has no substance. So you see clearly that there is no sense of separation and no doer there. There's no separate entity there whatsoever. Seeing that clearly is all that needs to happen. And if you see that clearly, and you see that there's nothing there now, when was there ever one? So, everything that's ever been done has never been done by any individual.

Once you see that clearly, everything becomes all-inclusive again.

James: When you say "to see that clearly," I feel like there's something critical that is not happening in me. I continually go over this in my mind—that I never chose anything and never did anything. And it goes so against my sense of experience. I understand what you're saying, but it's not like something that I know in my gut. The ramifications of non-doership are mind-boggling!

Bob: Well, let's go over it again. You're seeing right now? You're hearing right now?

James: [*Laughing*] I know all this from your books and CDs.

Bob: Go through it with me now. Do your eyes tell you "I see?" Do your ears tell you "I hear?"

James: No.

Bob: The thoughts come up and translate it into "I see" and "I hear." But can that thought "I hear" actually hear?

James: No.

Bob: Is the thought "I am aware" the actual awareness? Is the thought "I choose"actually the chooser? Is the thought "I think" the actual thinker?

James: No.

Bob: There's no entity there apart from that functioning intelligence energy—that "cognizing emptiness."

James: Well, even though I understand that, I keep wondering, "Could that really be possible? It seems so incredible.

Bob: Do you choose those thoughts?

James: No. They just arise.

Bob: Exactly. So you are not doing or choosing or thinking anything. These things are just what's happening.

Now, along with those thoughts there might be some insights coming up to show how everything is possible. Little insights and revelations will come up through the mind, which is the only translating mechanism we have. The insights will open you up to seeing what is. Just give it some time. Everything's going all right.

James: So, basically, however it's unfolding or being understood is fine?

Bob: Just look back on your life. Hasn't life unfolded many times in ways that you might not have wanted it to?

James: [*Laughing*] Yes, that's what happening now! It's unfolding in a way I don't like it unfolding.

Bob: You think it should be different.

James: Yes, I think it should be different.

Bob: In spite of all your previous thinking that it should have been different, it's brought you to this exact spot where you are right now.

James: So this must be fine? That's the point?

Bob: Yes. [*Laughing*] It's not going to let you down now. Like the old scriptural saying "Acknowledge Him in all thy ways, and He will direct thy path." So, just say, "Okay," and give yourself a little wink and smile, and say, "I know it's okay. You've got the reins; take over."

James: I see. Well, I felt like I had to get that question out of my system.

Bob: Good. But, there again, that wasn't any of your doing either. That's just what happened.

James: I can go to sleep now.

June 10

Bob: So, how are you going?

James: Pretty good. I was thinking about something Nisargadatta said: "Either you live in a world of desire and fear, or you live in freedom." I still live with desires and fears. They're not nearly as intense as they used to be, but they're certainly still here. And I wonder how much this understanding deepens.

Bob: Well, it can't actually deepen. You're already that pure intelligence energy, which you've always been. But, different insights come up through the mind. You might call it clearer understanding or better understanding. The essence is still the same. It's always been "one without a second"; it can't be added to, and nothing can take away from it. It's already That.

James: Recently a friend of mine said something interesting: "Many people think they're enlightened. Wait until they hear some bad news, like having cancer, and then see how real their liberation is."

Bob: Well, if they have the true understanding, they will realize that it doesn't matter because they were never born anyway. The fear of death disappears altogether. Naturally, the way you die gives some concern. You wouldn't want to be sick or in pain for a long time.

James: I've noticed that when I'm sick with a really bad cold, non-dual understanding doesn't make it a heck of a lot better. When that physical pain is there.

Bob: Yes, but even the intensity of that physical pain lessens a lot if you can stay with it moment by moment. If the mind is constantly judging and labeling the pain, then it can snowball and get worse and become overwhelming. But there's always a sense of peace or well-being in the background. Nothing's been touched there.

James: I've also been thinking about the fact that, in essence, nobody's better off than anyone else. I hear stories and read books where people claiming enlightenment say they "live in paradise," and things like that. Then, of course, I start desiring what they have. I want that paradise. But that must be nonsense.

Bob: Well, have a look at all that. Those are all experiences. They come and go. What you are is the experiencING. The experience and the experiencer are conceptual. But the experiencing is the actual.

The experience of silence is no better than the experience of chatter. They are both experiences. The experiencing, which they happen on, has never been touched. The experience and the experiencer are like reflections in a mirror. The mirror is the experiencing essence, which allows experiences to happen. It doesn't matter what your experience is.

James: That's where I start to get tangled. I would definitely prefer to have nice experiences. It doesn't seem like it's "all the same" whether I have a good experience or bad experience or flat experience. I want the good ones. That plays on my mind a lot, because I seem to have continual flat experience—nothing great, nothing terrible. Just flat. And I wonder, "Shouldn't there be some nice experience happening?" I understand intellectually that that would simply be another experience but . . .

When you say that we are the experiencING, is there a connection or a feeling to that? Or is it simply what is?

Bob: It's just what is. It's that "cognizing emptiness," if you like. It's pure awareness, or pure intelligence energy. Things appear and things disappear. And if a preference comes, that appears on it also. You couldn't have preference without that essence.

James: Is it purely conceptual about this "screen" or the "experiencing that's always there"? Does it give you some solace that it's there? Do you *experience* it?

Bob: You don't "experience" it, but stay with the subtlety of it and you'll see that in there is the uncaused joy, the uncaused happiness, the uncaused love. . . .

   This is not the pairs of opposites—love/hate, joy/sadness, pleasure and pain. It's the *uncaused* love and compassion. It's subtly there on its own. As you're sitting with that subtleness, it'll become more pronounced. Sitting with your essence gives it a chance to become more pronounced. And even though the so-called pleasure or pain and things are going on, there will always be that underlying sense of well-being. Nisargadatta puts it in the negating way: "There's nothing wrong anymore."

James: This sounds like what often happens to me at night. I'll be in bed waiting to fall asleep, or I'll awaken in the middle of the night, and this experience occurs where all thoughts have abated, and I'm with a kind of dramatic silence or subtleness. It seems like an experience. But it's not, is it? It's just what is.

Bob: Exactly. It's pure isness.

James: One night, this was happening and I noticed my shoulder hurting. And, honest to God, it became clear to me that the sensation was in fact a concept—an idea in the mind! Then I realized all existence is an idea.
   Why doesn't this happen more often?

Bob: [*Laughing*] Well, give it a chance. Allow it! You'll see it's happening all the time.

James: The next day I called Kerry and told him I had had an experience where I saw that the world is a concept.

Bob: You translated it as "I had an experience," knowing full well there is no "I." You know that there is no entity there that's doing anything at all.

James: If I had that dramatic silence or subtleness all the time, I'd be saying what many of these spiritual authors often say: "I'm living in heaven! I'm living in paradise!"

Bob: I don't know about these people's concepts of paradise. But, take the Bible: Adam and Eve lived in the Garden of Eden, which was paradise. Then they ate of the tree of knowledge of good and evil. In other words, the reasoning, or the thinking, mind came in. It put them in the world of sin and suffering. Prior to that, without the conceptualizing, or "the knowledge of good and evil," without the conceptualizing mind, they were in what they called paradise.

James: If these authors are writing books about how great their experience is, maybe they're having more of that subtleness than others.

Bob: They can't have more. It's all one. You don't even have to use concepts to describe it. Just let it be. And if it expresses in different shapes, forms, and patterns—which you can call bliss or ecstasy or whatever—you've still got to have some kind of opposite in order to describe it. Haven't you? You can't know what bliss is unless you know the opposite of bliss.

James: So the feeling of subtleness or pure silence that I sometimes have at night is no better than what I'm feeling now?

Bob: Not really, no.

James: [*Laughing*] It sure feels better!

Bob: Yes, sure. Intelligence energy can express in all kinds of variety and diversity. Just the same as some pain you have that feels worse than something else.

James: So the important part is the understanding that neither silence or mental chatter are any better. It's ultimately all the same.

Bob: Yes. If it's just what is, then there's no preference, partiality, or comparison. "What is" means unaltered, uncorrected, unmodified. Just as it is. No stance taken anywhere.

The only thing that will seemingly modify it or alter it is another concept.

James: Interesting.

Bob: It's no big deal really. It's very simple.

James: The problem is, when you've been on a spiritual path for so long, you constantly hear people say, "This experience is better than some other experience. . . ." There's a tremendous amount of conditioning that makes you want that "special" experience.

Bob: But you see there is no ultimate experience. Is there? The people who are so fascinated by experiences go on experiencing, and everyone can come up with a bigger and better experience. The mind is limitless in the experiences that are possible. When I was with Muktananda at his ashram, everyone was having kundalini experiences—energy rushing up the spine—for years and years. But all experience is in the mind. The answer is not there.

Come back to the basic simplicity of presence awareness. And see the subtlety in that. It's the uncaused joy, the uncaused love, and the uncaused compassion that is there. It's causeless. It hasn't got any opposites where one quality is going to flip into its opposite. Those qualities are just there naturally.

I often use the story of my days of drinking. I was eating so badly and smoking, and my taste buds were completely stuffed up. When I stopped all that and got on a health kick, I started eating sunflower seeds and things like that. And they were tasteless. I couldn't taste anything. After a few weeks, the taste buds began cleaning up, and I could taste things. I could taste the sweetness and the flavors, which I had been quite ignorant about. That's like the subtleties of the uncaused essence that come up. There's a sense of well-being that everything's okay, no matter what's going on. We've cleared away all the gross sensations. We're not concerned with them so much. We're starting to take notice of what's *really* going on.

James: May I ask what it's like with your students? I've heard that some teachers of non-duality have students who have been coming to see them for years and years, and I wonder what that's about.

Bob: Some come along and get hold of the understanding pretty quick. Others hang around for years. Some come along and can't grasp it at all. Then they go away and come back ten years later. I see them again after they've tried everything else.

James: I see.

Barb told me she does Bowen Therapy. It sounds really good. She also mentioned Sound Therapy and said that can even help autistic children.

Bob: Yes, it's very good.

James: I feel bad for the parents of autistic kids. How terrible not to have normal emotional contact with your children. I guess there are all kinds of experiences in creation.

Bob: Life expresses in all its diversity.

James: Who's making all these things happen?

Bob: You see, in actuality nothing ever happens. It's only an ilusion, an appearance.

James: But is there any intelligence behind it?

Bob: Of course. Look at how the universe is working. It implies intelligence, doesn't it?

James: It does. What confuses me is that there is infinite intelligence to creation, but at the same time there is so much negativity, and I wonder who would make this.

Bob: There again, James, when we see the negative things, it's only seen from our little perspective as so-called human beings. If you went to the moon and looked back on earth, where would a human appear from that perspective? We would be smaller than the microbes crawling around on your face right now. Every time you rub your face thousands of microbes die.

James: Yes. But if you were the person that Saddam Hussein was dropping in a vat of hot oil, for instance, things would certainly look pretty negative.

Bob: Well, that emphasizes what I've said about the reference point. When Saddam kills someone, he's probably protecting his interests. From his perspective, it's a good thing. From ours, it isn't. It all depends on the reference point.

Years ago, when Barb and I had a farm, we had a canary in a cage. Every day I'd hang it outside and bring it in at night. One day, I forgot to bring it in. The next morning I went out and all that was left was a few feathers and a bit of blood on the bars of the cage. A friend came by and said, "The poor canary. What a terrible thing that happened to him."

I said, "Yes, but it wasn't so bad for the owl that ate it!" The owl had a good feed. It was easy to get, but the canary had to suffer.

We see this constantly, and we call it negative. Life is constantly living on life. There's no death as we know it. Out of death, more life comes. This body dies, and immediately millions of enzymes take over and start eating it. Then the maggots and insects come along. The body will quickly be destroyed. Even the residual that's left goes into the earth, and then a blade of grass will grow. Then something will eat the blade of grass, and something will eat the thing that ate the blade of grass, and so on. There'll be positive and negative in all of that. Life consistently lives on life. Death never occurs really. It only does so to a particular reference point.

James: And nothing ever really happened anyway, actually.

Bob: Patterns of energy appear and play around for a while, and patterns of energy disappear. Just the same as a ripple comes on the water, and then there might be a big wave, or a big billow. But it's always and ever only been water.

Nothing's really happened to the water. It's just taken some different shapes and forms, and then it disappears back into water again.

So, nothing's ever happened. And you are in actuality that no thing—that nothing. And you can never go any further than that, James. All the saviors—all the Buddhas and Christs and Ramana Maharshis, or anyone else you want to name—have never gone beyond that "no thing." And I know for certain that I am that no thing. Don't you?

James: Yes, absolutely. But, I don't know whether to call that nothing or everything.

Bob: Yes. That's right.

James: It's something that's ever present.

Bob: Yes. You can't go any further than that. You are That.

James: I see. Well, thanks so much, Bob. We're certainly looking forward to your visit.

CHAPTER TWO

Sailor Bob and Barb Arrive

*

July 14, 2004

By the time Bob and Barbara arrived on a warm Florida summer night, the excitement my wife Vashti and I felt was palpable. The thought of having a teacher in our house who was steeped in the understanding of non-duality, and whose search had ended some thirty years earlier, left me feeling that I must be dreaming. In the thirty years that I had been on the spiritual path and participated in many movements, I had never actually gotten really close to any of the gurus. And it had been a long time since I felt as comfortable with a spiritual teacher's motives as I did with Bob's. So many of the so-called enlightened masters of our age had, in my mind, proved fraudulent. The pattern was always the same. Teachers began their movements with nothing but apparent love and compassion, and in the end left behind trails of scandals, greed, sexual shenanigans, and abuse of power. Indeed, for nearly fifteen years during my thirties and forties, I had wondered whether enlightenment was genuine, and if so, what it was worth since so many of these so-called gurus had little or no integrity and occasionally behaved so badly.

The issue of poorly behaved gurus was more than a pet peeve of mine when Bob arrived. From the age of twenty-one to twenty-seven, I taught meditation and participated intensely in a spiritual movement. After becoming disillusioned with my teacher for what I considered offensive behavior, I left. It was a painful affair, but nothing a few years of grieving could not repair. The issue, however, kept re-surfacing as more and more world-famous gurus were coming under scrutiny. For varying misdeeds, many gurus were being "outed" by their disciples through word of mouth, books, magazine articles, and so forth. By the mid-1980s I had become famous in metaphysical circles for writing the first clear Hindu/Vedic astrology book for the Western world, and I began practicing astrology for spiritual seekers all over the globe. As such, I began hearing first-hand stories from people who had been disillusioned or abused by their gurus in one way or another. Of course, there are two sides to every story, and, of course, not everyone believes the disconcerting stories about famous gurus that have been making the rounds for so long. But I did and still do.

Much of why I began believing was because I kept hearing extremely similar descriptions about the same teachers from different clients. Every time I heard stories of Guru A, the tales regarded sexual misconduct. All the stories about Guru B centered around lying and financial shenanigans. Stories about Guru C consistently revolved around disciples being traumatized in the name of "ego busting," while the teacher allowed himself to be worshiped and adored like a god. And so my process went. Most important, perhaps, was that so many of the incidents I heard about came from people who had been members of the inner circle of the guru involved. I heard from secretaries, chauffeurs, lovers, and close friends of these leaders. It was difficult to disbelieve so many unrelated people who, as I far as I could tell, had no reason whatsoever to lie.

Because I no longer felt devoted to any teacher, my main concern was not about any particular guru. It was about the nature and the authenticity of liberation. Mind you, I greatly respected most of the teachers who had occasionally behaved so badly for having written tremendously inspiring and genuine spiritual texts. Not to mention giving out all kinds of spiritual techniques and methods that helped many thousands of seekers improve their lives! Most of these gurus were, in my mind, clearly enlightened. At the same time, the stories I heard were terrible, in terms of integrity and morals. Thus, I was faced with quite a conundrum.

Throughout my search, I had many times read and heard that a person's level of awareness cannot be judged by his or her behavior. But I had never fully understood or believed that fact. I believed, somehow, that liberated beings behaved more or less perfectly, with impeccable self-control, and certainly not selfishly. I also believed that liberated beings were free from desires and personal preferences. These were, I now see, serious misunderstandings. As long as one exists in manifest creation—as long as one has a body and mind—there will be preferences. This does not mean there will be attachment to desires and preferences.

But preferences will certainly continue to arise, sometimes to be acted upon and sometimes not—depending *apparently* on one's choices and decisions, while *in reality* depending only on the proceedings of the illusory world we inhabit! When Bob arrived, however, I did not know all this. At that time, I expected liberated beings to behave, at a minimum, with honesty and integrity. Thus, I was happy when, upon meeting Bob, I found he seemed to meet my expectations. I was pleased that, like some of the other non-dual authors I had read, Bob was thrilled with his freedom to be "nobody." He was more than content to let go of the seemingly universal human obsession to find meaning and significance and personal advancement in a world understood to be illusory in the first place. Most enjoyable for me were the stories Sailor Bob told about his teacher, Nisargadatta Maharaj, throwing people out of his room if they insisted on treating him with devotion and awe. Nisargadatta knew that non-duality is about oneness, not "I am realized; you are not."

I perceived Sailor Bob to be a simple man with no ambition other than to help others awaken to the knowledge he had learned from Nisargadatta thirty years earlier. He had created no scandals, no great wealth, no power trips, and I doubted that at age seventy-five he was about to start. His sincerity and compassion were obvious both from his writing and our phone conversations, which he often ended by saying, "Love ya." Further, as already mentioned, I had experienced a strong sense of resonance from the instant I began reading his book. So, when Bob finally arrived, I felt like thirty years of prayers had been answered. I could not believe my luck.

Although I was happy about having unlimited access to Bob for his Advaita understanding, I was more excited about meeting someone who had been *living* non-duality for so long. I could easily gain Bob's teachings from his book and CDs. What I really wanted was intimate interaction. I also wanted to judge Bob's authenticity for myself. I needed to know whether the wonderful teachings in his books and lectures matched the man. Truth be told, I was also curious to see whether Bob was going to exhibit any of the many special "powers" that are often promoted as being connected to self-realization. But, for now, sitting in the Tampa Airport at 9:30 on a Wednesday night, I just wanted to meet this very special couple and get them to a bed as fast as humanly possible. Their entire journey from Melbourne to California to Chicago to Florida, including all the hours spent in airports, totaled a full thirty-seven hours of travel. How grueling.

When Bob and Barb finally walked into view, they were tired but smiling. The four of us hugged, and when my eyes finally met Bob's for an extended moment, I was struck by a peaceful sort of emptiness. His expression was unusually present—right here, right now. It was as if he was unaffected by the past hurts, complexes, opinions, positions, and stances that make up the auras of most human beings. Of course, I could have been projecting all of this. But I wasn't the only one with this reaction. In the next five weeks many commented on Bob's peaceful and free appearance. I was immediately impressed that Bob appeared to be living what he had spoken of in his book and lectures.

Early the next morning, our private talks began. Bob established a habit of emerging from the cottage around 6:30 or 7:00 a.m. and sitting on our back-yard deck under the fruit trees. I joined him there the first few mornings. Foremost on my mind was a problem that had plagued me for more years than I can remember. Why was life so badly designed? Who created a world where torture was possible? How could we live our lives enjoyably, knowing that death is right around the corner? How could we sleep well at night knowing that on any given day thousands of Africans are being murdered, having limbs hacked off, and/or starving to death? How could Saddam Hussein drop people in boiling oil or tie them down and send them head first into huge wood-cutting machines? What kind of creator would make such an existence, and why would He/She/It do such a dastardly thing?

These questions had haunted me for so long that by now I was unaware of how much damage they were doing to my psyche and energy level. For many years these questions had arisen nearly every night while I was waiting to fall asleep. And they had gotten worse since the Iraq War, which was now looking like the beginning of World War III.

Of course, many people simply adopt a selfish attitude and get along fine as long as they are not the ones being murdered, tortured, and so on. But I was not built that way. As long as anyone is suffering, I could not see how I was supposed to live happily ever after. Compassion aside, I always knew that what happened to others could just as easily happen to

"Sailor" Bob Adamson at a Longboat Key beach

Bob, Vashti, and Bob's wife, Barbara, at The Colony Restaurant

The Braha family—Vashti, Julian, and James—after one of Bob's talks

Bob and Dell, during a morning meeting

Emmett, Bob, and Kerry

Sailor Bob

Emmett, Bob, James, and Barbara

A father and son who came from Ft. Lauderdale to hear Bob speak

Kerry and Julian

The Adamsons and the Brahas at the beach

Sailor Bob

Vashti, James, Bob, and Barb in S. Fla. with James's sister-in-law, Liz Karabatsos, after two grueling days of hurricane evacuation

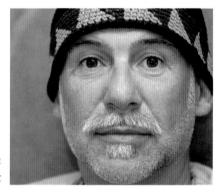

Dell, who kept Bob and Barb fit with Trager sessions twice a week

Vashti, Anne Feely (of Chapter 5), and Judy Seeger (of Chapter 3) in our living room

Bob and James

me. Thus, in 2004, with world affairs going downhill at breakneck speed, my dilemma was only getting worse. I hoped Sailor Bob could provide some answers.

After discussing the issue with him, I felt so much relief it seemed as if a hundred pounds had been lifted off my back. The morning after we spoke, Bob looked at me and said, "James, your whole countenance has changed."

I explained that our previous day's talk had had a very liberating effect, and I felt freer and more energetic. I explained that the dilemma had been with me for at least ten or fifteen years and that the relief was huge, actually life altering.

Bob helped me to see that all suffering other than physical pain (and even that to some extent) is due to mental activity predicated on duality and the false "me." Whenever suffering happens, there is always a concern about something in the past or future. In my case, this was especially true. I was perpetually contemplating my own death and its meaning, as well as the existence of torture. Because, if others were being murdered, raped, and tortured, that possibility existed for me. These were all mental worries based on future events, some that were possible and one that was certain: death. I now saw clearly that when such occurrences happen, they do so *in the present,* and our reactions at such time will be natural. If there is violence or danger, we will try to get out of the way. Our adrenalin will be racing, and our awareness will be remarkably in the moment—as anyone who has experienced a car accident (assuming it was not from behind) or violent attack can verify. When death comes, we will experience the event as everyone who has lived before us has also done. The same is true of any violent occurrence—the experience itself is not the main part of the problem. It is the mental anguish that comes before and/or after any so-called horrific event that is so distressing. But, for one who does not believe he or she is an individual, where is the problem?

Of course, there is the concern of physical pain, which does hurt in the present, and which is exacerbated by thoughts of fear. All human beings, no matter who they are, must endure a certain amount of physical hurt while in a human body. And for one who believes he or she is an individual, the experience is terrible because of the sense that "the pain is happening to me." On the other hand, for someone who has seen the reference point as false, pain is happening—pain is arising—but it is arising to no one. There is a significant difference. I am reminded of my one and only experience with a kidney stone, many years ago. For about thirty or forty minutes, I was bearing the agony without too much commotion. Pain was happening and I was handling it. After a certain point, however, I distinctly remember thinking, "I've been in pain so long. I can't keep this up forever." And that is when the suffering began. That is, not coincidentally, when I started vomiting. The thought of this severe pain continuing, for God knows how long, to a "me" was too much to bear.

Bob explained that when there is suffering, there is always a person focused on the mind, rather than the Now. There is always someone reflecting on a "me" and an "other." And there is always someone approaching life as if he or she is the center of the universe. In other words, there is always that damned reference point! I had read Bob's book *What's Wrong With Right Now Unless You Think About It?* several times and somehow understood it in relation to everything but my own anxiety about death and worldly horrors.

Right here, right now, I am fine. It's true that people are being murdered and tortured as I write. But, right here, right now, nothing is wrong. In the twentieth century alone, over a hundred million people have lost their lives in wars and holocausts, many in the most horrific ways. Yet the world is still here, and we are still having fun. There is plenty of beauty, joy, creativity, and happiness. How can this be? It can be because what happens in the world affects nothing and no one. The world is only an appearance, an illusion—like a reflection in a mirror. It is seen, but it has no real substance or lasting nature. If creation actually had an independent nature, wars and massive death would perhaps be devastating. But it does not. And, wars and death are constant. Clearly, the physical world is not who we are, and it is nothing to worry about. It is here only for enjoyment. And enjoyment, whether we like it or not, cannot exist without its counterpart—suffering.

As Bob often points out, nature resists nothing. Seasons come and go, night follows day, tides ebb and flow, storms rage and dissipate, volcanoes erupt, earthquakes change the landscape, and life continues perfectly. Only when we live life judging every moment of every day from the point of view of a mind-created reference point, do we start resisting—and therefore suffering.

This does not mean that we cannot strive to make the world a better place. Nor does it mean that we should repress desires to help out socially, if the spirit moves us. As long as we are alive, we are engaged in action. Inaction is impossible. Even reclusive yogis are engaged in meditation, contemplation, yoga, and/or caring for their bodies. Some seekers believe that when a person is enlightened, or awakened, he or she is inactive and has no desires. Nonsense. As long as there is a human form, there will be desires and preferences. But, to one who has seen the reference point as false, desires are of precious little significance and generate no suffering because they have nowhere to "take hold." If a person has seen through the false "me," desires arise but they dissipate quickly (sometimes almost instantaneously) because they have nowhere to attach themselves. Without energy, how can anything persist?

While discussing my fears of death and worldly violence, I was, of course, already aware that the universe is an illusion. But I was also aware that we *experience* the world as real. What I eventually came to realize was the profound power that results from understanding non-duality—our true nature. Although the world certainly seems real, the only thing we can know for sure is that we are; we cannot say we don't exist. The one and only constant in our life is presence awareness. *The present moment that is happening, right here, right now, and has been happening, right here, right now, for as long as memory serves is our reprieve.* It is that presence awareness, which we cannot deny and which is who we actually are, that reveals that we were never born and will never die. Understanding this, we are free, we are fearless, we are forever.

Successfully solving my dilemma was largely due to my trust in Sailor Bob (in the world of appearance, that is, since there is ultimately no cause of anything). After all, of what use would the entire preceding explanation be unless it is actually possible to live free, or relatively free, of the false reference point? In the years I had been studying non-duality, I had at times felt free of the false "me," while other times not at all—especially when contemplating death, politics, war, and torture.

Fortunately, I now had a living example of non-duality right in front of my eyes. And while his accomplishment may seem extraordinary, Sailor Bob is not. He is an ordinary, humble man who, after hearing Nisargadatta's teaching thirty years ago, simply stopped believing in a reference point. Bob avoids taking personal positions because he has seen that all positions and reference points are invalid. He sees like anyone else, but avoids labeling and judging. He feels, but fully understands that the feelings are not "his."

Seeing Bob live non-duality was immensely helpful in allowing me to stop judging war, violence, and death and to drop my own resistance to what is, right here, right now. It also didn't hurt that Bob was as compassionate as anyone I had ever met, yet was not suffering at all over worldly conditions. When we discussed the war in Iraq, he noted that all throughout the ages civilizations had come and gone, risen and fallen. He noted that oftentimes the bad guys toppled the good guys. Like anyone else, he had his own perceptions and viewpoints about the current war, but he expressed no intensity about it. As far as I could see, it looked like a movie to him. He felt bad for the people fighting and dying and would have preferred peace, but the possibility of a world war did not appear to disturb him. Circumstances, whatever they are, are just what is. Clearly, no one is dying because no one was ever born. Only bodies and minds appear to be born and die, but they are not who we are. Why suffer? Why resist? If killers are approaching, of course, run like hell. But, worrying and conceptualizing about some future calamity is simply wasted time and energy.

Although I would be probing and judging from the day Bob arrived until the day he left just how genuinely free he was of a "me," I was quickly impressed. Aside from the fact that at age seventy-five he was brimming with energy the day after traveling thirty-seven hours, he was simply so present. He never seemed to get "stuck" in anything, nor did he appear to react from past conditioning. So, when Bob explained that a person could be free from suffering even in the midst of tragedy as long as he or she stayed away from a reference point, I believed him and was able to grasp his reasoning.

There was also a phenomenon that occurred in Bob's presence that had a strong impact on me. It was something many of my friends also experienced. Whenever Bob spoke of being free of a reference point and looked me in the eye, I experienced what he was describing. I don't mean bliss or ecstasy or anything supernatural. I just mean that his freedom from a reference point was remarkably contagious. When he discussed presence awareness and steering clear of a reference point, all the clouds and distractions and "rubbish" that was usually in my awareness disappeared. When I mentioned this to Bob, after being aware of it for a week or so, he said he had heard the same thing from his students in Australia.

The pronounced appreciation of presence awareness that occurred after being in Bob's presence for many days was powerful. My two closest friends, who came to town about one week after Bob arrived, also noticed this. Bob and Barb were here for five weeks, but only during the final three weeks were the talks publicized. The first two weeks were reserved for rest and vacation. Early on, however, we discovered that speaking on non-duality, from early morning till late at night, seemed to be Bob's greatest pleasure. So for one full week, my friends Kerry and Emmett and Dell and myself would sit in my living room and bask in the knowledge. My wife, Vashti, who was often occupied with our five-year-old son, would drift in and out of the talks or listen from the kitchen whenever possible. We were all thrilled, and we all had the same reaction: *Seeking is over. I will never be the same again.*

When the week was up, however, and Kerry went back to Connecticut, he called a few days later to warn me: "James, there is a power source in your house. What you're feeling is real, and we'll definitely never be the same again. But I'm warning you. Bob is a power source."

What Kerry was saying was that being close to someone who had lived in such freedom for so long was having an effect on us, and we would be different when no longer in his presence. The habits of a lifetime are not easily dropped, and after a few days at home Kerry watched as his reference point reared its ugly head a few times. It reminded me of the story Sailor Bob tells of his awakening. In Bombay during the mid-1970s, Bob was visiting Nisargadatta's tiny flat on a regular basis to hear the talks on non-duality. One particular day, the teachings had a dramatic impact, and Bob suddenly understood that freedom cannot be gained from the mind or from experiences. Experiences, such as bliss, ecstasy, kundalini energy, and so on, no matter how great, will surely go just as they came. Freedom results not from any peak experience, but from understanding that who we are is presence awareness, that what we are seeking we already are, and, above all, that the reference point we have been creating is a phantom in the mind.

When Bob finally understood his teacher's message, he dropped the reference point and was left basking in presence awareness. But, as soon as he left Nisargadatta's house, horror of horrors, the mind and his false "me" came right back! Now, however, he knew that the reference point was a sham, and he could never believe in it again. From that day onward, whenever it arose, he simply reminded himself of its false nature and put no further energy into it. Thirty years later, Bob is a walking expression of freedom.

My point, make no mistake, is not to deify Bob (who wouldn't stand for it if I did), but to convey the enormous power that results from understanding. In 1976, when Bob finally grasped Nisargadatta's teachings, he was no different from any of the seekers now coming to my house to hear him. He did not suddenly break into an altered state of consciousness, where all thoughts ceased and bliss was rampant. He simply saw the truth of his real being. And when he fell back into old habits, he gave them no energy, which allowed them to fall away naturally—a phenomenon much like that of a fan that, once turned off, continues whirling some extra seconds or minutes until it runs out of energy (some teachers call this a "deconditioning" process).

There is a widespread belief among seekers, unfortunately promoted by many gurus, that enlightenment is a sudden, peak *experience* which once present can never leave. It is a terrible belief that sabotages the seeker from the very start. For one thing, nature is nothing if not diverse. Buddha gained his liberation when, after years and years of intense yoga and meditation, he finally gave up—and then freedom dawned. Others have awakened with very little effort, and some with none at all! There are many cases of liberation happening to people who had no knowledge of spiritual subjects or even the term "enlightenment." Some awaken gradually, some instantaneously. There are no rules. This is why, perhaps, when Nisargadatta occasionally encountered awakened men and women during his daily talks, he asked whether their apparent process had been sudden or gradual.

Despite what so many believe, awakening is not an experience. If all a person encounters is a wonderful occurrence of unity, God, peace, bliss, white light, kundalini energy rushing up the spine, and so on, the experience can and will eventually leave. It occurred in apparent time, it will leave in apparent time. At which point, the unfortunate seeker is left to chase the memory of an apparent past event, very likely until he or she dies. It is the *understanding* of one's infinite, non-dual nature that is crucial, not some beautiful experience. Certainly, a unifying or God-like experience may be an *apparent* catalyst for understanding to dawn. But that is merely an appearance. Experience does not cause understanding. There is no actual causation in the world of appearance. Nothing in a creation lacking an independent nature can be the cause of anything. Therefore, while a fantastic so-called spiritual experience may *appear* to cause a seeker's awakening or understanding, this cannot and should not be expected. If this is not instantly obvious, try asking the many thousands of today's seekers who have enjoyed so many of these experiences over and over, only to be left high and dry, never reaching their goal. Millions of seekers over the ages have practiced yoga, meditation, and arduous spiritual techniques, yet only a rare few have found liberation. Many, perhaps most, became seekers because of some dramatic spiritual experience that caught their attention by pointing them toward their true nature. Unfortunately, or should I say *damned* unfortunately, there simply is no real connection between experience and awakening.

Bear in mind that all those who have claimed to have had their lives transformed by enlightenment, or liberation, have consistently mentioned two salient points. One: Even after liberation, positive and negative emotions continue to occur, as do pleasant and unpleasant circumstances. Two: Once awakened, they realized that they had always been free. *They had been free even when they did not feel unity and bliss and peace and tremendous energy and so on.* They had been free even when they felt lousy and depressed. They had been free even when they were chasing liberation and thought they would never reach the "prize"!

Why were they free? They were free because, even though they had believed themselves to be in bondage and had believed there was a "me" who needed liberating, what they had really been was exactly what they were now—no thing, presence awareness, pure intelligence energy, and so on. They had been free in the apparent past. They were free now.

Most importantly, once the self-proclaimed liberated beings under-stood their true nature, experience became irrelevant. Once they understood their true nature, how they felt and whatever was experienced became entirely unimportant. Enlightenment is not an experience, no matter how many teachers promote it that way, and no matter how many people believe it. Awakening is not a description of feeling good or vast or infinite, even though feeling good and vast and infinite almost certainly will happen more often after awakening (when one stops resisting, good happens). Liberation is not about anything changeable. If it were, everyone on earth would have stopped seeking eons ago, since the only inevitable reality of our illusory lives is change!

This may shed light on why genuine gurus feel no compulsion to enlighten or change anyone. Out of compassion alone, they make their knowledge available. They do not force it on others, and they are totally unmoved whether anyone grasps their teachings or not. Some even leave society to lead hermit lives.

Despite what many believe, liberation never happens to any person, because liberation is the *falling away* (or seeing through) of individuality, and the simultaneous realization of one's infinite nature. Therefore, "you" and "I" will never "attain enlightenment" because it is the very idea of a "you" and a "me" that drops off. Further, whatever concept one has in the mind about liberation must be "false as hell," as Shakespeare's Othello would say. The concept of liberation is necessarily false because what we truly are is consciousness, pure intelligence energy, presence awareness—and this is "no thing." And "no thing" cannot be grasped by thoughts or concepts because thoughts and concepts are vibrations, or patterns of energy. They are "apparent" things. And a thing cannot fathom no thing. Any thought or concept one has of the nature of liberation is a phantom, pure and simple. Because it is infinite and unbounded, presence awareness can only be defined by what it is not! This is why Advaitan teachers tell seekers to avoid like the plague any guru who gives you something. Seek out only those who help you to strip away. And note that this prohibition includes those who give out *techniques* designed to strip away. This is because once a person begins practicing spiritual techniques, there is generally no end in sight. Those who practice techniques in order to find presence awareness, *which exists in plain sight right here, right now*, are nearly always doomed to spend their entire lives seeking. One need only note the dismal success rates within spiritual movements.

When teachers give credibility to the claim "At one time I was in bondage, and now I am free," time is implied, and time does not exist. Time "apparently" exists, but that is merely because of a memory—a concept in the mind. No one ever experiences anything except in the present moment. Even on Alpha Centurion, light years away, it is right now. Liberation is not something to be gained. It is simply something to be appreciated and acknowledged right here, right now. Presence awareness, or unboundedness, which is who we are, is ever present. There never was a time when it was not. It cannot be gained. It cannot be lost. As Sailor Bob would say, "Full stop."

There are some seekers who simply love chasing enlightenment. Such seekers cherish meditation and adore altered states of consciousness and believe they lead to ultimate freedom. Certainly, there is nothing wrong with living a life of continual seeking. In the world of appearance, no life is any better or intrinsically different than any other. Those who love the path more than the goal (consciously or unconsciously) and wish to keep their apparent search toward enlightenment going often refer to what they call "the final understanding." They believe that, until the mind-created reference point, or false "me," has *completely* disappeared, awakening is still a goal to be enjoyed somewhere in the future (as if there were such a thing!). This philosophy or belief, make no mistake, is the polar opposite of non-dual teachings. If what I am saying seems paradoxical, it is. Of course, I was initially a seeker, and, of course, I went so far as to bring Sailor Bob to America so I could get his teaching. But, within the teachings of non-duality, one learns to *stop the search* in order to find one's real self. In my very first phone conversation with Bob I grasped the fact that what we are seeking, we already are, and that the search itself is the problem. If who we are is consciousness, or awareness, or no thing, there is nothing to do but *be* that consciousness. Consciousness is not actually something to be found. It is who we are. Neither can consciousness be touched. It is limitless and unbounded.

Non-duality is the understanding of the inherent oneness of all existence. The very idea that some special people are It or have got It, and others are not It or have not got It, is a travesty cultivated by apparent individuals still believing in their own false reference point. Of course, I also originally believed Bob had It and I didn't. That's what searching is all about. But Bob disabused me of that error quickly. Whether or not one realizes one is presence awareness is actually irrelevant. We are all It, know it or not—even like it or not! Knowing our immortality does not make us *essentially* different from one who does not know it. But obviously, one who understands his or her true nature is relieved of a great deal of psychological suffering. There is also, generally, a pronounced ease and grace to life. But living a life of well-being does not make a person intrinsically different from one who does not. There is no "final understanding." There are only different apparent experiences in a world that only appears to exist. A person who experiences ecstasy or bliss twenty-four hours a day for twenty straight years, if such a thing is possible, is no more oneness than a person who suffers massively. One who appears constantly stuck in his or her false reference point is no less presence awareness than an enlightened yogi meditating high in the Himalayan mountains.

For those who still cling to the idea that awakening is some kind of dramatic experience, consider the following passage from *I Am That* by Nisargadatta Maharaj:

> Your expectation of something unique and dramatic, of some wonderful explosion, is merely hindering and delaying your self-realization. You are not to expect an explosion, for the explosion has already happened—at the moment you were born, when you realized yourself as being-knowing-feeling. There is only one mistake you are making. You take the inner for the outer and the outer for the inner. What is in you, you take to be outside you and what is outside you take to be in you. The mind and feelings are external, but you take them to be internal. You believe the world to be objective, while it is entirely

a projection of your psyche. That is the basic confusion and no new explosion will set it right. You have to think yourself out of it. There is no other way."

What a statement, to anyone who believes liberation is an experience: "You have to think yourself out of it. There is no other way." Clearly, if the conditioning of the mind brought apparent duality into our lives, then only a deconditioning process would allow us to remember our oneness!

One can only guess why certain memories remain with us, while so many disappear entirely. For some reason, one of my earliest memories is of a time when I was actually constructing my identity. As I was trying to piece together my place within my family, I distinctly remember thinking, "I am James. I am the small and cute one." Whatever other attributes my family heaped upon me, I cannot recall over fifty years later. But the process of initially constructing who James was, based on mental concepts, I have for some reason never forgotten.

Once again, however, I have gone beyond my story. It was early morning on July fifteenth, when I noticed Bob sitting motionless on a chair in my back yard. My schedule was clear for the next five weeks—my first long vacation in twenty years—and I had warned Bob that I wasn't going to let him off easy. I had told him via e-mail that I intended to press him hard for his knowledge. I said it jokingly, but there was plenty of truth to the statement. After years of reading books on non-duality, there was much I understood. But there was also much I did not. More than anything, a sense of certainty was missing. It was the certainty I was after, which I hoped would help end the continual habit of approaching life through the false self center—the mind-created "me." Between his book, the talks on his CDs, and our phone conversations, Bob had already said everything that needed saying. But, like so many seekers, I still had lots of doubts. My understanding felt intellectual, rather than experiential—something many students of Advaita complain about. Bob had already displayed incredible patience and compassion in our phone conversations, and I was more grateful for that than I can possibly express. I knew that in the next several days I would be pressing him on many questions he had already answered for me in detail, and more than once. With some issues, I simply needed repetition—lots of it.

With others, I needed to see his face, to see that he believed what he was saying and knew from experience whereof he spoke. I wanted his *wisdom*, not his concepts. Armed with a tiny cassette recorder and a mass of determination, I made my way toward dear Sailor Bob.

*

July 15 – Day 1

James: You say that the reference point is false. Can't we say that the mind, or thoughts, are the reference point?

Bob: Yes, but thought has no substance; you can't grasp a thought—it has no independent nature. Can you have a thought without awareness? Is a thought independent?

James: No.

Bob: So, the thought is believed to be the reference point because we've never questioned it. As soon as that "I" thought comes upon a little child, he believes "this is what I am." He goes through his reasoning, and if he wasn't good at school that day, he thinks, "I'm not good enough," or "I'm not smart enough." He adds all these thoughts to form that mental picture. But that "I" thought on its own can't be grasped. It's nothing. The reference point, or self center, is just a bunch of images. It's got no independent nature. We're being driven by a phantom.

James: Ever since I've been studying Advaita, I've been wondering this: If it's not us doing things, who's doing it? We're being lived, right? Who's living us?

Bob: [*Laughing*] James . . . who wants to know? That's your false self center again. That's the ego again, thinking you and I are so great that we're doing the thinking, or something "out there" is doing the thinking.

In nature, there's just *one* movement of energy!

James: Did something create all this existence?

Bob: It isn't created; it's transient. As our reference point, we think of a life of billions of years, and we can't *conceptualize* it. But nothing's ever been created.

James: So, this conversation is not happening?

Bob: Well, it's happening in the appearance. If a cloud comes along, is it attached to the sky?

James: No.

Bob: Well, that's just like the concepts that come into your mind. What happens to the cloud in the sky? It comes along and then blows away. Use the metaphor of "space-like awareness." It's like space, empty. But, instead of being empty in a void, like space, it's *"cognizing emptiness."* It has that capacity of knowing. It's imbued with a natural intelligence—not like the intellect that knows this and that. But pure intelligence, the same intelligence that is functioning in the universe, is keeping the stars in orbit and causing the wind to blow and all that. The pure intelligence is making the trees grow, and it's beating your heart and growing your fingernails; it's doing all those things right now. It's causing your thoughts to happen. But that's just like clouds in the sky, not attached anywhere. It just comes and then moves on. The energy is constantly vibrating.

James: I have this concept that there is this consciousness, or oneness.

Bob: Yes, you have a *concept*.

James: From this oneness sprang the appearance, right? That makes consciousness the creator, no?

Bob: Just take the ocean and the waves. On the ocean, a ripple or a wave appears. The wave may rise and splash or spray, but, what is it? It's only water. It's never been anything other than water—appearing as difference.

James: Okay, so what's happening now between you and me is consciousness appearing as a conversation.

Bob: Don't try to conceptualize consciousness. That's only a label we put on it. It's emptiness that has the capacity of knowing. I don't mean knowing this or that, or the intellect. But knowing that you *are* right now. That's prior to thought. Just that pure knowing, which you can't negate.

James: So, it's emptiness that is capable of knowing?

Bob: It's not one that is capable of something. The two are actually one and the same. "Cognizing emptiness" or "emptiness cognizing." That's all.

James: What is cognizing?

Bob: Just seeing.

James: So, it's just cognizing. There's no intelligence behind it?

Bob: Well, you can say that cognizing is intelligence. Knowing is intelligence. Not the knower and the known, but pure knowing. So it's the activity of knowing.

Right now, that knowing that you are is with you, isn't it?

James: Yes.

Bob: Now, knowing is not the knower or the known. It's actually what is happening now: knowING. So, it's going on right now. That knowing is an activity, and activity is energy. So, pure intelligence energy is activity of knowing. That's all it is. The world appears and disappears in that knowingness. The knowingness is just purely knowing. The appearance and disappearance can only be conceptualized from a reference point—from an erroneous belief! For example, take seeing. You're seeing right now. Then the thought comes up, "I see." But the actual seeing was happening before the thought. With the thought, you've created a pseudo-seer. When you say, "I see the tree," you've created a pseudo-object—a subject and object in form. But can there be a seer or a seen without seeING?

James: No.

Bob: Those are just labels that we attach. Like the thinker and the thought. Always remember what Nisargadatta said, "You try to grasp it with a concept and you fail. And you are bound to fail, because you can never grasp it with a concept." You must stop trying to conceptualize everything.

James: So everything is just happening?

Bob: Exactly. It's all happening by itself, as itself. And nothing is happening!

James: How do you explain that nothing is happening?

Bob: Using the metaphor of space-like awareness, all this manifestation is the content of space. There's nothing you can think of that's outside of space. So the appearance is the content of space. If space is nothing, can something come from nothing?

James: Why does it feel so real?

Bob: [*Laughing*] To *who*?

James: To my thoughts.

Bob: Yes, and the thoughts are part of the appearance also! In essence, the appearance is real because it is made of presence awareness, which is real. Look at how a mirage appears real. Or the blue color of the sea. Within intelligence energy, patterns are forming and displaying as this manifestation.

James: For so many years, I've wondered how there could be a God that could allow all the horrible wars and torture and so on. But if the manifestation is an appearance, none of this is really happening. Right? Nothing is tragic, correct?

Bob: That's right. The people were never born, and they can never die. They're just patterns of energy. They appear, play around for a while, and then disappear. In fact, they're still just the one intelligence energy. It's never changed.

James: I have a question about spiritual experiences. Sometimes, usually late at night in bed, I suddenly feel infinite or vast—without any boundaries or limitations. The next day, I'll tell my wife or my friend Kerry, "I had an experience." But, actually, what has happened is that the feelings and thoughts that are usually going on have disappeared. The unboundedness I sometimes experience at night is actually always present, isn't it.

Bob: Yes, but as soon as you labeled it an experience, then you've "taken delivery" of it from the reference point.

James: Yes, I understand that.

Bob: What happened was just experiencING, which the experience and the experiencer appear on. If your senses are wide open, and you're not labeling everything, then you're just seeing what is. And you'll see the wonderful, magical display of it all, appearing and disappearing, without attributing it to a "me."

James: Does life appear particularly interesting to you?

Bob: Again, to be interesting or boring, it has to be from a reference point. Sometimes there are periods of silence, even long periods; other times the chatter can be going on. I don't prefer either one. The so-called silence that seekers talk about, I couldn't care less about. Any more than I care about the chatter. They're both experiences. I am that in which the experience takes place. And that's constantly and always ever been the same. It is no thing. It's no use trying to grasp it as a thing; it contains all things.

James: Now, when you make that statement, like Nisargadatta did, that you are that in which everything takes place, I understand it. But I can't say that about myself. I am constantly taking delivery of stuff. You say you don't care whether there are lots of thoughts or no thoughts. I can't do that.

Bob: If I took delivery of the reference point, it would be the same. I'd be thinking, "I shouldn't have done this," or "I shouldn't have said that." But I've seen through the reference point. I've seen clearly. So, what comes up, comes up. That's what I mean when I say, "I couldn't care less." It's not me. It's just that there's no preference, there's no partiality, no comparison. It's just what is: unaltered, unmodified, uncorrected. The Buddhists talk about "what is." Just the seeing—the actual functioning. The only thing you'll ever alter, modify, or correct is a thought.

James: So, we're going to have thoughts. The point is not to take delivery of them.

Bob: Yes, and there's no one to *not* take delivery of them. Just seeing and recognizing.

James: Yes, well, you can say all this and write the books, and people will hear you and say, "Well, Sailor Bob can do that, and that's great for him. But I can't do that." It seems to me that the significant part is conviction. I understand what you're saying, but I don't yet have the full conviction. . . .

Bob: *Who* doesn't have the conviction? You've got that concept of you, and so you think things should be different. You're seeing right now?

You're hearing right now? That knowingness that you are is with you now, right? You can't negate that.

James: Right.

Bob: So, what's this rubbish about not having the conviction? You go off on some conceptual thing. . . .

James: Right, but why don't you go off on some conceptual thing?

Bob: Because I've seen that the reference point is false. Do you see what you're doing? I'm pointing it out to you, and you're going into the ifs and the buts and all. You're going into the future. You move into time again. Time is a mental concept. You move into a so-called imaginary future. Or you go back into the past. But you don't live in the future and the past. Everything happens in the Now. It's like a cloud over the sun. It's blocking out the knowingness of the Now. These ideas that "I don't have this" or "I'll get the conviction in the future" are keeping you away from it.

James: So it's right here, right now?

Bob: Yes, it's immediate. There's nowhere to go.

James: Well, yesterday I got really angry at someone. A lady wrote me a letter that really bothered me.

Bob: That was yesterday, never mind the past. . . .

James: When it happened, I thought to myself, "Wait a minute; there is no James." And still the upset remained.

Bob: Yes, because when you say, "There is no me," that's become a reference point. You might have seen there's no James last week or last month or yesterday. But that's dead, like all your other thoughts. You have to see it right now. Instead of simply saying, "There's no me," have a look. Investigate, in the Now. Look and see if you can find a self center or a "me."

James: Well, at the time I got upset, I stopped and said to myself, "Who am I? I am presence awareness." That was clear to me. And still upsetting thoughts continued.

Bob: But you were putting the concept "I'm presence awareness" on it. Without that concept, it's simply "I am." Full stop.

James: I tried being aware of the present moment. I looked around the room without labeling anything—just being aware. . . .

Bob: Without labeling anything, you just take in the whole thing. You notice that seeing is happening spontaneously, hearing is happening spontaneously, immediately.

James: Well, in any case, I still have to answer her letter.

Bob: That's fine. Just do what you have to do. Let happen whatever happens. You might write to her while you're pissed off. Or you might tell her off or whatever. But there's no "you" that's doing any of that. Whatever occurs is just the way it happens.

James: I see. Can we talk about this non-doer issue? That's very conceptual for me.

Bob: Well, I'll show you. You're seeing right now, aren't you?

James: Yes.

Bob: You're hearing right now. Is your eye saying to you, "I see"? Is your ear saying to you, "I hear"?

James: No.

Bob: So the thought comes up to translate "I see" and "I hear." But can that thought "I see"—can it see? And can the thought "I hear"—can it hear?

James: You're telling me something that I've read in your book, or heard you say, twenty times. . . .

Bob: Well, listen to me right now. Can the thought "I see"—can it see?

James: No. The thought is garbage. It's just a translation.

Bob: So the thought has *no power whatsoever*.

James: If the thought has no power, then there is no doer?

Bob: The thought "I am aware"—is that the awareness?

James: No, of course not.

Bob: The thought "I choose"—is that the choice maker? The thought "I think"—is that the thinker?

James: So, if the thought has no power, there is simply no doer?

Bob: Of course not. You see, thought has been so closely aligned to that intelligence. But, in fact, all it does is translate. It translates into words and labels that we communicate with. *Thought is so closely aligned to pure intelligence energy that it's come to believe that it is the pure intelligence energy.* Now, when you see that the mind and the thoughts have no power, do you fall apart? Do you disappear?

James: No.

Bob: You realize that the living is going on quite effortlessly, without thinking. What's wrong with right now, unless you think about it? You pause from thinking for a moment, and you still haven't fallen apart. You're still hearing, seeing, tasting, and life is still going on. You're not relying on the thinking.

James: Yes. Bob, you have students who have been coming to you for years. What's their story? Why don't they eventually "full stop?"

Bob: Well, they don't. . . . The same as you're going on right now. [*Laughter*] But, there are also those who come along and see it right away.

James: So far, there is no "full stop" for me. My mind keeps going on and questioning. The mind keeps wanting a reference point.

Bob: You're trying to stop the mind. But once you see it's rubbish, just like the mirage on the road, you're not bound by it.

James: Well, something is happening. Yesterday, I had that annoying letter from that lady, and I knew that my reaction was nonsense. So it only bothered me for an hour or so, and then it was gone. A few years ago, it would have upset me all day long, maybe longer. It's gotten better.

Bob: Yes, it will.

James: But I don't like that "it will" part. That's in the future.

Bob: That's true. But you will drop it quicker. The habit pattern is to see everything from a reference point. You've done that not once or twice, but constantly—day in and day out for all your life. We've hypnotized ourselves. But when you've questioned it and seen the falseness of it, you can no longer believe in it. Just like you can no longer believe there's any water in a mirage.

James: Earlier I asked you if you find life exciting or boring. I asked because it seems like sometimes, when I am remarkably free of the reference point, everything suddenly appears new and fresh and amazing. Do you have judgments about the way life looks?

Bob: I don't have judgments, but judgments come up.

James: What do you do with them?

Bob: They're not mine. Who's to take delivery of them. They come up and then they go. The whole pattern just goes on.

James: So, even the people who appear to take delivery of thoughts, they're not really taking delivery—they're just appearing to take delivery. Right?

Bob: Yes.

James: So the people who are suffering massively are really no different from us. It's insignificant whether anyone awakens or not. You know, it's hard for me to grasp sometimes. It reminds me of an expression my father used to say: "It doesn't go through my head."

Bob: *Don't try to conceptualize it.* Stay in the experiencING and then you'll enjoy it.

James: Bob, I *love* the thinking process, and that makes me want to conceptualize everything. Look at the magnificence of creation: math, science, art, millions of creatures, open-heart surgery, and so on. I always want to know who made existence. And the creation isn't even real!

Bob: It's like a reflection in a mirror. What's making all these reflections? Why is this reflection better than the other one? [*Laughing*]

James: Life is so miraculous. There are millions of cells in the body constantly replacing themselves. Do you ever wonder how or why?

Bob: The hows and the whys are finished. Those would be movements *away* from it.

James: Because everything's already happened?

Bob: Just be with the happening, and little insights will come up. And you'll get answers that are satisfying.

James: When you had the experience with Nisargadatta where you suddenly understood what he was saying. . . .

Bob: I understood him, and I realized, "I'll never be trapped in the mind again." Then I walked out the door, and I was back in it! [*Laughter*] But it was never the same again. Of course, sooner or later the reference point would come up again, but then I'd realize, "Wait a minute; this is the same old nonsense," and I'd see through it. Sometimes, like you said, it would hang around a few hours or a few days, and then it's gone.

James: When did you see Nisargadatta?

Bob: In 1976.

James: Was there much of a difference in your experience of life in 1976 than ten years later because your experience had deepened?

Bob: It doesn't deepen. But the stuff that is covering up presence awareness just drops off. It can't deepen, because it's purely That and That alone.

James: If, for example, you had an upsetting experience in 1976 like the one I had yesterday, wouldn't there have been more annoyance than if it had happened in 1986?

Bob: Sure. But even in 1976 there was an immediate change. I was in India at Muktananda's ashram, and I had a routine there. I was loyal to the guru and very earnest. I was chanting and meditating and all the rest. I was doing it all very religiously. Then, after seeing Nisargadatta, I had nowhere else to stay but the ashram. Even though I had to go back there, all interest dropped off. I still went through the motions at the ashram in order to live there. But where it had previously meant everything, now it didn't mean anything. So, I continued that practice. It's like the old Buddhist saying "Before enlightenment, chop wood, carry water. After enlightenment, chop wood, carry water." The difference was, before, it was "me" doing this meditation and yoga and whatever. And, "I should be doing this. . . . I shouldn't be doing that. . . ." Afterward, all the doing was happening, with no commotion.

And then we returned to Australia; we bought a farm with 700 acres of land and lots of goats. Soon after, we lost the farm due to floods, and I got very sick. I caught Rush River fever. So everything was kicked out from under me. The Rush River Fever was really bad for a year or two.

And yet, while all that was happening, there was always a sense of well-being inside. If all that had happened before, it would've driven me mad; I'd have probably shot myself. So much anxiety and stress. That sense of well-being is always there now.

James: Simply because of knowing that there is no "me"?

Bob: When you get yourself out of the way, that subtle essence expresses through you as well-being. As Nisargadatta puts it, "I can only say it negatively—there is nothing wrong anymore." You can't say it's a high or great or anything. And you can't say it's wrong or bad. It's just what is. There's a sense of well-being present. It's an "uncaused joy," if you like—an uncaused happiness, an uncaused love and compassion.

James: How do you make a decision? Sometimes a problem arises and I say, "Oh well, that's just what's happening." Other times, I think, "I don't like that. I'm going to stop that." How do I make a decision whether to try and alter something or just let it be?

Bob: *You* don't. Decisions are made; choices are made. There's no decision maker, no choice maker. Preferences are held.

James: This reminds me of the decisions I make when I trade stocks. One day, I'll call my brother and ask him whether he thinks a certain stock will fall. He says no. Then I think, "He's wrong. What does he know?" A few days later, I call and ask a similar question. He gives his opinion and I think, "He's right. I better listen to him." So, he gives his advice, and then a thought enters my mind to accept or not accept—for no clear reason. Obviously, there's no "me" making a choice. It's so clear.

Bob: You learn to rely on an intuitive, spontaneous sense. That's what we lose—what they call the "sixth sense."

James: But the intuition isn't actually "me" either, is it?

Bob: Intuition comes up from pure intelligence and tells you what to do. But then we refer it to the "me" of past memory, and it loses its spontaneity. If we act spontaneously from our intuition, things work out.

James: The other day, I was thinking about death and reincarnation. I know that Advaitans don't believe in reincarnation because there is no actual self center to be reborn. If all that's ever born is the body and the mind, and the mind dies at the point of death, then it makes perfect sense that no one has ever returned from the dead. Of course, we hear miraculous stories and all that. But I don't know anyone who actually has returned from the dead, and I don't know anyone who knows someone who has done that.

On the other hand, the day my father died, one of my brothers had an interesting experience. My brother was resting in bed and suddenly felt my father's presence. He heard my father say, "Don't worry about anything. Everything's fine." My brother asked him something, and my father answered, "I have to go visit Mom now."

But in death the mind dies. It's finished.

Bob: Yes, that's all that was born.

James: So, what about the miraculous stories of very young children who start talking about "the old house we used to live in." The parents have no idea what the kid is talking about. And then they go to some town the kid has mentioned, and all the details of the town are remarkably accurate. Then the child takes them to a house and starts describing all the rooms accurately, even though he's never been there in this lifetime. What's that about?

Bob: It's all in that consciousness, or awareness. It's all in that pure intelligence energy.

James: What is?

Bob: The whole manifestation. Everything that's ever happened. Every life that ever happened. Everything is contained in pure intelligence energy—in the Now, in the moment. Reincarnation implies a future, and there is no future. Ancients have said it's omnipresence, it's timeless.

James: So I could know what's going on in New York right now because it's all here.

Bob: Yes. But, you're not tuned in on that, are you?

James: No.

Bob: That's how you get child prodigies and people who have lived these so-called previous lifetimes. They're simply tuned into something that is happening.

James: The reason I ask about reincarnation is because I'm an astrologer. When I look at horoscopes, I see what's going to happen in people's lives and in their apparent futures. And it works fairly well. Not 100%, but maybe 70% of the time, which is darn good. As astrologers, we assume the conditions of people's lives are as they are because of what they did in past lives. But I know that from the point of view of nonduality there is no past and future. If everything is happening in the Now, then there is no past life or future life. I get that, but I must admit that I still think that in the world of *appearance* there may be past lives.

Bob: Who is being reborn?

James: Well, that's something I can't answer. I can't find a self center or a "me," so I have no answer. But, at the same time, it doesn't make sense to me that a person could be born with great artistic talent by sheer accident. Or that a person could be dirt poor or have terrible love relationships, and so on, simply at random.

Bob: Even astrology confirms the oneness of life. You're not separate from the stars.

James: That's true. At the moment a person is born, the stars are indicating what that person's life is, and will be. They're connected somehow. Human beings are microcosms of the macrocosm.

Bob: And life continually lives on life. There's just one intelligence energy vibrating into different patterns. Just like the ocean comes up in different waves, but it all goes back into ocean.

James: Doesn't it amaze you how real everything seems?

Bob: It's truly amazing.

James: And yet there is no meaning to anything?

Bob: How could there be? Nothing ever happened! [*Laughing*] It's just the play, as they call it.

James: But it's so counterintuitive. Nothing ever happened, and you came to America. Nothing ever happened, and we're having this conversation.

Bob: Look, you go to sleep at night and then you start to dream. In that body that's taking an active part in that dream, does it have eyes that see? Does it have ears that hear? Can it breathe?

James: No.

Bob: When you wake up—puff, it's gone. Nothing ever happened.

James: So a dream is exactly the same as our life?

Bob: Yes. And a dream can't take place out of sleep. It's contained in sleep. Well, our existence can't take place outside of awareness.

James: The students that come to you for years and years and still don't fully get it . . . It doesn't matter, right?

Bob: It doesn't matter. I know they're already That, whether they do or not. A lot of them get to a reasonable place, where they can live without lots of psychological problems happening. But then sometimes they forget it, and they get hooked again. Then they come back.

James: But it's not actually better if a person understands anything or not. Whether there is suffering or not.

Bob: That's why they say there's no difference between a Buddha and an ordinary person. In essence they're both the same, no matter how they're expressing.

James: And you believe that story? [*Laughing*]

In most religions I've studied, they say that the purpose of life is happiness. There was a void or an absolute that somehow, God knows how, had an impulse to enjoy itself, to make something happen. And that's existence. But that implies a reference point. There's a void or an absolute that was bored or something and decided to have fun. That's ludicrous because it has no boundaries.

Bob: Yes. It has no beginning, so it never decided. It has no beginning and no end. It's just what is.

James: When you saw Nisagadatta, was there one particular thing that he said that made the significant difference?

Bob: He pointed out that the only way you can help anyone is to take them beyond the need for help. He'd show you your true nature, and you don't need anyone or anything from that moment on. And I haven't needed help from that day to now.

James: He showed you your true nature?

Bob: He pointed it out. That's all he could do. He couldn't do a damn thing for me, just the same as I can't do anything for anybody else. I can point, and whether or not anyone looks at that pointing is up to them.

James: Well, something you're going to hear a lot in your talks here is this idea about the "final understanding." Ramesh Balsekar says that people can have some knowledge but lack the complete, or final, understanding. You're probably going to hear this concept over and over while you're here.

Bob: What's he talking about? If he knows existence is omnipresent and timeless, what can be final about it? It's right now. It's always been right now.

James: Well, you know what he's talking about. He's talking about those students who come to you for years and years and are not in the "full stop" mode that you're in. Right?

Bob: Well, that's how it is. Whether they know it or not, I know that they're there.

James: So you think it's an irrelevant concept?

Bob: Yes, because it's implying there's a "you" that's going to get something in some future time.

James: In the world of duality, it hurts if someone is squeezing my head or punching me.

Bob: Yes, until you wake up. Just like things seem to hurt in a dream.

James: Well, that's what he's talking about—the final understanding. Some people are having this illusion that they're in pain, and some are not.

Bob: Ramesh wrote a book *The Final Truth*. Did you read that one?

James: No.

Bob: Well, after a few hundred pages, he comes to the last page, and on the top it says, "This is the final truth," and underneath there's a blank page! [*Laughing*] That was good. Ramesh is very good, although he does move into dualism now and then in his talks.

James: There's a ten-page piece on non-duality called "Clarity" by Nathan Gill that is awesome. It's on his website.

Bob: Oh yes, I know that one.

James: Also, there's that wonderful book you told Kerry to get called *Awakening to the Dream* by Leo Hartong.

Bob: Yes. That's excellent, too.

James: Bob, I want to come back to the issue of conviction. In the 1980s, I participated in lots of EST seminars. The courses are about self-development and mastery of living and that sort of thing. And it was very much about intention and commitment. It had a huge impact on my life. In the world of appearance, there's something that a person brings forth to create results—intention—to make something happen. Nothing occurs without intention. Before you arrived, I was thinking, "When Sailor Bob gets here, I really want to get what he has to offer." You're laughing at me. . . .

Bob: What did I say in my book?

James: You said, "*Who* is there to get it?"

Bob: Start from the fact that you already are That. It takes away the idea of a seeker. All you have to do is scrape away the rubbish that is stopping you from seeing it. Just dismiss anything that comes up that seemingly takes you away from it. You're left with what you already are. The idea of wanting to get something implies time, and time is just a mental concept.

James: Yes, of course. Spiritual seeking gives real meaning to the word "absurd." The message of non-duality seems so simple. How did it get so lost and mistranslated? Why is there so much about meditation and techniques and yoga and all that?

Bob: Non-duality is too simple for the complicated mind. The mind's nature is to divide. The mind can't understand or conceive of non-duality—one thing. Thoughts are vibrations, movements. That's why you'll never find the answer in the mind. Seeing that, it's full stop. You don't go looking there. And there's no way out of the mind except by full stop. Whichever direction you go in the mind will still be in the mind.

Within Buddhism, there's a teaching known as the Dzogchen scriptures—Dzogchen means "the great perfection"—and they have one very important statement: *The great perfection is non-conceptual awareness*. All the concepts that anyone has about awareness are like clouds covering up the sun. You don't see the awareness for the concepts. It doesn't mean your concepts have to stop. But a concept is a concept. And the concept is not the fact, not the thing.

James: How does all this affect reaction? You know how people get their buttons pressed? Does that go away?

Bob: I call that response. There'll be responses, but who is responding? If you take delivery of something from a "me," you suffer accordingly for it. You think you should've done something or you shouldn't have done something, and you carry it on. But, as I say, when you're not believing in the false reference point, response will be there and then be gone almost immediately. There might be something that needed to happen. You don't know. You don't fixate on it. But if you're judging from the way you think things should be, then problems arise.

Consider this, James. The definition of "phenomenon" is "that which *appears* to be." The definition of "noumenon," which is the unmanifest, or no thing, is "that which is." So, the universe we see is appearance. But the real universe is the unmanifest.

James: That's the "reality."

Bob: That's the reality. No thing. So, no thing has ever happened. Any happening has to be a thing. Energy, or belief in something, doesn't care which way it goes. Just like the current in an electric motor. Turn the switch one way, it goes forward. Turn it the other way, it goes in reverse. Electricity doesn't care. The vitality, the living essence, doesn't care whether you think in dualism, stuck in the mind, or anything else. It just goes where the energy, or belief, goes. But if you question all your beliefs, you'll find belief is only a reference point. It's not the actuality. A belief can never be the actuality. The actuality is this present moment. Presence awareness. You can't negate it.

James: It's the only thing you can know.

Bob: It's *no thing*. It's the knowing itself. There's no "you" to know. It is knowing itself. Just like the sun is shining. It doesn't need any light to shine on it. It's self-shining. You are self-aware. Awareness itself is like the sun shining. It's self-lighting or self-knowing. That's what you can't negate. *Non-conceptual, ever-fresh, self-shining presence awareness. Just this and nothing else.* That's a Buddhist term. Keep the simplicity of it and you can't go wrong. It's so simple that the mind can't grasp it. It tries to work it out and conceptualize it.

Sometimes we get the idea that all concepts should disappear, or all thoughts should stop. No. Just understand that a concept is a concept. The concept is not the thing. You have concepts about yourself, and others have concepts about you. So, you couldn't care less what someone thinks about you. It's only conceptual. They don't know the truth about you. And your concepts about yourself are not the truth. By not indulging the concepts, you're left with the truth, with who you really are.

James: People keep seeking. That's all some want to do with their life is seek.

Bob: That's right. Seeking, seeking, never finding. Because the seeking is in the mind, and the nature of the mind is to divide. It'll keep you seeking forever. Thirty years you were seeking with meditation. And still seeking. You're an intelligent person, and you worked out many other things in the mind. But when it comes to self-understanding, you've never worked it out. Eventually your intelligence will tell you, "Maybe I'm looking in the wrong place." Once you realize that, you don't look there anymore. It's pointless.

*

July 16 – Day 2

James: What was your childhood like?

Bob: I had a reasonable childhood. We grew up on a farm. We didn't have much money, but we did all right. We lived off the land and ate rabbits. It was nice. Then I quit school at fourteen and left home.

James: You were a sailor, right?

Bob: Yes, I went in at the age of seventeen. I was drinking so much alcohol in those days. After I left the Navy, I was shearing sheep for a while. I worked on construction sites on dams and worked in gold and copper mines for a while. And then I went back to sea, on the coastal boats as a Merchant Marine. Then I got kicked out of that. I was unemployed and unemployable.

James: How long were you a drinker?

Bob: From about age fifteen until about thirty-two. At that time, I didn't believe in anything. I was an atheist. When I got into the AA fellowship [Alcoholics Anonymous], they had this program and they used to talk about God. Each person had their own understanding. I managed to stop drinking there, even though, if it were up to me, I would have kept drinking. Circumstances had gotten me into AA. I was pretty angry then, and people steered clear of me. After a while, a fellow handed me a book called *Sobriety and Beyond.* In the introduction, it said, "We alcoholics are given a second chance." That hit me. And then it said, "How well do you use that second chance?" That also hit me. And it came to me at that time: *There's only one way I can use it—to find out what it is that's given me the second chance. It's none of my doing, so maybe there is such a thing as God or a higher power. Maybe.*

And that put a little chink in the armor. A little "maybe." That "maybe" has taken me to where I am today.

James: Now that you've completely seen through the reference point, the false "me," is it possible you could go back to drinking?

Bob: Well, of course, anything is possible. But there's no point in doing so. People have asked me, "What if you could go back to drinking without becoming addicted to it?" And I tell them, "What for? Why would I want to drink? What could it give me that I haven't already got?" When I used to drink, I would get that high from it, that elusive high. I was always drinking more and more to find that elusive high. And, of course, I would drink so much I would go past it. It was elusive. But with non-duality, you get that natural high that's constantly with you. You don't need any stimulants or anything else. Desires for things fall away of their own accord. As long as someone thinks they're getting something out of drugs or alcohol, they'll continue taking them.

James: I see. What's your schedule like these days?

Bob: Well, I get plenty of phone calls from seekers. Three days a week, I have talks that last a few hours. Some times there will be a few people and other times there may be ten or fifteen.

James: I was very impressed with Nisargadatta's book *I Am That*. It had a big effect on me, and at the time (but not now) I liked the fact that he said we could *do* something. He said that we should try to stay with the "I am." He said that his guru, before dying, had told him not to forget that he was infinite and unbounded. And to always remain with the "I am."

Bob: Yes, but it depends on what you think that "I am" is. He means that you should stay with that sense of presence. He doesn't mean the thought "I am."

James: I know. Lots of people think he means we should keep saying, "I am, I am, I am."

Bob: He's referring to that sense of presence that expresses through the mind as the thought "I am." It's presence awareness.

James: People get confused.

Bob, how old were you when you were seeing Nisargadatta?

Bob: I was around forty-eight or so. I was staying in Muktananda's ashram.

James: Were you telling others about him?

Bob: Yes. In fact, at one point Nisargadatta said to me, "You're the cause of all these Westerners coming to me."

James: Because you were telling people?

Bob: Yes. I went there about a week after Maurice Frydman died. He was the one who made *I Am That*. He translated Nisargadatta's tapes and put them into book form.

James: Had you read the book before meeting Nisargadatta?

Bob: I was in a bookshop. People had pointed me to *I Am That*, but I had ignored them. And the shopkeeper said, "You've got to read this book." I read a few pages, and I hotfooted it there straightaway! I hadn't read the book at that stage, but what I read in those few pages really hit me. My understanding was bordering on what I read, and I was sick and tired of the experiences in the ashram. I had all sorts of kundalini experiences, but I wasn't getting anywhere. We'd go into Bombay and there would be Westerners there, and some would be going to one guru and some to another. And I'd say, "Well, you should go to see this man."

James: How far was the ashram from Nisargadatta's flat?

Bob: Fifty or sixty miles. We were in a little village that had formed around Nityananda, Muktananda's guru. There was nothing there really. Nityananda lived in a little hut, and they built the ashram around him. When Muktananda came along, he built his ashram a bit further down the road.

James: I see. I have friends who read *I Am That* and other books on non-duality who enjoy them and agree with them and then go on searching and meditating and chasing enlightenment. They want the experiences that so many people talk about. All those great feelings and all. I can't fathom what they're doing. Anyway, I'm getting it. I'm getting it.

Bob: [*Teasing*] What's this "getting"?

James: Well, you know.

Bob: I am That—not "getting" it. Whatever can be gotten or lost is not you. Whatever can be forgotten or remembered is not you.

James: How about if I said, "I remember I am That"?

Bob: No good. There's an "I" remembering. See, there's a knowing that you can't negate. That's the actuality—not a "me" remembering some past thing. There's a knowingness that you can't negate. You don't need a word for it. You know that you are. You can't say, "I am not." Just knowing, knowing, knowing. Seeing, seeing, seeing.

James: So I can't say that seeing, seeing, seeing is happening more and more?

Bob: That implies a time when it didn't happen. Just seeing—right here, right now. Knowing—right here, right now.

James: *Awareness* of knowing is happening more and more?

Bob: [*Laughing*]

James: They're all false.

Bob: You don't need anything; you just are. Look, you woke up this morning. You opened your eyes, had some thoughts, took a shower, did some work, got into some discussions, and the day went by. But has that wakefulness changed?

James: No.

Bob: Everything has taken place on that wakefulness. It's come and gone. Without the wakefulness, could anything have happened? You are that infinite space every day—that "naked awareness," or wakefulness. Without any adornment. Everything else is adornment on it. Like clothes on the nakedness. Just that simple wakefulness. That's who you are.

James: Less thinking?

Bob: Doesn't matter how much thinking. That's still adornment. That comes and goes. In essence, even the thoughts are that, too. They couldn't be anything other than wakefulness because they are the *content* of wakefulness. The content can't actually be different, but it's *appearing* as different. Just like all this manifestation is the content of space. Space is nothing. So, can something come from nothing?

James: No.

Bob: So the content is nothing also, but it's appearing as something. Just like the blue sea appears to be blue. That's why they say "cognizing emptiness." When you look inside yourself, you see there's no self center. So, what must be there if there's nothing in there? It must be empty. It's empty, but hearing and thinking and seeing are still happening. So it's that emptiness of self that's cognizing. There's nothing there but emptiness itself. And that emptiness that is "space-like" contains everything. It makes you laugh.

James: You can't really talk about it. It just is.

Bob: As soon as you open your mouth about it, you're in duality. You can only talk in concepts. The word is not the real. You can say, "water, water, water," for the rest of your life, but you'll never be able to quench your thirst like that. The map can never be the territory.

James: There's something I read in Advaita books that I don't understand. They say that what we're looking for is actually beyond the "I am." What are they talking about?

Bob: You know that you are. That sense of presence expresses through the thought "I am." You don't have to go around saying, "I am, I am, I am." So, "I am" is a primary thought. Are you thinking "I am" right now?

James: No.

Bob: So, are you seeing? Are you hearing? Are you functioning?

James: Yes.

Bob: That is beyond thought. It is without the labeling. That's beyond the mind. People say, "Go beyond the mind." And they search for years and years trying to find out what's beyond the mind.

James: We're living beyond the mind.

Bob: Exactly. In the immediate experiencING—the seeing, the hearing, tasting, smelling, touching—the living beyond the mind is happening. It's happening prior to any labeling, prior to any thought. All the mind does is label and conceptualize. We're always living beyond the mind. And that question "Who am I?" that seekers are always using . . . People spend years and years searching with that. If you pause for a moment and ask, "Who's asking this question?" then you realize that the questioner is the very question itself! If that question is not being asked, then there is no questioner. So, no questioner and no question . . . and where are you?

James: Back in presence awareness.

Bob: That's right. Simple as that.

James: By the way, I heard that when Ramana Maharshi told seekers to use the question "Who am I?" as a spiritual inquiry, he was mistranslated. According to Ramesh Balsekar, as I understand it, the actual translation should have been, "Who is this me?" It has a somewhat different meaning.

Bob: Oh. Do you remember what I said in the beginning of my book? "I am not speaking to any body. I am not speaking to any mind. I am speaking to that *I am* that I am."

James: That confuses me a bit.

Bob: Yes, it might. Look, I can't speak to your body. Your body can't hear me.

James: Can you speak to my mind?

Bob: No. Because there is no mind. Mind is just a collection of thoughts which have no independent nature. I'm speaking to that life essence. I am speaking to that *"I am"* that I am. That sense of presence. In that way, we communicate.

James: So this is presence speaking to presence. . . . Can presence speak to presence?

Bob: Presence is resonating with presence. It's not a matter of speaking. It's self-knowing.

James: Bob, regarding politics and worldly affairs, does anything bother you?

Bob: Well, it's like the Biblical statement "A thousand shall fall on your left side, ten thousand will fall on your right side. But it doesn't come nigh your dwelling place." I see the world going on, but it doesn't come near me.

James: I noticed that. Nothing hooks you. Is it fun?

Bob: It's just what is.

James: People are very upset about the happenings in the world—all the suffering. I understand the world is illusion, but if I were a person in Iraq right now, it would be pretty bad.

Bob: Well, how does it all come about, the idea of suffering?

James: From a reference point.

Bob: It's always connected to the primary dualism—"me" and the "other." If you've seen through the reference point, the mind-created "me," then who is all this so-called suffering happening to? Events are happening, but not to any person. Also, people are constantly adding to their suffering by imagining the problems of other people.

James: Like me. I'm always concerned about the horrible wars in Africa and the terrible suicide bombers all over the world.

Bob: That's right. Everyone is worried about all the people being killed. But they don't stop and think about the fact that if you look in the obituaries in Melbourne, two hundred people die every day.

James: So, if a person is free of the reference point, then they're just watching what's happening?

Bob: Yes. You've removed the cause of your suffering. But you can't actually help others unless you can help them see that their reference point is false. It's invalid.

James: Are you saying that if a person in the midst of war were free of the reference point, they would have no concern about tomorrow?

Bob: Of course, they would be concerned. But there would be no *vested interest*. There would not be an imagined problem anymore. There would only be whatever is happening—whatever is in the moment. What is your experience? Do you have any psychological suffering?

James: Not when I'm aware that my reference point is false.

Bob: That's right, because you've removed the cause. The "me" is the cause, and the effects are the anxiety, fear, depression, anger, or what's going on the world. These are all relative to that cause—the "me."

James: I've heard so many times that if you could stop your mind, you would have peace.

Bob: You don't want to stop your mind. When you see it has no power, no independent nature, it's finished. It can't exist on its own. It's not substantial. It couldn't exist without awareness.

James: That means it has nothing to do with who I really am.

Bob: That's right. It's a phantom. A rainbow couldn't be in the sky without the sun and the clouds. It can't stand on its own. It's nothing.

James: Where are the thoughts coming from?

Bob: As I told you, it's "cognizing emptiness." And if you have a look, you'll see that there is no place that a concept can attach itself to. It's like a cloud appears in the sky. The cloud isn't attached to the sky. But there couldn't be a cloud without the sky. If energy or belief goes into a thought, that stops it from leaving. That's resistance or conflict. It's no longer free to go. When you're walking down the street, try looking without labeling. No fixating on thoughts. Something you read in lots of books is this idea of being thought-free.

James: You can't. The idea is not to get attached to them.

Bob: People think they have to force out every thought. But, in fact, being thought-free means *just let the thought be free*. Let it do what it likes. Let it float around and then leave. No thought has ever lasted. Where are yesterday's thoughts?

James: Look at thoughts that we were so attached to years ago. Where are they now? And yet people kill for thoughts.

Bob: When you realize how transient they are, you don't bother with them anymore. You're not bound by them. Thoughts are vibration. Vibration is movement of energy.

James: It's the habits though. Somebody will say something nasty, I'll get upset . . .

Bob: But you recognize them as habits, and you just let them fall off. "Me" is the cause of all your problems. Investigate and see that there's nothing with an independent nature that is "me." Then you see that cause is false. It's fiction. Can there be an effect without a cause? An effect can't exist without a cause. And the cause is always that false "me," or false self center. See that it's a fiction and the effect will drop away. If there's no "me" to be affected, where can the effect take place? It's so simple, we miss it.

Experience, however sublime, is not the real thing. By its very nature it comes and goes. Self-realization is not an acquisition. It is more of the nature of understanding. Once arrived at, it cannot be lost.

—Nisargadatta Maharaj, *I Am That*

CHAPTER THREE

Bob Meets the Locals

*

Knowing that Bob would need a few days to recuperate from his long journey, I planned his first meeting with locals for Saturday night—three days after he had arrived. This was not a formal meeting. Those were planned for the last three weekends of his five-week visit. Saturday night was simply a small gathering of neighborhood friends who were interested in spiritual matters. I did not tell guests that Bob would be giving a talk because at that time I did not know Bob loves to speak about non-duality all day and all night long. My intention was simply for Bob to meet my friends and vice versa. Bob, however, immediately knew he would be speaking, which was what we were all hoping for.

I also invited my dear friend Emmett Walz, who lives on the East Coast of Florida, about a four-hour drive from Longboat Key. Emmett and I have been friends since high school, and he has been a seeker since our college days. He had participated in many of the same paths as me, such as Transcendental Meditation, yoga, EST seminars, Lifespring, macrobiotics, and so forth. For the past seven or eight years, however, he had been especially enjoying his daily meditation sessions and going to a month-long meditation course in the mountains at the end of every year.

Emmett had read Sailor Bob's book and felt it was quite profound. He had also read other books on non-duality that I shared with him, and was moved by many of the teachings. He had several times shared passages from Nisargadatta's books that had resonated powerfully with him. I was thus stunned when Emmett passed on the invitation to the party. He said he was busy and planned to visit on one of Bob's three publicized weekend talks. I strenuously objected, actually got right in his face, pleading, "Are you crazy? There's an awakened teacher coming to my house, and you're coming for one weekend? What's going on?"

Emmett responded with a seemingly intelligent answer. He said, "What's he going to do, James, *give* me enlightenment?"

This was something I could not directly refute, since liberation is, of course, nothing one person can give to another. On the other hand, being in the presence of someone who has been liberated for thirty years was nothing to take lightly. And so, after arguing for five or ten minutes, I relented and the conversation ended. Annoyed and confused, I told Vashti that Emmett must not be feeling well and would perhaps rethink his decision the next day. How someone who had valued self-realization more than anything for the better part of his life could turn down an opportunity like this was beyond me. Fortunately, the next day Emmett called to say he had changed his mind and would take time off work to come for the weekend. After a few days with Sailor Bob, Emmett decided to take lots of time off and wound up staying in our house for two straight weeks, as well as one or two other weekends. It was a joy having him.

If some of what I have said seems contradictory, it's because it is. Of course, it is true that there's nothing we can do to attain liberation because there is actually no independent entity within us and because nothing in a transient creation can possibly be causative. But it's also true that there are things that *apparently* help. One is hearing or reading non-dual teachings and being in the presence of someone who has gained the understanding. And if this seems paradoxical, it's because it is. Paradox is at the core of this teaching, as indicated by its being called a "pathless path." Advaita asserts that any seeking is counterproductive because unboundedness, or pure intelligence, is who we are, and any searching necessarily takes our attention *away* from that. However, in order to let go and realize our true nature, we generally need to understand certain premises. In other words, paradoxically, we need to seek in order to find out that the search is the problem. Also paradoxically, we need to seek to find out that our apparent bondage is a fiction. This is why Advaitan teachers allow seekers to hear their teachings, despite the fact that one could, if one wished, correctly call every Advaitan guide an outright fraud for teaching! And most teachers acknowledge this. Bob always begins his lectures by saying, "I can't tell you anything. I can't teach you anything. I can only point with these concepts."

Within the world of appearance—where most people believe they live—it appears to be necessary for seekers to seek and for teachers to speak. Where Advaita differs from other teachings is that it emphasizes that it is critical for seekers to realize that, in order to reach their intended goal, they must *stop* searching and clearly see that what they are seeking, they already are. That is, like it or not, the only way out of this mysterious game of hide and seek that consciousness is playing with itself. More to the point, it is the only way out of the game of hide and seek that *we* are in fact playing with *ourselves*!

In Emmett's case, when he said he knew no one could give him enlightenment, he knew, conceptually, that seeking is a problem. But this was not the motive for his statement. Until a certain point within our interactions with Bob, seeking was clearly happening for both Emmett and myself. Emmett's statement was simply an expression of his lack of urgency in meeting Bob. Which was why I argued so forcefully with him. Knowing that Emmett was still in seeking mode, what could be a greater opportunity than to be with a living master? What could be better than speaking with the man Emmett had already acknowledged as having written one of the best non-dual texts he had ever read? Thus, my surprise and subsequent argument with him.

Regarding the paradoxical nature of a pathless path, newcomers are often plagued with frustration. By the time Bob arrived at my house, I had been reading non-duality books for nearly four years and had already grappled with the same issues that many readers of this text may now be struggling with. Despite all my questioning during Bob's five-week visit, however, I had essentially given up my struggle within two days of his arrival. Of course I questioned everything and presented every doubt I had until the instant that Bob left. But my "process" actually ended within the first two days.

How can that be? Because the moment I decided to trust Bob's words, a visceral reaction occurred, and a decision was made to give credence to the real world, the world of consciousness, of non-duality. The moment I decided to trust the results of my investigation into what is real—whether or not it *appeared* real within the dream world in which we all live—a letting go of attachments to apparent realities began. When that happened, my fate was sealed.

Ten or twelve days into Bob's visit, during a conversation in which I forcefully argued certain doubts about life in the world of appearance contradicting reality (presented in Chapter Five), Bob gave one of his most profound teachings. He said, "Well, what are you here for? To talk about the appearance, or understand reality?" His question was more essential than I realized at the time. Many people study non-duality for years and years, and never end their search. In nearly every case it is because their new understanding of reality contradicts their life in the world of appearance. For such seekers it is perhaps too challenging, scary, or counterintuitive to set aside their apparent experience long enough to give ultimate reality its full due and consideration. Ironically, when one does set aside the apparent experience long enough to fully appreciate non-duality, one finds there is, in essence, no contradiction. Both worlds are, in essence, the same. This is because illusory existence is made up of the same underlying consciousness that comprises everything. The net result, as Bob always says, is that "everything becomes all-inclusive." In the same way we know that the dream that took place during sleep last night was illusory, we also know that, within our experience, the dream happened.

In any case, Emmett arrived on Friday, a day before the party. Below is a conversation with Sailor Bob, Emmett, and myself. If it seems odd that within the talk I am occasionally attempting to teach Emmett so soon after asking Bob so many basic questions myself, it is for two reasons. One: I had been studying non-duality much longer than Emmett. Two: After discussing non-duality with Bob non-stop for a day and a half, I simply could not help myself. I should also mention that within my previous years of study I had actually encountered the answers to many (perhaps most) of the questions I was now asking Bob. But the answers were, for one reason or another, unsatisfying. I apparently needed to hear them from someone living non-duality. Fortunately, I wanted answers badly enough to ask until I found.

*

Emmett, James, and Bob

No Resistance to What Is

Emmett: Do you prefer one thing to another? Does it matter what happens to you?

Bob: You see, that very word shows we already know this innately. When something "doesn't matter," it doesn't concretize. When something doesn't matter, you're not concerned with it. The same thing with when you say, "I don't mind." But when something does mind, you focus on that, and it does matter.

James: In other words, the problems are always in the mind.

Emmett: So, how do you pursue something? Do you pursue anything?

Bob: Well, there's no "you" there. There's no entity to do anything, but things will happen spontaneously. The universe is functioning as it should. And you are that universe. Whatever you're attracted to will come to you, and whatever you're repelled by won't come to you. So you just go with the flow. There's no resistance to what is. Resistance is conflict, and conflict is disease.

Emmett: When conflict arises . . .

Bob: That's resistance, and it's recognized from the point of no resistance. You can't do anything about resistance. But what happens is that intelligence will recognize it from the point of non-resistance. From the point of non-resistance, you'll notice a very subtle relaxation.

Emmett: Yes, I have that. When I become conscious of resistance, I start to relax and I feel my shoulders drop. Everything settles.

Bob: Yes, at that point you're there.

Emmett: But sometimes the resistance comes back.

Bob: Yes, but in knowing about the effects of resistance, the point of non-resistance will come up more and more. Because you're seeing the falseness of staying in resistance.

Emmett: Is that non-resistance with you pretty much all the time?

Bob: Yes. Just the same as it is in the universe. As in the microcosm, so in the macrocosm. This universe functions in the pairs of opposites just the same as the mind does. But you don't see the forces of nature in opposition to one another.

Emmett: Yes, nature flows effortlessly no matter what happens. From our perspective, it looks like terrible things are happening in nature—earthquakes, hurricanes, animals killing each other, and so on.

James: That's all caused by our reference point. If we could stop our minds, everything would be great.

Bob: And, you don't need to stop it.

Emmett: In your book, you said that stopping the mind is no better than having lots of thoughts.

Bob: That's right. It's a matter of understanding the mind. It has no substance or independent nature. You can't have a single thought without the underlying consciousness. Thoughts are just a fiction. The mind is a fiction in which we get bound up. Remember the scriptural statement "Know the truth and the truth will set you free." You're free of it. Simple as that.

Emmett: In my past efforts of going to meditation courses and all, I'd become completely disconnected from all the problems. Then every-thing's great.

Bob: You see, that meditation is always from the point of somebody trying to get somewhere else. When you realize that the somebody trying to get something is a fiction, you realize there's nobody to meditate and nothing to meditate on. From that viewpoint, you're never out of meditation. You're in the "natural state," which has no beginning, no end, and no in-between. What you are is already whole and complete. You're omnipresent. Sitting and meditating is becoming. It's a mental concept. You have some concept of a future time when you'll get something.

Emmett: The mind tends to drop away more often, which is nice. But when you come back, you're still that seeker—waiting.

James: It doesn't matter that thoughts are coming, as long as you recognize them for what they are—illusion.

Bob: Recognize them and then be finished with them. But they'll always be there to some extent. As long as you have a body, you'll have thoughts, and you'll still think in the same way. The nature of thinking is in the pairs of opposites, which is dualism. You can't think in another way. Past/future, painful/happy, hot/cold, and so on. In understanding it, you're no longer bound by it. Let the mind do what it likes. It's not you. It's an appearance that comes and goes.

Emmett: And eventually there comes an understanding . . .

Bob: Not eventually. That implies time. It's immediate, right now. That knowingness is right now; you can't negate it. Forget this rubbish about "eventually" because that will keep you bound. Just realize now that under no circumstances can you say, "I am not." That knowing that you are is constant. The term "eventually" implies that there's something you've got to get. You can't go any further than that—the knowing that you are. That is "no thing" that you can ever grasp or conceptualize in the mind.

Emmett: See, that's the problem.

James: You have to stop looking in the mind. You can't get it in the mind.

Emmett: That sounds like not looking at all.

Bob: That's right. The answer's not in the mind. *The only way out of the mind is full stop.*

Emmett: Looking back, does it seem like you've always known?

Bob: Yes. We've always known. It just hasn't been recognized. We've ignored our true nature. That's why it's called ignorance. We ignore our true nature and go into the appearance. Now you recognize, you re-cognize your true nature.

Emmett: But you do see a distinction regarding what you know now and what you knew before?

Bob: You see, "before" is a fiction. It's just like when you wake up from a dream. What are you going to think about the dream? When you realize it's been a dream, you dismiss it. The sixteen years I searched, the knowing was actually there even though I didn't know it—no matter how it appeared.

James: If you look at anything in existence without thinking, there are no problems. It's the thinking that creates the problems.

Bob: Thinking is labeling. If you're not labeling anything, you're knowing what everything is. You're knowing what everything is before you label it.

James: I've been looking for answers in the mind my entire life. There are no answers there.

Bob: We've all done that.

Are the Scriptures Mistranslated?

Emmett: Bob, so many people have written about enlightenment in scriptures, and much of it sounds different from your teaching. Are we misunderstanding them? Are they mistranslations?

Bob: In many cases, they are mistranslations. Look at the story of Moses on the mountain. He goes up and has an experience. And he asks God, or whatever, "What shall I tell the people? Who should I say sent me?" And the answer comes to him, "Tell them the 'I am' sent you. My name is 'I am.'" And Moses realizes he is that "I am." Of course, the people think he's talking about something other than that. When Jesus said, "I am the way and the truth and the life," they thought he was talking about himself. But he was talking about the same "I am"—that sense of presence that Nisargadatta spoke of. That's the way.

Isaiah said, "Be still and know that I am God." Break it down—be still and know. Break it down further—be still. Break it down further—be. And Christ said, "Which of you by taking thought can add one cubit to his stature?"

Emmett: A cubit?

Bob: About a foot and a half. You can think as much as you like, but you can't make yourself an inch taller. So the scriptures get garbled. People write from duality, and so they add and detract to what the sages were saying. Essentially, all the sages are saying the same thing. They're saying life is non-dual, one without a second; there is only That. It's omnipresence, omnipotence, omniscience. Omnipresence means total presence, not a future and past. Total presence. Omnipotence means total power. Omniscience means total intelligence, total knowingness. Total—nothing other than that. In the Dzogchen scriptures, they mention non-conceptual awareness. They tell you in one sentence, "The great perfection is non-conceptual awareness." They call it "non-conceptual, ever-fresh, self-shining presence awareness. Just this and nothing else."

That's what comes down from all traditions—the non-dual, the one without a second. It's only when it gets translated and garbled into the many . . . People translate it, and they can only do it in dualism. So we miss the simplicity of it.

James: It's too simple.

Bob: We're used to working things out in the mind. But when it comes to pure intelligence, the mind can't grasp it. The mind is a thing, and it can't understand no thing. Presence awareness contains the mind. The mind can't contain it. That's why it says in the *Bhagavad Gita*, the sword can't cut it, fire can't burn it, wind can't dry it, and water can't drown it. Presence awareness contains all of those things. None of those things could contain or grasp it. They wouldn't exist without it. So it's pointless. Stop the search. Stop the search right now.

Emmett: Was there a final moment when you got the understanding?

Bob: There was never any final moment. When I was with Nisargadattta, I just realized what he was saying—that I had always and ever been That. I couldn't have been anything else! The seeming sixteen years of my search disappeared like a dream. I realized that the sixteen years didn't matter. Anything that was previous didn't matter. Anything in the future didn't matter. The actuality is right now. I can never live this moment again, and neither can you. If I'm not living totally in this moment, if I'm not seeing, hearing, tasting, touching, smelling fully—if I'm locked into the mind instead—I'm not actually living. When you're totally aware, totally alert, you're really living. This is the actuality of this moment. It can never happen again. You can recall the past, or you can imagine the future. But you're wasting all your energy in the recollection and the imagination, because they're stopping you from seeing what is happening right now. So if you're aware, if you're awake, then be that.

Emmett: There are descriptions of the final realization that talk about bliss consciousness. . . .

Bob: Yes, those are all experiences. They're not It. Anything you can experience is not It. Anyone you would like to name, Christ, Buddha, Mohammed, and so on, have never gone beyond "no thing." And I know that I am that "no thing." Nobody can go beyond that.

Emmett: Can you be there *and* have the bliss? [*Laughing*]

Bob: You can have bliss, but the bliss is just experience. I have no preference for silence and peace, any more than chatter. They're both experiences. What they are being experienced in, or on, is that essence which I am, which has never changed. And can never change. The definition of reality is that which never changes. [One interesting dictionary definition of reality is "that which has necessary and not contingent existence.] All the rest is transient. It's coming and going. Anything that's transient—that comes and goes—cannot be reality. Reality is "no thing."

James: When you were seeking, didn't you come across writings that spoke of how blissful it is when you reach that state?

Bob: Yes, of course.

James: So, they were basically teaching a misunderstanding—a mistake. Right?

Bob: Yes. They can have experiences. I've had all sorts of experiences. I've had visions. I've had kundalini where all sorts of *kriyas* [bodily positions that occur due to intense energy rushing up the spine] have taken place spontaneously. I've had bliss and great highs. I've seen different colored lights. But these things are not what you're looking for. Those experiences will come and go. What you're looking for is the "no thing" that you've always been and always will be. And you don't have to go anywhere to find it because you are that. And that will bring you the sense of well-being you're looking for.

James: Are you talking about a sense of well-being that's always been with you your whole life, or something that began after you understood Nisargadatta's teaching?

Bob: Something that has always been there but was never recognized. It was ignored. But it was always there. It's too simple for the mind to grasp. The subtlety of it is too much for the mind. When you stay with the "no thing" or the "I am," you start to notice the subtleties in it. You see the uncaused peace, the uncaused joy—not the opposite of sadness or the opposite of turbulence, not love or hate, but the uncaused love. It's a natural compassion that's innate within you. That starts to express. And it has no opposite because it's uncaused. It's just what is. That's your natural state. And that's what *Nirsarga* means—the natural state. You become childlike. It doesn't mean that all sorts of dramas don't happen. But because the sense of knowing that you are has been recognized, you can't get away from it. You can't negate it. You can't lose it. You realize you've always and ever been That. It had no beginning and no end. No birth, no death. No time, no space. It can't be conceptualized. You are That—right *now*.

How Do I Act, If I'm Being Lived?

Emmett: I've been thinking a lot about this idea that I'm being lived—that choices are being made, but there's nobody making the choices.

Bob: Yes. There are choices being made—*seemingly* by a choice maker. There'll still be preferences and beliefs being held. But there's no entity that they can latch onto. When you realize that there's no center here . . . What must be here if there's no self center?

Emmett: Nothing.

Bob: That's right. It's empty. If there's nothing here, and yet you're still hearing and seeing, then it must be that emptiness itself that has that capacity of cognizing. It's emptiness itself that is cognizing. When you see that, you realize that nothing here [*pointing to self*] is seeing, but seeing is happening. Nothing here is hearing, but hearing is happening. Emptiness has no center, no circumference, no beginning, and no end. So, you're not even here. There's no specific place you can locate yourself. *You're everywhere!* Space has no center, no circumference. It's everywhere. And that is what you are.

Emmett: Yes, that's a rough one for me.

Bob: It's a rough one for a "me." But take the "me" out of it, and where are you? It just is. Take the "me" out of it, and notice that you're still seeing, still hearing and thinking. So, your essence is still functioning. And though it's appearing as something, if there's no reference point, it must be, in essence, the same intelligence energy appearing as something different. You'll realize that all the patterns of energy are appearing as something substantial and solid, in some shape and form. But they can all be broken down into subatomic particles—which science then breaks down into space, or energy, or nothing. So, their essence is "no thing."

You are "no thing." That "no thing" has the potential to encompass all things. Everything has come from that "no thing." Something can't come from nothing. So, in essence, though it appears as something, it's still "no thing" patterning as some thing. And you are That. And don't forget it! [*Laughing*]

Emmett: When I consider this understanding, I always wonder how to apply it. How do I be a reference point anymore? How do I be an individual in the world, and how do I be human anymore? Choices are happening, but now I understand they aren't my choices. So, how do I live?

Bob: Have you seen that the reference point is false, that it has no substance or independent nature?

Emmett: Yes. The reference point doesn't even exist.

Bob: If it doesn't exist now, when did it ever exist?

Emmett: It never did.

Bob: So, why are you asking how to live your life *now*? You will live it now just as you lived it before—except you no longer believe in the "me." This shows you that you're being lived. You were lived as this limited individual. Life has taken you where it wanted to take you. Now, it's turned you around to this understanding. The livingness continues. That's why I say to act as if you're already that oneness. You've already lived as if you're a human, and you've won Academy Awards at that. [*Laughing*] Why not act as what you really are? You'll find it much easier! [*Laughing*]

How old are you?

Emmett: I'm fifty-four.

Bob: You're young enough to be my son, too. [Bob often calls James and Kerry his "sons."]

Emmett: How old are you?

Bob: I'll be seventy-six in a few days. Now, son, listen to what I'm telling you. . . . [*Laughing*]

Emmett: I notice from your book that when people ask you questions, you never get thrown off course. You always bring them back to the presence awareness, which is who they really are. That's obviously a realized reality for you. And, I sometimes get the glimmers. . . .

Bob: You know why? Innately, you already know this. That's why it resonates with you. All the thinking of thoughts is just like the clouds over the sun. The sun's always shining, and then there are little breaks in the clouds that resonate with you. And hearing it—though this is all conceptual—there is a sort of rejoicing in the recognition of itself. It starts to open up those meridians. Because you know it, but you've been waiting to hear it. Ever since we learned language in the first year or two, we've ignored our reality. It doesn't like being ignored. That's a concept too, of course, but it likes to hear about itself. It likes to recognize itself, so it can flourish. The seed stays in the ground until the water comes, and then it will burst and sprout. And then it will bring flowers or fruits.

Emmett: It seems so bizarre that there are billions of people, and so few ever realize truth.

Bob: Well, look at how many seeds a tree produces and how few seeds ever make it to full-grown trees. Very few sprout. But in one little seed, there is the potential to cover the earth in trees.

Emmett: Something different happens for the seed that sprouts. There's a different reality for the person who has the understanding. Your mind knows about your awareness of reality. Your mind knows something that it didn't know before.

Bob: It knows that it has no power—that it's nothing.

Emmett: It's just a useful tool.

Bob: Yes. That's exactly what it is. The mind is a movement of energy.

Thought is subtle word. At the spoken level, word is sound. Sound is a vibration. A vibration is a movement of energy. That vibration always vibrates in the pairs of opposites—past, present, future. So, the mind is very limited. But it's a wonderfully creative instrument. This house was an idea in somebody's mind at one time. So was this clock. But the mind can also be self-destructive. It makes us think we are limited human beings. Sometimes the thoughts tell us we're no good, we have low self-esteem, and so forth. We're anxious and fearful. So it's not the enemy. It's a matter of understanding it, allowing it to be creative with beauty and art. But, when the mind gives limitations, it's important to see the falseness of it.

*

That Night

Later that night, Bob and I spoke alone. After a few minutes, we were joined by Vashti.

Is Non-Duality Just Another Belief?

James: Bob, I can feel my search coming to an end. But I also can envision times when I will get stuck in the mind again.

Bob: Yes, you can get caught in the old habit patterns. But when you see the falseness of them, thoughts will come up that these are just habits. And you'll realize this the wrong way. Full stop. Give up the reference point.

James: I feel so much open space from relieving my problem with world suffering. That issue was with me for so long.

Bob: That problem doesn't exist in the natural state. There's no problem in nature at all. It's not even in Julian [James's five-year-old son], but it's starting to be. He's starting to talk and reason a lot now. So, the conditioning starts to come upon him. So far, he couldn't care less about thinking. He's having fun playing.

James: He doesn't care about the killing in Iraq.

Bob: No, but when the reasoning starts, he'll start asking why this and why that. And he'll get answers from school and society, and he'll get conditioned like everyone else. So, the natural state is functioning, but it gets clouded over with thoughts and labels. And we start functioning from that learned stuff. It's all words and labels. It's not "the real." The natural state is beating your heart and growing your hair.

James: Last night I was wondering whether my new understanding—the understanding of non-duality—is just another belief. Am I just starting another belief system? Is this just a different kind of conditioning from what I was given as a child?

Bob: Yes, but look at where you go for that. You go into the mind to try and work it out. That's taking you away from presence awareness again. Just stay present without all the labeling and conceptualizing. Of course, concepts will keep coming up. Just see them for what they are. The answer is not in the mind. It never will be. This is not about beliefs. It's about knowing that you are.

James: Basically, anything that comes from the mind is rubbish. Even the concepts of non-duality are rubbish. What is useful is living in the moment, in the natural state.

Bob: And that's happening by itself!

James: We can't get out of the natural state! But we can think about it and label it and conceptualize it. And that's the problem.

Bob: That's right. You didn't say, "I'm going to take another breath right now. I'm going to beat my heart now." That just happened.

James: There was a wonderful Indian guru called Papaji who used to say that if you want to do any sort of practice or meditation, try living without thinking. I never understood what he meant until now. I think he was talking about living without trying to label and conceptualize everything at every moment.

Next week Kerry is coming here for six or seven days. We were talking about how he might not have enough private time with you when you go and stay with him for a week in Connecticut. Now I have to laugh because I've spent a total of two days with you and . . . [*Laughing*]

Bob: That's all you need.

James: Of course, we had lots of phone conversations. But, really, after you get the understanding, what more can you do?

Bob: That's why I don't have "followers." People can get it in one talk if they're ripe. Especially if they've looked at it before.

James: Well, I certainly think that's a gift of yours—being able to convey the understanding so well. So many people read and study Advaita, and they keep going back to see the teachers, and they keep searching. I find it perplexing that so many people keep coming to see you for years and years. Unless it's just to be in your presence.

Bob: It's not necessary to be in anyone's presence. Some people keep coming and some don't. I started my teaching with alcoholics and druggies. This was when we had our health-food store, and it happened to be close to an AA chapter. They used to come in the store, and I knew I could help them. One thing led to another, and then I wound up talking to lots of them about non-duality. These people were in the same place I had been 16 years earlier when I was an alcoholic—full of their minds, full of the self center, and all the rest of it. And many of these people had never done any searching at all, so it was quite hard for them. Some of them got relief almost immediately. But they don't get it fully. They get some understanding and then get stuck in their minds again.

James: I'm sure some people are a lot more serious than others. In my case, I had certain doubts. To some extent, I felt like non-duality just sounded like more words—more concepts. I had been so brainwashed that the nervous system had to get purified, and you had to have certain experiences. I'm sure you know the word "*darshan*," that is used in India to indicate being in the presence of someone who is living the enlightenment. When you see someone who's liberated, it has a powerful effect in giving one faith in what is possible. That's one of the main reasons I wanted to see you. I had to know whether you were actually living what you spoke of in your book.

There's No One to Be Aware

James: I love politics. So I watch lots of news shows. And all they ever show these days is killing, beheading, and car bombings.

Bob: And corruption.

James: And corruption. Many seekers won't watch television because of all the negativity and all the news of death and war. When you analyze it, though, something isn't right in our suffering about all the death. Death is what's happening. It's always been happening, and it's never going to stop. So why are we so freaked out about it?

Bob: That's right. People often come to me complaining about war and people dying in Africa. I tell them, "Yes, you're all concerned about it because it's brought to your attention. But you pick up the morning newspaper, and how many of you look at the death notices? Every day in Melbourne about two hundred people die. Nobody takes any notice of that." [Note: In the world of appearance, there is a massive difference between a person dying peacefully of old age and a child being blown up in a terrorist attack. But within the context of consciousness, or oneness, there is no difference whatsoever. One possible solution to this problem is to decide where you wish to live: in the world of appearance or in the world of reality.]

James: Nisargadatta said there are worlds colliding in space, and people on earth are worried about all the deaths over here. It's that damned reference point again.

Bob: It's the reference point that makes us think we're so important. When you have the understanding, then the Biblical statement starts to become real: "A thousand shall fall on your left side, ten thousand will fall on your right side. But it doesn't come nigh your dwelling place." You see everyone carrying on, and you're just not interested anymore. It doesn't come near you. It doesn't touch you. Whatever little does, you can handle quite easily. The solution comes up. It's amazing, really. You see the chaos and trouble going on in the world, but it doesn't touch you.

James: When I first looked in your eyes at the airport, I noticed that there doesn't seem to be any worrying going on. That was my first impression. Most people's faces reveal so much anxiety.

Bob: So, Emmett's still into meditation?

James: Yes. He still loves it, and he thinks it will bring liberation. I suspect that's going to change in the next few days. Emmett and Kerry and I all taught TM for years, and we went to long meditation courses and all. But, about four or five years ago, the meditation just fell off for me. It just didn't seem to have any effect, other than rest for the body. And that's not what I was looking for. Some people have the nature to enjoy meditation and solitude. Some people go live in caves. I could never do that.

Bob: There's no one to meditate, and nothing to meditate on. There's a natural meditation going on all the time. You don't have to sit with your eyes closed. It doesn't start and it doesn't end. It's there all the time.

James: That would be living the natural state, without constantly thinking and labeling.

Bob: The functioning happens. And then that silence comes automatically. But you're not looking for the silence anymore. Before, we constantly strained to find the silence. . . . And it's impossible because the very act of looking makes silence impossible.

James: Almost every time I've read a story of someone who awakened, they tell a story of some incredible spectacle. And it makes the reader look for some super intense experience. It keeps them searching. When people come here in a few weeks to hear you speak, I can guarantee that some of them have gone to this teacher and that teacher. And after they see you, they'll go see a bunch more teachers.

Bob: That's right.

James: They're coming to see "the enlightened guy who'll maybe give them enlightenment." The question is: when they are offered the understanding, will they take it?

Bob: That's right.

James: Some of them will say, "No, I want to search. No, I want some great experience."

Bob: [*Laughing*] "No, the next one will know better. I'll go to the next one when he comes. He'll know more."

James: It's not so much that he'll know more. It's that this is way too simple. It can't be it. But it is it. One thought that comes into my mind a lot is about purpose. I think, "What's the purpose of all this life? Oh yes, there is no purpose. . . . What about the purpose? Oh, yes. There is no purpose." It comes up a lot. What did you call existence—a ripple or a blurb on the emptiness?

Bob: An appearance. Like a cloud arises in the sky, the appearance arises on the emptiness. There's a metaphor the Buddhists use: "space-like awareness." Or "cognizing emptiness." The sky is empty, you see. And the sun is in the sky. The sun shines of itself. The sun cannot know darkness. But it can't know light either because it has nothing to compare itself to. It's self-shining, and we are self-aware. There's no one to be aware. Awareness is self-shining, like the sun.

The sun evaporates the water and forms a cloud. When a cloud comes upon us, we think we can't see the sun. But the sun has never left the sky. And the sun itself has caused the cloud by evaporating the water. Then, the sun stirs the air or blows the cloud away. So, none of those clouds are attached to the sky. If you look at the thoughts and try and see what they're attached to, you'll see they're not attached to anything. They just arise on that "space-like emptiness" and play around a while and then disappear. But people believe that there's some reality to them, and then they fixate on them and keep them there.

James: Bob, do you often feel infinite? Do you have feelings of infinity, like an experience?

Bob: That would be a concept. You would have to get a concept of what infinity is. Right now is infinity. Right now is eternity. What do you have to feel or think about? It just is.

James: That means you have that all the time.

Bob: It's always the background, yes. All the feelings, senses, and emotions are still there. Nothing goes away, as far as that's concerned. Prior to having the understanding, they would get locked in and carried around for long periods. Now, they come up and quickly disappear.

Vashti Takes Back Her Power from the Mind

James: [*Speaking to Vashti who has just entered the room*] We're talking about the appearance of creation and how it happens.

Bob: We're talking about intelligence energy. I don't mean the intellect.

I'm speaking of the intelligence functioning in the universe. It's not something separate from creation—it's intelligence itself displaying as all this manifestation. It's beating your heart, maintaining the seasons, and so forth. It's one essence, one taste. That energy is a subtle pulsation or vibration. And that is the activity of knowing—the knowing that you are. That knowing is the immediacy, because it's a happening. If it's something that is *known*, then it's something that is dead or over.

Vashti: So, are you always conscious of infinity?

Bob: Not as a concept of infinity. But it's all one anyway, and knowing that there can't be anything other than that. . . . What the ancients said was true, as far as I'm concerned. Existence is omnipresent, all presence. It's omnipotent, all power. It's omniscience, all intelligence. It can't be anything other than the one. The idea that there is "me" and other is a movement away from that.

Vashti: I know that. But I forget it a lot, when things come up.

Bob: Yes, but what can be remembered and forgotten is not you. The remembering and forgetting appears on the knowing. You wouldn't be able to remember and forget if the knowing wasn't there. So, the knowing is there but is seemingly obstructed by clouds.

James: The remembering and forgetting is from the mind. Bob is talking about something other than the mind. He's talking about the knowingness. The remembering and forgetting is in the world of duality. What I'm now realizing is that we've been asking you this question of whether you experience infinity *from our reference point.*

Bob: [*Laughing*] You're seeing it.

James: In fact, infinity is all that really is.

Vashti: [*inaudible question*]

Bob: Look, you're seeing right now, aren't you? Is your eye saying to you, "I see"? Is you ear saying to you, "I hear"? The thought comes up and translates it into "I see something; I hear something." But ask yourself, can that thought "I see" actually do the seeing?

Vashti: No.

Bob: And the thought "I'm aware," is that your awareness?

Vashti: Wow. I see.

Bob: So you see that thought has no power at all. So you see that you couldn't have any thoughts at all if you didn't have awareness. If that basic knowingness weren't with you, how many thoughts could you have? None. The mind has no power. The power is coming from that pure intelligence energy. It enables the mind to appear on it. The mind itself is nothing.

Vashti: So I've been feeling the power and attributing it to the mind?

Bob: Yes. You are the power. Even your expressing where the power is coming from couldn't exist without that life essence. Thought is just a translator. It translates in words and concepts, and you have to understand that the word can't be the real thing. The map can't be the territory. The word "water" will never quench your thirst. The word "me" is not what you are. And the thought "I am" is not you either. That's the primary thought. Awareness, or consciousness, is your true nature. It is constantly with you. Under no circumstances can you say, "I am not," because you have to exist to be able to say it.

James: You have a big smile on your face, Vashti.

Vashti: It feels good! So, of course, it would seem like things come and go. I lose touch, and I forget. The mind is always . . .

Bob: Yes, the mind is dualistic. It can only function in the interrelated pairs of opposites. If it's not past, which is memory, then it's future, which is imagination and anticipation. And within that range, it's constantly functioning in the good/bad, pleasant/painful, happy/sad, loving/hating, positive/negative, and so on. Life is only a vibration, or movement of energy, and it gets translated into words or labels. This whole manifestation is that dualism. If there wasn't silence, there couldn't be sound. If there wasn't day, there couldn't be night. So, the entire manifestation is only an appearance. It's just vibration, or patterns of energy, appearing on that emptiness. We take the appearance to be real. But it's not. You are the essence on which the vibrations appear. And that's not in the body. The body is in that.

That's why you can't grasp it in the mind. It's not in the mind. The mind is in that. The mind is a thing. What you are in reality is the no thing in which all things appear. You are that infinity, omnipresence, omniscience. We put limitations and boundaries on ourselves by words: "I'm not good enough, I've got low self-esteem," and so on. Things we've learned. These are all added to the primary thought "I am," which you don't actually need in order to know that you are. We add to that "I'm not good enough," and form a mental image that is seemingly concrete, substantial, and real. And that becomes a reference point which everything is evaluated from. Everything is relative to that reference point. Things are either good or bad from that image of ourselves, pleasant or painful from that image of ourselves. When you understand that that reference point is invalid—it has no independent nature and can't stand on its own without consciousness or awareness to support it—then you're free of it.

Vashti: That frees up a lot of energy.

Bob: You see, you have the five senses: smelling, touching, tasting, hearing, and seeing. But most of our awareness is taken up with thinking. And so much of that energy goes into past and future concerns. Even though we're using the senses, we focus more on the mind. When you are totally focused on what is happening in the moment, when you're with your five senses, thinking can never be a problem. Energy is freed up. Something that would have been a problem with lots of thinking can be easily seen through.

Vashti: And then all of the five senses work better.

Bob: There's a saying, "Be utterly awake with the five senses wide open." Actually, you are always wide awake. You don't have to do anything to make that happen. And they say, "Be utterly open with un-fixated awareness." And that's the key to it. You're not fixating on anything—fixation is resistance. Allow thoughts and everything to flow. Just like nature. Nature's not worrying about the next season. It's not worrying or resisting anything. The pairs of opposites are constantly functioning in nature. When we take a reference point and try to alter or correct things, that's conflict and resistance. And that resistance stops the flow of energy. That causes all kinds of problems.

*

Saturday Night Party

On Saturday night, eight or ten friends gathered at our house to meet Bob and hear him talk. Bob covered essentially the same topics presented in this book. Only one or two attendees were familiar with non-duality, and reactions were therefore somewhat different from those at the formal talks that came later, which drew people from as far away as Arizona, Chicago, and Seattle. Those people had experienced a powerful resonance with the teachings in Bob's book and were very keen on meeting a living expression of Advaita. They were serious about making use of Bob's teaching and were, like me, finally getting answers to longtime questions.

At the Saturday night gathering, it became clear that many people don't take to Advaita right away, even when very interested in spirituality. This, of course, is not surprising. As must be obvious to anyone who has read this far, non-duality is an extremely counterintuitive paradigm. Its teachings contradict habitual beliefs perpetuated since one's earliest memories. People hearing for the first time that their self-identity is nothing more than a bunch of thoughts and mental images have much contemplation ahead before making any use of the fact. Even if one is deeply familiar with the concept of enlightenment, the idea that one is "being lived" and has never made an independent decision or choice in one's life may well bring some resistance.

As it was, no one at Saturday night's lecture appeared to be dramatically affected. A few from the crowd returned for more of his talks, but none that I could tell, except Emmett, experienced significant life changes due to non-dual teachings. Of course, my friends had a good time and enjoyed the talk. But clearly none were bitten by the non-duality "bug." This surprised me in some cases. Here I was, taking advantage of what I then, and still, consider the greatest spiritual opportunity of my life. Within days I had seen my understanding of non-duality deepen dramatically and impact my psychology in a wonderful way. I was thus taken aback when two very close friends were not grabbed by Bob's talk.

These were friends who were interested in spiritual matters and with whom Vashti and I had enjoyed many philosophical discussions over the years. Of course, I was being drenched in the knowledge all day long. They were not. Still, I was surprised.

One friend appeared to have a difficult time grasping that the mind could be contained by something outside itself (consciousness, or "no thing") and not the other way around. He kept looking for the reality Bob was speaking of within the mind, where it can never be found. Others asked questions about love and harmony and how to make the world a better place—not exactly issues which receive much attention from a teaching that considers existence perfect as it is, and nothing more than an appearance anyway. A few that I spoke with afterwards seemed to understand what Bob was saying but, as far as I could tell, weren't about to let the knowledge impact their lives. This brought home the fact that there is nothing one can do to gain liberation. Despite apparent causes, the understanding, or the knowingness, either happens or it doesn't.

Within the world of appearance there are all sorts of possible explanations as to why some people are moved by non-dual teachings and others are not. They are ultimately all false, of course. Aside from the fact that there cannot be any real cause in an imaginary world (that is, a transitory world with no independent nature), bondage itself is false. Therefore, liberation does not exist. People may believe they are limited and mortal, but this is no different from believing that ocean water is blue, or that a mirage can quench someone's thirst. We are all free. Who we truly are (presence awareness, consciousness, space, "no thing") has always existed and will always exist. It is just that some are aware of the fact and others are not. This is why, as mentioned earlier in this book, genuine teachers make their understanding available but have no vested interest in whether anyone grasps it or not.

For example, months after Bob went home, I asked him how many had fully grasped his message and was stunned when he replied, "A few." I said, "You mean a few, as in five or ten, over nearly thirty years of teaching?" He said that plenty of people had gotten some benefits from his message, but only a few had grasped it fully. Only a few had gone "beyond the need for further help," as Nisargadatta puts it. He added quite happily that the number was increasing because of his recent visit to America. He had encountered many ripe seekers at his talks here, some of whom had since traveled to Australia for further sessions with him.

My point is that Bob had spoken to several thousand people over a thirty-year period and at age seventy-six was still going strong despite so few truly grasping his teaching. This is no problem for Bob because he knows that everyone actually is free—whether or not they know it. Manifest creation is simply a dream, or appearance, and is actually carrying on exactly as it should, no matter how horrendous it sometimes seems. Existence is one movement of energy, comprised of consciousness. It is oneness appearing as many. What occurs within the appearance is no more important or significant than the dreams we experience during sleep, which are real to us when happening but unreal when they are over.

The teaching that the world is a dream-like appearance is unquestionably difficult to fathom when a person believes he or she is a separate individual. When one feels separate, everything that is seen as "other" somehow gains greater weight and authenticity. When the sense of separateness falls away, however, and one recognizes one's true nature as infinite and unbounded, that which is physical and transitory stands out as changeable and therefore unreal. Paradoxically, one may also feel a greater sense of connection to everything—even the world of physical objects—because of the pervasive sense of oneness that is ever present. One sees the physical as false or illusory because it is changeable but knows that it exists by virtue of the underlying oneness—the unbounded consciousness that is who we are. At least, that has been my experience in the months since Sailor Bob left.

But one should not necessarily expect to feel exactly what I have just described—that is just my experience. That is my perception. And while there are certain common denominators among those who have recognized oneness, perceptions vary from person to person. One of the biggest problems that has arisen over the centuries is the confusion created by different so-called realized souls describing their own unique experiences. It cannot be overemphasized that awakening shows up differently in different nervous systems. For example, while the world of appearance has recently lost much of its reality for me, I have not felt the bliss and ecstasy for hours on end that some have reported. While I am now experiencing a startling amount of effortless fulfillment of desires—something utterly unknown to me before—I have yet to see the miraculous disappearance of reactions that can occur. I have experienced a great lessening of reactions, but nowhere near what some describe.

Different ideas and concepts will also resonate more or less with different people. In the year or so leading up to meeting Sailor Bob, my friend Kerry and I often spent several hours a week on the phone discussing non-duality. When Kerry first encountered Advaita, he was struck like a thunderbolt by the reality of non-doership. Non-doership is the feature Buddha described when he made his famous statement, "Events happen; deeds are done; there is no doer." This is the same point Sailor Bob frequently makes that, since no one can find a self center within, there is no individual present. What we are is consciousness, presence awareness, intelligence energy, space, or "no thing." Thus, there is no one *doing* anything. As Bob says, "We are being lived." This truth, which powerfully impacted Kerry's life the instant he learned of it, had precious little effect on me until I met Sailor Bob. I can't count how many discussions—and arguments—Kerry and I had about the non-doership issue during the year before Bob arrived. My favorites were when I spoke of doing something in order to speed up the awakening process (a completely absurd notion in the first place), and Kerry, like Bob, would ask, "But *who's* going to do that?" To which I would answer, "The same person who picked up the phone five minutes ago, so we could have this discussion!"

In my case, for a very long time the truth of non-doership paled in comparison to the understanding that time is a mental concept. From the moment I recognized the falseness of past and future, life was never the same. I felt immediate and dramatic relief from all the mistakes, indiscretions, and bad behavior that had accumulated over fifty years of living. I am talking about the mistakes that were constantly in my awareness and had plagued me on a daily basis. When I realized that the only actual reality is the present moment—right here, right now—it became immediately apparent that my past had happened in appearance only—literally in a dream. I was freed from the weight of guilt and regret I had been carrying. (Note: This does not mean I am not fully responsible for any present action taken. And it does not mean that I will be spared moments of upset or regret if and when "future" mistakes are made. It means that once an occurrence is seen in hindsight, it is clear that it was illusory.) Kerry, on the other hand, was far more moved by non-doership than the conceptual nature of past and future. Non-doership provided him with relief from his past mistakes the instant he realized there was no Kerry taking the actions that appeared to be his. Thus, he appreciated a certain understanding I did not, and vice versa.

Here's another example of the profound differences in people's experiences. For the last year or so I have enjoyed somewhat habitual experiences of pure silence and stillness in the middle of the night. During these periods the usual intensity of thoughts and feelings have dramatically abated while presence awareness has been glaring. The more this has happened, the more sense it has made to me that these occurrences were consistently happening in the dead of night when activity had ceased. It made perfect sense, that is, until Vashti told me that her clearest experiences of presence awareness always happened during the day, in the midst of activity!

Why do different people have different experiences and perceptions? That is simply what is. One can, of course, go on forever, citing all kinds of apparent reasons: different backgrounds, genetics, socioeconomic upbringings, spiritual techniques, and so on. But ultimately, these distinctions are false. They can be true only in the world of appearance. More importantly, the point is moot because awakening is not based on experience. It is based on understanding. If liberation—freedom from apparent bondage—were based on experience, what would the criteria be? Would it be the ability to raise people from the dead, which Christ and some yogis are said to have done? Would it be intense psychic ability, which some so-called realized souls have to a great degree, but others do not? Would it be the ability to live for 500 years, as the Indian saint Babaji has supposedly done? Would it be the ability to look into someone's eyes and give them an instantaneous experience of oneness—something H. L. Poonja (also called Papaji) did for disciples? Would it be the ability to appear in two different places at once by creating an ethereal body, as Ramana Maharshi reportedly did when he met Papaji in North India while simultaneously speaking to his disciples in South India? Would it be the ability to stop a train engine from starting, as Neem Karoli Baba did? Would it be the ability to heal people of illnesses, as Nisargadatta did, simply by being in their presence? Would it be when one's sense of individual identity has so disappeared that one no longer answers when one's name is called out? Would it be the ability to stop one's heart or enter *samadhi* (a deep meditative state where all thoughts and bodily activities—even the heart—stop) for hours at a time? Would it be when no desires or preferences arise—including the desire for lobster or chocolate, or the preference that one's child lives a happy life?

It would be none of these. Because, for one thing, many miraculous powers have been achieved by individuals whose sense of separation and seeking have not abated. More importantly, as long as life functions in its apparent evolutionary fashion, there will always be bigger and better experiences with no end in sight. For thousands of years, sages and seers have stated over and over that there is no experience that proves a person's liberation. Experience is not what is needed. We can never get enough of what will not bring eternal peace!

Although experiences and perceptions are likely to deepen and intensify in apparent time, the most one should expect from non-dual understanding is the falling away of the sense of separateness, the end of the sense of seeking and becoming, and the end of undue concerns over past and future. (Of course, there will always be some thought for the future while living in the world of appearance. One needs to pack necessary medicines before going on a hiking trip in the woods, one needs to prepare for a test, and so on.) And, of course, one should feel the peace and joy that results from all these. As mentioned in the Introduction, if these shifts have not occurred, understanding has not happened. But keep in mind that these effects need not necessarily become permanent in one instant. The habits of a lifetime did not disappear instantaneously for Sailor Bob Adamson, nor for many whom Nisargadatta deemed liberated and asked whether their understanding had come suddenly or gradually. What is necessary is simply to see that the reference point, the false "me," is a mind-created phantom and to remember this fact when accidentally getting lost in it. What is necessary is to fully understand that what you are seeking, you already are. What is necessary is to realize that because existence is, in essence, oneness, all reference points are false. This means that all viewpoints are false, including the idea that Advaita is the best spiritual teaching or that one thing is better than another. As the sixth-century Zen scripture the *Hsin Hsin Ming* puts it, "A mind that sees good and evil is a diseased mind."

Within the world of appearance, it seems that the seekers who have the most difficult time with non-dual teachings are the ones who listen from their intellects, rather than their hearts. When the heart is open to the teachings, a kind of surrender can take place, which seems to be essential. There is nothing one can do to surrender, and yet for those who become self-realized, surrendering somehow has occurred. The problem with trying to surrender, of course, is that since we cannot find a self center, who is to do the surrendering?

Because all reference points are false, the teachings of non-duality—which can only be presented in words and concepts—are as invalid as any other point of view. As the Taoist scripture says, "The Tao that can be spoken is not the true Tao." However, within the world of appearance where our "experience" occurs, realizing oneness produces positively remarkable effects. At the very least, it brings the end of psychological suffering. But in order to grasp the teaching and begin to unravel the conditioning of the false "me" that has been developed over the course of a lifetime, there is an apparent need for openness. It is the kind of openness one demonstrates when consciously trying to appreciate another person's point of view. It is, in a sense, an act of generosity or perhaps a kind of faith.

Who can say why one person will have this openness and another will not? In my own apparent process, I seemed to need to be with a teacher I trusted, a teacher who was patient and willing to explain certain issues again and again until I could grasp them. Most of all, I seemed to need to see someone living non-duality before I could let go of my safe world of old conditioning and accept a teaching that seemed logical spiritually, but was massively counterintuitive. Although I had read four years' worth of books and heard plenty of CDs before meeting Sailor Bob, my life had not yet been greatly affected. I agreed with what I read, but only a few of these truths deeply impacted my thoughts and habits, and certainly not enough to end my nagging sense of separateness. In reality, my eventually getting a fuller understanding is simply what happened. Any explanation of my apparent process is nothing more than words and concepts. In the world of concepts, however, let me say that it did not hurt one bit that Bob expected me to grasp his teaching. Naturally, I have no way of knowing what on earth, if anything, Bob expected. But it seemed to me then, as it does now, that Bob expects everyone he speaks with to recognize the same reality he does.

In terms of being ripe for grasping non-duality, there are no rules. Some people with no obvious spiritual or philosophical background understand the teachings immediately and have their lives radically altered. Others, like myself, are ripened in the traditional way. First, I had a background of thirty years of meditation and mysticism. While that carries a certain amount of baggage with it, it also means that only a few of the non-dual concepts were jarring. Second, I had concluded years earlier, before finding non-duality that I was no longer interested in self-development, better experiences, and so on. My main desire was liberation. That was no small thing. Most seekers believe that self-development and liberation are connected and try in vain to "purify" and fix themselves, hoping ultimate freedom will follow. It will not. It will not because there is no end to purifying or perfecting oneself. The apparent evolutionary nature of life guarantees that one can go on forever getting better, smarter, healthier, happier, and so on, without attaining the one thing that really matters: liberation. That much had become obvious to me after engaging in all those years of spiritual, healing, and self-development practices. And so, several years prior to Bob's visit I had stopped trying to fix myself. And at this point, although I was better for all my self-development, I was still suffering. I worried about the future, about how my son would fare when I died, about worldly affairs, about what kind of God would allow torture, and I still feared death. Worst of all, the nagging sense of separation that had existed since early childhood had not budged.

I was as familiar as could be with the physical world and its transitory nature and dearly wanted to know the other side of the equation—the side that sages and seers have spoken and written about. I definitely had the strong desire for liberation they claimed was essential. And, although I had ended my formal meditation practice, I had occasionally been practicing a certain inquiry of my own, which was, in a way, a precursor to Nisargadatta's advice to be with the "I am" and Bob's teaching of being with presence awareness. This was nothing complex or intricate, but merely an attempt to make sense of what I had learned about other people's awakenings. So many of the people who had attained freedom reported that when they found their true selves they realized they had always been free. If this was the case, I thought, then *I must be free now*, despite feeling limited, mortal, fearful, and enslaved by God knows how many concerns. So, I would occasionally sit with eyes closed, trying to perceive where this great freedom was in just "being." And though this appeared to result in nothing, it may have been a worthwhile part of the apparent process. At any rate, suffice it to say that I was lucky.

What follows is a two- or three-minute sample of Bob's twenty-minute Saturday night talk, followed by excerpts of questions and answers. The entire talk is not included because much of it was similar to talks already transcribed in these pages.

*

Saturday Night Talk

Bob: What I speak about is based on what the ancients have told us. In Hinduism they call it Advaita, which means non-duality, or one without a second. In Dzogchen Buddhism they say, "Non-conceptual, ever-fresh, self-shining presence awareness. Just this and nothing else." In Hebrew scriptures they say, "Hear, oh Israel, the Lord our God, the Lord is One." There is no other than that. Most traditions speaking about God, or the Supreme, say it's omnipresence, omnipotence, omniscience—total presence, total power, and total intelligence, or total knowing. If what they say is true, it's total. It doesn't leave room for you, me, or anything outside of that or other than that. But over the years, this all gets garbled and mistranslated.

Take this body, for instance, which I believed was who I was. If you investigate, you'll see that the false can't stand up to investigation. What's the body made up of? It's made up of the elements—air, water, fire, space, earth. All those elements are what makes up the universe. And they can be broken down into subatomic particles—into nothing, into space, into emptiness. And that is the same with everything in manifestation. So everything is made of the same essence. I use the term "the natural state," or "presence awareness," or "intelligence energy." I don't like to use the term "God" because people come from different religions, and everyone has a different concept about that.

When I was with Nisagadatta, years and years ago, I was in a bad way. And he said to me, "The only way I can help anybody is to take them beyond the need for help." And he did just that by getting me to look to see for myself whether what I believed myself to be was true or not. And when I investigated in the way he pointed out, I found that I wasn't what I believed myself to be. And I haven't needed help from that day to now. That doesn't mean that dramas and problems don't come up. All sorts of things have happened to us [Bob and Barb] over the years. But with that release from the bondage of self, there is a sense of well-being. It's innately within you. And you all know it, and you've had glimpses of it all your lives. But we've ignored it because we've been so focused on looking outwards. That's why I say that when you hear this, it will resonate, because it's your natural state.

The Knowingness Prior to the Mind

Emmett: What about the suffering and the bombing going on in the world? Are we not affected by that?

Bob: The problem is all based on that false self center you believe yourself to be. If a child has a warm, loving family around, he feels more secure and less vulnerable. In old times, families gathered and formed into tribes. The stronger my tribe, the more secure and less vulnerable I would be. Today, people form into nations, and nations go to war with other nations because of that insecurity and vulnerability. They're always frightened of what the nation next door will do. Then they think, "We'll get them first, before they get us. Then we'll be stronger and less vulnerable." All our problems are based on that idea of a self center, an individual, a separate entity. But if I know that there's no identity here [*pointing to himself*], I must certainly know—whether you do or not—that there's no identity there [*pointing to people in the audience*]. So, if there's no identity here, and there's no identity there, what could I want of yours? Why would I hate you? Why would I feel insecure? That's where every problem arises from—that primary dualism of "me" and "other." Every "ism" arises from that: capitalism, communism, Catholicism, Hinduism, Buddhism. They all arise from that idea of a separate identity.

Emmett: This seems to suggest that there's a being or a reality that we realize we are—that oneness—and yet the body and mind continue. So we still have a protectiveness over that. We're not going to allow that body to be damaged if we can help it. So we're still acting with respect to that self as ours.

Bob: Yes, and that self will continue and procreate and so on. The Hindus have a phrase, *sat chit ananda*, which means "existence consciousness bliss." This is not three things, but one and the same thing—three aspects of it. It's another way of explaining that "being" which you can't negate, "knowing" which you can't negate, and "loving to be." That's the blissful aspect, "loving to be." We'll do anything to be, rather than die. Loving to be is an innate functioning. It's keeping us going.

Emmett: So, even when you're aware of that self that never dies . . .

Bob: It was never born.

Emmett: It's eternal. And yet you act in this world in a way to maintain that which appears to be vulnerable to death?

Bob: It's not a "you" that acts. Activities simply take place. What was born was the sense of "I." The little child knows that she is, but she has no sense of "me" or "I." When she cries for food or for her mother, she does that naturally, but she has no self-identity yet. Eventually, she is conditioned to believe she is a separate person, or individual. And that's when the "I," or sense of a self center, is born. Well, it's that "I" that dies. The ancient scriptures tell you that. In the prayer of St. Francis, it says, "Make me an instrument of thy peace. Where there's hatred, let me sow love." And he goes through many of the opposites, until he comes to the end of it. Then he says, "It's only by dying that I can have eternal life." Well, he's not talking about carking it [Australian slang for dying]. He's talking about dying to that self center. He's saying that only then will he be an instrument of peace. St. Paul says the same thing. He says, "I die daily." He's talking about dying to that sense of individual self.

Have a look at when your body started. There was intelligence energy in the sperm and the ovum in which you were created. When the intelligence energy in the sperm and ovum operated, it doubled a cell that had started out single. If you had any beginning, that single cell would have been it. Even before that, the intelligence energy was in the food that your mother and father ate. And you can go back before that, until the energy was in everything. It's never had a beginning. And when will it ever end? When this body dies, disintegration occurs. There are a million enzymes that come into play and start to devour it. And worms and maggots come along and eat the body. So life is continually living on life. It can't know death. With the birth of the body, there was one sperm that made it into the ovum. What about the millions of sperms that didn't make it? They were life too. When you have a disease in the body, those bacteria or microbes have as much right to life as we do.

Emmett: And we have the ability to appreciate all these things because of mind.

Bob: Yes. Of course.

Emmett: When the mind is lost, when we die, that intelligence doesn't experience in an individual way anymore. And that's the basis for my fear of death.

Bob: Now, you say that, without the mind, you won't know. But you're knowing right now, aren't you?

Emmett: I am.

Bob: But without that *thought*, are you still knowing?

Emmett: Yes.

Bob: That's prior to that thought, isn't it? That knowingness. And you are still seeing? You're registering everything in this room right now? You're hearing sounds, feeling your backside on the chair?

Emmett: That's also by virtue of the nervous system.

Bob: That's right, but the nervous system is a translation too. But without that life force, nothing could exist.

Emmett: They both need to be present. That's what I'm trying to work out. What kind of existence is there without the body-mind mechanism present? There's pure awareness but no individuality anymore. So, for all intents and purposes, there really is death!

Bob: What are you now? What's your current image of yourself? The idea that you're a separate identity is nothing more than a mental image, a mental picture without any substance and without any independent nature.

Emmett: So you are confident that when you leave this world, your awareness of your true nature somehow lives on, and there is no death or loss?

Bob: There's no one here that was ever born. What was never born can never die. The ancients call it "cognizing emptiness." I look within and can't find a center. There's nothing there. But yet there is still seeing, hearing, and all the functioning. So it's that emptiness itself that has the capacity of knowing. The emptiness is universal, and it has intelligence, or knowing. The functioning is happening on that emptiness.

Emmett: I get it, every now and then, when you explain it. I get it for a moment—and then it leaves me.

Worry, Fear, and Loving to Be

Susan: When you came to understand this, did it make you feel hopeful or despairing?

Bob: I felt freedom from the bondage of self. I was no longer bound to this entity that was full of pain, anxiety, fear, self-pity, guilt, and remorse. In seeing this, I said, "I'll never get caught in the mind again." And then I walked out the door [of Nisargadatta's flat] and naturally was right back in it. Because it's become habitual. But in seeing it, it was never the same again. Once you see something as false, you can never believe it again.

Susan: Do you ever worry?

Bob: Thoughts will come up. There are still emotions and feelings. But where before they were like a snowball rolling downhill, gathering speed—with increasing anxiety and suffering and fear—now they come up, play around for a while, and disperse—just as is. Unaltered, unmodified, uncorrected. That's the play of the functioning of consciousness, awareness, intelligence energy. Just as clouds aren't anchored to the sky, these thoughts aren't anchored anywhere in here [*tapping his chest*].

Martin: If you were in a dire situation, and someone attacked you, how would you react?

Bob: I don't know, until the time comes. . . . Naturally, I would defend myself. I could be trying to escape. There would be some response, certainly.

Martin: Why defend oneself? I've read stories about Zen teachers having normal reactions to dangerous situations, and the disciples are disappointed. They think the master is supposed to be beyond it all. Of course, it makes sense that if you're in the moment, then whatever comes up is fine. On the other hand, it seems that if you've gone beyond this illusion, it would be a matter of indifference.

Bob: Yes, but to whom? If there's anyone to have indifference, he's back in the self center again. It's not a matter of being indifferent. Whatever activity takes place is only taking place by this image—this mind-body organism, or this pattern of energy. The pattern of energy could attack; it could be destroyed; it could do whatever functioning happens. People have this idea or image about how a so-called master should act, instead of simply seeing what is.

Martin: From my perspective, or the students with the Zen master, it seems that any attempt at self-defense indicates that the teacher only had an intellectual understanding and that he was caught defending himself. That would seem to indicate that the teacher had a sense of self. But, if I understand you correctly, there simply is no self.

Bob: There is no self. As I said earlier, there is a "loving to be" that everyone has. If you take that attitude of "Why defend yourself?" it would extend to "Why would you eat? Why keep this life going at all?" It's just a natural instinct to keep going. Look at nature. Why would an animal run away from a lion? Because it wants to be. It wants to live.

Martin: And what about fear?

Bob: That's just a feeling or emotion that comes up. Many times, we label it fear from a past, similar experience when it's actually not fear. As soon as we label it fear, anger, or anxiety, we're loading it down with those past things, which makes it worse than it actually is. If I dropped a snake at your feet right now, you'd be up and probably out of this room immediately. When you got out of the room, because of the adrenalin pumping and goose pimples or whatever, you'd say, "I'm scared." But it's just an emotion or reaction that got you out of a certain situation. You've named it fear and loaded it down with that label. Instead of seeing it as it is, we immediately label it and load it down with past events. And it becomes a lot worse than it actually is. Labeling is the cause of all kinds of problems.

Emmett: There's the loving to be, which causes the response, and then we attach the label to it, which has nothing to do with the actual reality. Like an animal. It doesn't have fear. It just has an appropriate response to circumstances.

Bob: Look at how animals act. The lion chases the herd of antelope, and it catches one of them. Fifty feet down the track, the antelopes have stopped and gotten back to their normal life, which is eating. If it was us, we'd be checking behind ourselves all day wondering, "Is he still coming after us? Has he gone away?" We'd be worried and concerned about it all day, instead of immediately getting back to life. Things can come up, and you let them go when you stop labeling everything. Lots of experiences happen without labeling. You've heard stories of car crashes where someone is stuck, and a person lifts up the car to save the victim. You ask the person, "How did you do that?" They say, "I don't know." You ask, "Why would you do that?" They say, "I have no idea." I watch a lot of documentaries. They once showed a pack of wild dogs chasing an antelope. Then all of a sudden, the pack just veered off and left it alone. There was a sure feed for them, and yet they just stopped. Why? Innate intelligence just directed them. There are all kinds of things like that happening constantly.

With the understanding of non-duality, many scriptural statements start coming true. Like the one, "A thousand shall fall on your left side, ten thousand fall on your right. But it doesn't come near your dwelling place." Much of the world's activities don't come near here. I go out and see the world's chaos and madness and all that's going on, and somehow it doesn't come near. The other one: "Acknowledge Him in all thy ways, and He will direct thy path." Just open yourself and listen to that inner essence, and you'll find yourself going here, there, and everywhere and doing what needs to be done quite effortlessly. I call that effortless living. And yet, you'll see this body/mind making a tremendous effort sometimes. But the results so easily and effortlessly fall into place.

Regarding labeling, there was a fifteenth- or sixteenth-century Japanese Zen master named Bankei who said it quite simply. He called the original emptiness, "the unborn Buddha mind." And he said, "Everything is perfectly resolved in the unborn. Why exchange the unborn for thought?" And that's what we do. From our perspective—from our invalid reference point—what's going on in the universe might seem chaotic. But from further out there, billions of light years away or whatever, you'll see that it's actually a very orderly chaos. It all depends on the reference point. And if you see the falseness of the reference point, why have one?

Everything is Valid in the Appearance

Martin: Bob, what's your definition of mind?

Bob: There's really no such thing as mind. Mind is just a collection of thoughts that we call mind. And thoughts, of course, have no independent nature. They come and go. We get lost in the appearance. The appearance is still going to appear. As long as we have this body, we're going to continue to think in the same way—in the pairs of opposites. We can't think in any other way. It's a matter of understanding it. And seeing through it—having no bondage to it.

Martin: Do you believe in reincarnation?

Bob: Reincarnation implies there is some separate entity who in some future time can reincarnate. If existence is one without a second, if it's non-dual, if it's omnipresence, omnipotence, and omniscient, who is there to reincarnate and when? All that exists is right now. Patterns of energy appear and patterns of energy disappear.

James: How about in the world of appearance? Could we appear to reincarnate?

Bob: Everything is valid in the appearance. There can be telepathy. . . .

James: So, in the appearance there can be reincarnation.

Bob: There could be, but it's appearance only. There's no entity to reincarnate. For reincarnation to exist, there has to be that belief in a separate entity.

James: Well, we've just heard you talk, and you've explained that we don't really exist. But we look around the room, and we certainly appear to exist. So, in the world of appearance where most of us live [*group laughter*], there could be reincarnation.

Bob: Well, some people seem to believe in that, don't they.

James: I'm not talking about belief. I'm just saying that in the world of appearance there could be reincarnation. Right?

Bob: But, who for?

James: Well, in reality, there's no one to reincarnate. In reality, you and I aren't even sitting here talking. This whole conversation is just an appearance. So, even though there's no conversation happening, there is one appearing to happen. So, couldn't there be an appearance of someone living and dying and then returning.

Bob: All appearances and all possibilities exist.

Emmett: [*Laughing*] We got one in, James!

James: [*Group laughter*] We got the reincarnation going! There's hope that we can come back.

Judy: Where does that put astrology, for that matter?

Emmett: [*Laughing*] Don't even bring that up.

James: Oh, forget it. For the past few years every time I would do a horoscope reading and tell the person about their past lives, I'd be thinking, "There are no past lives." But, hell, the person I'm talking to doesn't even exist! So, what do I care about past-life information?

Bob: Well, in the appearance, everything is valid. It's just that it's understood to be appearance.

Clouds Aren't Attached to the Sky

Martin: Bob, what would you say to an atheist, who doesn't believe in any orderly universe? I was reading a book by a Harvard professor who was defending Darwinism. And he said existence was based on algorithms. He was trying to get rid of the idea of supreme Intelligence. It was too close to the idea of God or a divine being. But, I couldn't follow what he was saying.

Bob: As you say, he was trying to defend an "ism"—Darwinism. You see, there's a reason that I say that you'll never find the answer to life in the mind. Because the nature of the mind is dualism. The mind continually divides. Thoughts are always functioning in the pairs of opposites. The further you go into the mind, the more division there will be. The mind just keeps dividing into something else, something else, and something else. We're all intelligent people here. And you've worked out many things in the mind. But when it comes to understanding truth or reality, you've never found the answer. Why not? Surely it must eventually dawn on us that we're looking in the wrong direction. There's only one way out of the mind, and that's full stop. You can come up with all kinds of theories in the mind, but you'll never find the answer there. The ancients have already told us: "There's nothing simpler than one."

If you ask yourself, "What's wrong with right now if I don't think about it?" you have to pause thought for a moment there. And you realize you can't say a thing about it—good, bad, pleasant, or painful. The important thing is that you still are—in that pause without a thought. You still are. You're still hearing, seeing, and so on. But you haven't got a concept about it. As soon as I open my mouth, I'm conceptualizing. And that's not It. That's why I started this lecture saying, "I can't teach you anything. I can't give you anything. I can only point with these concepts." It's up to you to look into what I'm saying. It's up to you to see a concept as a concept—to see that the word is not the thing. The map is not the territory, but it points out the way.

Martin: What happens if we are the map? How do you explain to the map that the map is not the territory? That seems to be the problem.

We're all the maps, but we think we're the territory.

Bob: Now you're going into the words I was using to try to illustrate. You're dividing and carving that up, you see. That's yet another track in the mind.

Emmett: Is there anything we can *do* in terms of coming to know this reality? We're here listening to you with the hope that "once I hear Sailor Bob speak a few times, I'm going to have something more and finally know it."

Bob: Just realize what I said earlier. Realize that you were never separate in the first place. Start from that. What you're seeking, you already are. Start from that point, and then instead of striving and struggling to get some place, all you have to do is scrape away the rubbish that's stopping you from seeing it. Investigate the rubbish that comes up, and see if this is true or not.

Emmett: That investigation of the rubbish . . . There's a clearing away process that is something that the mind is doing? Who is doing that process?

Bob: No, it's just a matter of seeing. If you look at something, you see. There's no one to do the investigating, really. If it's moved to happen, something will resonate with you, and that activity will take place.

Emmett: When you say resonate with "you," you don't mean the false reference point, right? You mean our essence, or the presence awareness that is who we really are, correct?

Bob: Yes. Something will resonate with that which already innately knows it. It re-cognizes itself. The cognizing emptiness that has been ignored for so many years will re-cognize itself.

Martin: Is the re-cognizing like cleaning away a cataract, so the eye can see? It sounds like the seeing is where the action is. It sounds like the mind is in the way of seeing. And then when the mind is removed, the seeing becomes more crisp. Is that what it was like for you after you got this understanding?

Bob: I'll use a metaphor here. Consider the sun shining in space. On that space, a cloud appears. It appears that the sun is gone. But, actually, the sun is always present. And it's the sun that forms the cloud by evaporating the water. As soon as the cloud thins out, the sun is seen again. When you investigate, you realize that the sun never leaves the sky. It's self-shining. "Self-shining" means it doesn't need another light to manifest its light. And the sun can't know darkness. The further out it shines, the further darkness will disappear before it. And it can't know light either because it has nothing to compare itself with. It's like that pure intelligence energy that you are. This awareness that you are is self-shining, ever-fresh presence awareness. Just this and nothing else. It's self-aware. It doesn't need any mind to grasp it or say, "I'm aware." That awareness is there prior to any thought.

Martin: As far as your personal life goes . . .

Bob: There's no person. [*Group laughter*]

Martin: Well, before 1976, was it cloudy relative to after seeing Nisargadatta? Or was it the same reality? For me, using your metaphor, it's like I'm living in Seattle. It's cloudy all the time. [*Group laughter*] I'm wondering if you're living in Florida where it's always clear and sunny. Or is it like Seattle for you, but you're just aware of that fact.

Bob: To go back into the past, which is all conceptual, I was just the same as you. There were clouds constantly covering the sky. I believed that those clouds were actual—that they were real. There was no concept of any sun being there. It was total ignorance. I was completely ignoring my true nature. But, through investigation, I realized—I saw—that the sun was there, and that no clouds are attached to the sky. Before that, I thought that the clouds were substantial and had some independent nature. Once I saw that the sun is always there and the clouds come and go, then the false beliefs simply stopped.

No "You" to Make a Difference

Susan: When you saw all this, was it like a rebirth for you, like you were being born anew?

Bob: I can give it all kinds of descriptions, but those are just labels. They're not the real thing. There was a great sense of relief and release.

Susan: Was there some particular thing that Nisargadatta said to you. . . .

Emmett: [*Joking*] That's what we want to know—what he said to you!

James: He said the same thing as Bob, in different words.

Bob: When he told me that I was not the body or the mind, I understood what he was saying. There was a seeing of it. And then I thought, "I'll never get trapped in the mind again." And as soon as I walked out the door, the mind came back with the same old rubbish. Because it's habitual. Those habits were reinforced day in and day out for the forty-eight years before that. But, after I saw what he was saying, every time the mental rubbish would come up, I would say, "Wait a minute. I saw this was false." And that would happen more and more frequently. As the years passed, less and less energy was going into the mind. Without energy, nothing can live. So the hypnotism was broken. Energy doesn't care which way it goes. Like an electric motor, if you flip the switch one way, the motor turns left. Switch it another way, the motor goes to the right. It doesn't care. Well, it's the same with this. If you put your energy into erroneous beliefs, that's what will grow.

Susan: Do you believe that human beings can effect change?

Bob: I've got no belief. A belief is a reference point. A belief is never the actuality. There are no human beings that can do anything. But activities are taking place through the appearance of so-called human beings. That's what's happening.

Susan: Do you vote? Do you feel like there's a capacity for change, that one person can make a difference?

Bob: You see this all the time. People who are into ecology protest and stop the trees from being destroyed. Civilizations rise, play around for a while, and like everything else, they eventually disappear. Forests are cut down so cities can be built. Then after a few centuries or whatever, nature may destroy those cities, and forests come back. Nature takes over.

Susan: Do you believe in free will?

Bob: No.

James: May I say something? Bob has come here to speak. That's happening in the appearance. So, in the appearance he's doing something to help us. And we're here listening so we can get something. In the appearance, that looks like free will. But that's all in the appearance.

Bob: But there's no one speaking, and no one to get anything.

James: In reality, there are no people here doing anything. There's no self center in Bob or me or you. I can't locate an independent nature inside. All I can find are a bunch of thoughts and images. In that sense, there's no one here. But in the appearance, he's speaking, which implies he would like to help us get the understanding and make our lives better. If we want help, he's here to do that. The other day, Bob asked, "How's Emmett? Did he understand what I was telling him?" So, in the appearance, all that helping and fixing stuff is going on. It's just that Bob is talking about what's really happening, not what appears to be happening.

Barb: You can do everything that the mind thinks is making a difference, and you're achieving nothing because there is no "you."

Bob: Activists are created. Nelson Mandelas and Mahatma Gandhis are created, but there's no independent nature in any of those so-called people. They are being lived. Their lives are happening the way they are happening. It's only their minds that can attribute their actions to them—to a "me."

Barb: This creates a tremendous freedom. And if I'm moved to do something, I do it. But it's just a happening. There's no "me" that's actually here. Why is one person moved to skyjump out of airplanes or go live in the forest to study apes? That's just what happened. The same with Bob's speaking. I never thought he would start speaking. But, it happened. And his coming here to America is fascinating, the way that happened.

Bob: [*Laughing*] I had no intention of coming here. None.

Barb: He refused at first. But here he is in America, talking.

*

Two Private Talks

During the next few days, I recorded two private talks. The first is between Bob and me. The other is with Bob, Dell, and myself. For some reason, I was consumed with the notion of cognizing emptiness, as if there were some hidden meaning in the term. Eventually, I came to realize it is just a label for the phenomenon of consciousness manifesting an apparent world.

Bob and James – July 18

Bob: In one of the scriptures, they're talking about manifest creation, and it says, "Nothing is seen, yet it is seen." What you're actually seeing is "no thing," yet the whole thing is seen.

James: What do you mean I'm seeing "no thing"?

Bob: What are you?

James: Nothing. I'm space, or emptiness, or consciousness.

Bob: What are you seeing?

James: Nothing. Creation that doesn't exist.

Bob: You're actually seeing no thing, yet it is seen. It's all appearance. Can something appear from nothing?

James: No. Existence is an illusion.

Bob: This is all space.

James: So, in reality, we're seeing nothing.

Bob: Yes. Yet it is seen. You're seeing it as an appearance. But you know the truth about it. Just like you know that blue water in the ocean isn't really blue. In the *Hsin Hsin Ming*, it says, "Emptiness here, emptiness there, yet the infinite universe stands ever before your eyes."

James: So, what we're seeing appears real, but we know it isn't. Now, is the intellectual knowing of this significant or important?

Bob: It's not an "intellectual" knowing. An intellectual knowing is some *thing*. What's the only true thing you can possibly say about yourself?

James: I am. I exist.

Bob: There is a knowing that you are. You can't negate that. Pure knowingness is going on. Now, who or what is knowing that? Pure emptiness, or no thing, is knowing that. There's no entity there. That knowing is the cognizing emptiness. That's pure intelligence.

James: It's knowing itself?

Bob: No. There's no discrimination of itself in there. It's one without a second. It's pure knowing.

James: So, when I'm seeing nothing . . .

Bob: No thing. There's no object. Pure subjectivity.

James: So, this is an understanding.

Bob: Yes. Understanding is all. Now that you understand, you get back into life. You've seen through the illusion. You don't have to get into concepts about all this.

James: My concepts have been working overtime.

Bob: [*Laughing*] *Your* concepts? Who's taking delivery of them?

James: Let me say it another way. Concepts have really been appearing in the last twenty-four hours.

Bob: [*Laughing*] Who says so? Who says so? Me, me. You see the problem?

James: Yes. As you're walking around, is there a knowingness that you're looking at yourself?

Bob: There's just a knowingness. Things are appearing on that knowingness. For example, when one gets a pain in the body, it doesn't appear in that emptiness. It seemingly appears as some object out here. It's like an object. The person is aware of the pain. He takes delivery of it and says, "It's my pain."

James: So, I'm seeing the pain in the same way I'm seeing that table. Like they are outside of me, when in reality they are me.

Bob: Yes. It's one taste. The whole lot. Non-duality, one without a second. Full stop.

James: Bob, you don't actually see the emptiness, do you? You just understand that everything is space. Correct? I ask because we hear all kinds of things. We hear about celestial perception and people seeing auras and energy, and all that.

Bob: It doesn't matter whether they do see these things. Whether they're having some experience or not, they're still seeing emptiness like you and me. Actually, they're just saying, "My experience is better than your experience." Whatever is happening for them is still appearance or emptiness—no matter how great or ecstatic the happening.

James: So, we've been conditioned to crave some spiritual experience. We have to let go of that, don't we?

Bob: The whole conditioning is to look outside yourself—not realizing you're complete already. We're conditioned that the more we gather, or learn or experience, the more whole and complete we will be. That's what the search is—a search out there, away from reality. We're That from the very start, so there's nothing we have to search for. All we have to do is see what is false. And then the false drops off. You're always one without a second.

James: I realized today that when I'm in bed trying to be with presence awareness, or the "I am," I'm actually looking for more and better experience. I already feel complete, but I'm thinking it'll be more complete, more fun, more interesting, more this or that. It's ridiculous.

Bob: Totality is totality. Omnipresence means total presence. Omnipotent means total power. Omniscience means total intelligence. What can be added or taken away from that? This is what the ancients have told us from way back. It's all That. Nothing to seek. We just have to see that our beliefs were false.

James: At night I often feel this incredible silence and stillness, and it feels wonderful. So then I go looking for it. But that's just good feelings. What good are they? They come and go. I've had plenty of good feelings in life. They're transient.

Bob: It's just more experience.

James: People are always telling me to go try this or that spiritual technique. "You'll feel great." Well, I don't want to feel great. I don't want to feel bad. I just want the end of the illusion—the end of duality.

Bob: You want "what is." You want what is right now.

James: Exactly.

Bob: Visible emptiness, audible emptiness.

James: That's what it truly is.

Bob: It's just like the reflection in the mirror.

James: It's a matter of understanding that.

Bob: That's all.

James: What about desire? You've said desire is just a fixation in the mind on an object.

Bob: If a desire comes up, instead of doing something, just be with the attraction—be with the desire. See how it unfolds, without doing anything or adding anything to it. Without translating it into any concept. Just let it be. Just be with it.

James: Let's say two people in love break up, and one of them is heartbroken. What is he or she to do?

Bob: Just be with the desire, with that feeling of attraction, but without conceptualizing a separation by saying, "I haven't got it." Even though they're not together, even though they're seemingly apart, just leave that feeling of attraction there. Let it be and see what happens.

James: So, if the person is feeling the heartache or the yearning, they should just be with it.

Bob: The feelings are all being translated by the mind, and then they become a knot in the gut. Or an ache in the heart. The mental has affected the body. But nothing physical has happened. The mass of energy has accumulated there, and you keep fixating on it and it grows. It's a psychological effect, and it will dissolve if you just be with it, without resistance. When you have some anxiety or knot in the stomach, if you look for it in the body you'll find it has no core or self center to it. You focus your mind on the spot that hurts. If you stop the worrying energy from going into the problem, it must disappear because it's not real. It's only a thought-created thing. Thoughts can't be in two places at the same time. If the intensity of the thinking is in the investigation of it, you'll see that instead of the problem growing, it dissolves. I've had plenty of students come to me with these kinds of problems. I tell them to go into the feeling and investigate it. Some students actually refuse. They're afraid the feelings will be too big or hurt too much, so they keep resisting the problem and it continues. Or, it gets worse.

This is what people generally do with problems—they resist them.

And so, they persist, instead of just playing around for a while and then leaving. But the people who are able to go into the problems and focus on the feelings find that the problems quickly dissolve on their own. It might come again later, of course, out of habit. But once you know the falseness of it, you know how to handle it when it comes back.

James: I see. Can you tell me about the "cognizing emptiness" again. I have a hard time with those words.

Bob: Cognizing emptiness means it has that capacity of cognizing, or knowing. Otherwise, there would only be a void or a vacuum. Nothing could ever appear—ever. But it's *cognizing* emptiness. It has that capacity of cognizing, or knowing—which is intelligence. It's intelligence that manifests as this creation. The fact that the planets go around in orbit and the seasons come and go in an orderly way implies intelligence operating everything. The same as it's beating your heart and growing your body. That's the innate capacity of the emptiness.

James: This seems kind of unfathomable. If it were just emptiness, it couldn't materialize?

Bob: There would be no manifestation or appearance whatsoever.

James: I have a sense of what cognition means. But I still don't completely follow. There's emptiness and then there's *cognizing* emptiness.

Bob: Not two. Just one.

James: I understand. You're saying that if there were just emptiness, there would be no cognizing. But I never understood how it made an appearance in the first place. It just did?

Bob: A subtle vibration.

James: You're saying that by virtue of the fact that emptiness did cognize, we call it cognizing emptiness?

Bob: It is cognizing. You're knowing that you are, aren't you? That is a cognition, or intelligence.

James: Would I know that I am even if I didn't have a mind and body?

Bob: The knowingness would exist, but there would be nothing for it to express through. There would just be pure emptiness. There would be static.

James: How do I know that I would be knowing if I didn't have senses?

Bob: If there weren't a pattern of energy through which it expresses and experiences, you would be the nothingness—which is what you are in essence, anyway. It would be like the knowingness of deep sleep. You would be unaware that you are aware. In deep sleep, if there's a stirring or movement, you wake up and are suddenly aware that you were unaware—and then the world appears. It's only in wakefulness that you can be aware that you were asleep.

James: So if I'm awake, I can become aware that I am.

Bob: You don't become aware. You are aware. Becoming implies time. Awareness is wakefulness. They're the same thing. Consider the concept "space-like awareness." Can space know space?

James: No.

Bob: Awareness can't know itself if awareness is all there is. So the subtle vibration vibrates and creates the pattern of your body. Now, when you look outside yourself, what's the first thing you see?

James: Space.

Bob: And where are you seeing it from?

James: From my eyes?

Bob: No. What are you?

James: Emptiness, or space.

Bob: So, it's space seeing space. If that pattern that you are didn't exist, could space see space?

James: No.

Bob: Awareness vibrates into different forms and patterns and cognizes itself.

James: Well, can we conceive of . . .

Bob: We can conceive of anything—of any possibility. But you don't need to conceptualize. That's why they say in one sentence, "The great perfection is non-conceptual awareness." When you go into the mind, you're back into the trap again. You're back in duality.

James: If I stick with my experience of knowingness, of knowing that I am, then I'm okay.

Bob: It's not "your" experience of knowingness. It's the experiencing essence. The knowing is experiencING. You can't move away from it. You can produce all kinds of concepts on it, but they're only happening in the moment also.

When we use the terms "enlightenment" or "awareness," they're all concepts too. You don't need any labels. The basic fact is, you are. You are your own proof—not as a "you"—because that knowingness is not particular to that point of perception. You as an object are in the awareness also. That body/mind you call "you." Just the same as to you I am an object. To me, you're an object. Everything is objective, but what it's appearing in is pure subjectivity. And that can't be objectivized. Got it? [*Laughing*] Don't forget it!

James: I know that I am prior to thought. I know that I am.

Bob: Take all that off and what's left?

James: Knowing.

Bob: That's as far as you need to go—knowing. You can't fall out of that knowingness. You can't get away from it. You can't say there was a time when you were not. You can go back into memory and say, "I don't remember." But you can't say there was a time when you were not, because time is a mental concept. There's no such thing as time. It's just a mental concept.

James: If I'm here now, I was always here. Actually, I can't say anything about "was." Past doesn't exist.

Bob: Get the "I" out of it. You are the "now-ing." Take the "k" off knowing. "Now-ing" and knowing are the same thing. Knowing this actuality is happening now, and the Now is happening now.

James: Nisargadatta says something like, "People think that the world is ancient. It's not. It rises with your consciousness."

When this body dies, there'll be no more individuality.

Bob: Now you're hypothesizing—going into some future time. You're believing that the world is ancient. You're putting more time on it.

James: I'm talking concepts now. Is it correct to say the world exists because I am? Isn't the appearance happening because I exist—I mean "me" as source.

Bob: When is it happening?

James: Now.

Bob: Fine. So, is the world ancient?

James: No.

Bob: So, what are you talking about, "when you die"?

James: The world isn't even here. Stay with me for a minute. Let me finish the question. I am consciousness, or knowingness. When this appearance of James . . .

Bob: As soon as you say "when," you've moved away from omnipresence. You've gone back into time again. You're into mental concepts again.

James: Well, I want to ask this. Please just stay with me so I can ask this. Some day, this appearance of James is going to die. We both know that. When that happens . . . in the world of appearance . . .[*laughing*] Look, Bob, you and I are here—we exist—and Nisargadatta isn't. So, you know what I mean. Okay?

Bob: Okay.

James: Let's say that one moment before James's death, he wants to know: the moment that the body dies, does the illusion cease to exist?

Bob: When did illusion ever appear? Does an illusion have any reality at all?

James: No. It's an illusion.

Bob: You're talking about an illusion within the illusion, and you're worrying whether it stays or disappears!

James: Let's not say that I'm worrying about it.

Bob: You're looking in the mind again—trying to get the answer in the mind.

James: The answer's just not there.

Bob: You've got to see that, James.

James: The answer's not in the mind.

Bob: There's no point in caring about that. You never existed in the first place.

James: Nisargadatta was never here!

Bob: No. And neither are you! You were never here.

James: That's why I'm having trouble. It's crazy to ask the question because I'm not here.

Bob: Exactly. That's one of the biggest problems. We see the falseness of the world, but not the falseness of ourselves. We are appearing in the world also. We're not something separate from the world.

James: [*Laughing*] This illusion never happened, and I'm asking whether the illusion will go away.

Bob: Yes.

James: The reason I asked is because Nisargadatta said that the illusion only exists because "I am."

Bob: Because of the sense of presence—that knowingness.

James: Why was he talking about the world of appearance? The damn thing doesn't even exist! He's confused me.

Bob: Don't let him. Give him away. Ultimately, the world is not. Like the reflection in the mirror. You see the reflection of a chair in the mirror, but is the chair there? You can't say it's not, can you? It appears to be there. But, when you try to touch the chair, there's nothing there. You can neither say it is, nor it isn't.

James: I see.

Bob: It cancels itself out. It neither is, nor is not.

James: The same as creation.

Bob: Right.

James: Ultimately, once you open your mouth, it's rubbish—it's duality.

Bob: That's right. All he could do is point. As soon as Nisargadatta opens his mouth, it's rubbish, and as soon as I open my mouth, it's rubbish because it's all conceptual.

James: But you can point the way.

Bob: The mind can tear anything to pieces. The mind just keeps dividing. It can divide forever. That's the problem sometimes with highly intellectual types. They miss the point. It's their loss.

James: The simpler the person, the easier to get this. In my case, my habit is to keep asking questions from my reference point. Because the reference point is false, many of the questions I ask are absurd. It's amazing how long it takes for me to see it.

Bob: But you're seeing it. The more the reference point comes up and the more I kick it out from under you, the more you'll see it. And then you'll start kicking it out from under yourself.

James: Well, you're sure pretty good at kicking it out from under me! Nisargadatta said that in the beginning days meditation can be good. It loosens the mind.

Bob: Most people who make it to non-duality have gone through that already.

James: Some people haven't done any meditation or read any spiritual books, and yet they can be ripe for the teaching.

Bob: Exactly. Nisargadatta felt that seeing him six or seven times was enough. I feel the same way. It's actually simple.

James: Yes, but for people who have been in spiritual movements for a long time, there's an awful lot that has to be broken down. These teachers have told us for years and years to expect bliss, perfect health, perfect relationships, no desires whatsoever, no reactions to anything, and on and on. You come here and say those are just experiences, and they're irrelevant. . . . That's pretty startling.

Bob: If people just think about the title of my book, that would be enough: *What's Wrong With Right Now Unless You Think About It?* You have to pause and stop thinking. And you realize that you haven't fallen apart or disappeared just because you stopped thinking. For our living-ness, we've relied so much on thought. But the livingness goes on without thought.

James: Nisargadatta told Stephen Wolinsky [author of *I Am That I Am*] that he should be able to get the teaching in about six or seven days. Then, after the week was up, he told him to leave.

Bob: That's right.

James: Bob, someone sent me an e-mail from a spiritual teacher regarding "final realization" and "partial realization." The teacher said he doesn't acknowledge or recognize such a thing as partial realization. There is only the possibility of either no realization or final realization. Does this make any sense?

Bob: No. Because there's no realization possible. *Who* realizes? It's just a matter of seeing that there is no seeker. It's seeing the falseness of the seeker.

James: Could someone *finally* see the falseness of the seeker?

Bob: You can see it at any time. Just by a little investigation. There's nothing final about it.

James: I think he is addressing the people who say that they *had* realization, but then it disappeared. He's correct that they're talking nonsense. But to say there is such a thing as final realization also seems like rubbish.

Bob: If he's saying that there was a process of getting it, and then the process ended, this is false. There never was a process. The seeming process was an erroneous belief.

James: Yes. Bob, what is your sleep like? Is it any different from mine or anyone else's?

Bob: I don't think so.

James: I ask because I've heard a concept that people who are enlightened are awake during sleep.

Bob: These are just experiences. They have nothing to do with awakening. Look at what Molly [one of James's neighbors] was saying. She was in a coma at the hospital and was suddenly aware of everything in the room.

James: Yes, she was in a coma. Her eyes weren't even open. So, what was doing the seeing?

Bob: Just the seeing itself. The eyes can't see anyway.

James: The eyes can't see?

Bob: No. If the life force was out of you, your eyes wouldn't see anything.

James: So, the eyes aren't ever seeing.

Bob: No.

Bob, Dell, and James – July 21

Bob: What's your background.

Dell: I started seeking in 1972. I started with TM. And I've tried lots of other meditations and things. I've been grasping for a long time. So, how does one surrender to that process of grasping?

Bob: What's the *you* that you're talking about? Have you ever looked into that?

Dell: I'm working on it—since reading your book.

Bob: You know that you are, don't you? You can't negate that. That knowing that you are expresses through the mind as the thought "I am." The person that you think you are is just a mental picture. It has no independent nature. You couldn't have that mental image of yourself if you weren't conscious or aware—if that knowingness weren't there. So, that ego, or false self center, which is a reference point that everything is evaluated from, is a fiction. And you've been living with that fiction your whole life. The idea of separation is a fiction based on that idea of "I." What you're seeking, you already are.

As soon as the "I" idea comes on, it's always functioning in the pairs of opposites. If it's not past, which is memory, then it's future, which is anticipation and imagination. Within that range, it's vibrating in the pairs of opposites: good/bad, pleasant/painful, happy/sad. Everything is judged from that image of yourself—which is a dead image of the past. It's not a valid reference point, because it's from the past. It's dead. What you're seeking, you already are. You can't get out of this present moment. You can recall the past, but can you live a moment in the past? Of course not. You can only recall the past in the present. You can imagine the future, but only in the present—right now. So, this is the actuality—this moment. This is the only moment you can ever live. You can go back and recall the past—looking for enlightenment and all this nonsense, which we've been doing for years. And in doing that, we've missed the obvious. The present moment. So, have a look at this. Investigate it. You'll find that you're left with what you are—pure presence awareness.

Dell: How do I stop all my desires from coming up?

Bob: *Who?* Have a look again. When you say, "How do I . . . ," who are you talking about? Have a look and question that. You see. What is desire? A thought. It's a fixation on a thought. If you're not fixating on a thought or idea, the thought is free to flow. You see, the fixation is a blockage of energy. It's resistance to what is. Any resistance to what is, is a conflict. You can't stop a thought. It's just a matter of understanding that thought has no substance or independent nature. There's no entity within you with any power that can stop or do anything. But the seeing of this is important. The recognition of resistance must occur from the point of non-resistance. In that moment of non-resistance, you're *there*. You can only recognize that you're in resistance from non-resistance. For example, if you're totally insane, you don't know it. You only recognize your insanity from the point of sanity. In that recognition of resistance, from the point of non-resistance, you'll notice a very subtle relaxation. And after a while, doing it more often, it becomes more pronounced. In that moment, there's a letting go.

Dell: But how do you let go of it?

Bob: You can't. There's no *you* to do anything. It's just a matter of recognition—watching and being aware in the moment. As soon as you say "how," you're looking for a formula, and you're relating it again to a self center, a reference point.

Dell: Where does the recognition come from?

Bob: From the pure intelligence energy. You're knowing that you are right now, aren't you? You're seeing everything in this room? Where are you recognizing that from? Thought? Isn't it prior to thought? You're seeing everything before you think, aren't you?

Dell: Yes.

Bob: That natural knowing, or pure intelligence energy, is what you really are. The emptiness, the cognizing emptiness, suffused with knowing, suffused with intelligence. That's why I call it "intelligence energy," rather than the term "God," or "spirit." Because everyone has different concepts about God. It causes confusion. The intelligence energy I'm talking about is the same intelligence that functions in the universe. It keeps the stars in orbit, tides coming in and out; it beats your heart, digest your food, and so on. You don't have to tell your cells to grow. The "I" can't do anything, but we believe it can because our focus is in that thinking.

Dell: For the last six months, I've been doing a lot of meditating and self-inquiry. Ramana Maharshi told people to ask, "Who am I?"

Bob: And have you found anything?

Dell: No.

Bob: No, because there's nothing there! You'll never find the answer in the mind.

Dell: That's where I've been looking. Because of our past conditioning, we're looking for the answer. And there is no answer.

Bob: That's right. The mind is dualism. It's vibrating into pairs of opposites.

Dell: If we can't find the answer in the mind, where can we find it?

Bob: Full stop.

Dell: Where's full stop?

Bob: Right now. Without a thought, have you stopped seeing? Have you stopped hearing?

Dell: No.

Bob: You haven't stopped being or fallen apart just because you stopped thought. Full stop is prior to mind. Without thought, you still are.

Dell: How do you stop thoughts?

Bob: You don't stop them. You can't stop them. But understand what thought is. When you ask yourself, "What's wrong with right now if you don't think about it?" what do you do? You just pause and have a look. In that pause, in that instant, there's no thought. And what do you realize when there's no thought? You realize you can't say anything. You can't say it's good, bad, or anything. You haven't fallen apart. You're still that basic knowing that you are—that presence awareness that is prior to the mind. So you see the difference between the thinking mind and that reality—that pure intelligence. It's constantly there, but we ignore it because we're so focused in the mind. We think the mind is doing everything. It's not.

You want something like round-the-clock ecstasies. Ecstasies come and go, necessarily, for the human brain cannot stand the tension for a long time. A prolonged ecstasy will burn out your brain, unless it is extremely pure and subtle.

—Nisargadatta Maharaj, *I Am That*

CHAPTER FOUR

Intimate Talks – The Fun Begins

*

For the next several days, Vashti and I showed Bob and Barbara some of the sights of Longboat Key, Sarasota, and St. Petersburg. We took them to the beach, the St. Petersburg Pier, and the local bookshops we often enjoy. Occasionally, Bob would have a talk in our house with one of the locals, which I generally sat in on. In these sessions, Bob gave his usual pointers, and the students asked whatever questions they had. And during our sightseeing trips I peppered Bob with questions throughout the day. It was during these meetings—particularly at breakfast for some reason—that Vashti got her questions answered. This is why so few of her dialogues show up in this book. Vashti, incidentally, loved staying up till midnight crocheting and watching movies with Bob and Barb. And Bob loved seeing Vashti crochet as it brought back memories of his mother doing the same.

On Thursday night, Vashti boarded a plane for New Hampshire, where she was attending a crochet conference. Although a crochet-lover from way back, Vashti had just begun to design patterns professionally. The conference was, in one sense, a present I gave to her for being so agreeable to my bringing Bob and Barb here. A few months back, Vashti had been anguishing over whether to attend the August Chicago conference or the July New Hampshire one. Each conference had certain benefits that the other did not, and the decision was therefore difficult. Knowing this, I told her to go to both and not to give the cost or time away from the family a second thought. I would be forever indebted to her for letting Bob and Barb stay with us, and I told her so many times. Not that she needed persuading. Vashti was extremely excited about meeting Sailor Bob and hearing his teachings. She was also thrilled that we would be meeting seekers from all over the country who would come to hear him talk. Vashti and I actually enjoyed many laughs over the countless times people would ask her how *she* felt about having visitors and seekers in the house for a full five weeks. As if anyone had to twist her arm. By the end of Bob's visit, Vashti's spiritual search—which started at the age of nine when she started meditating—came to an end. Her fear of death (which I was totally unaware of) also ceased, as did many spiritual illusions and misconceptions. In the end, having enjoyed two crochet conferences and all the wonderful spiritual knowledge, Vashti claimed that she was the biggest winner of the summer of 2004.

By far, the most fun part of Bob's visit was the week my two closest friends, Kerry and Emmett, joined me in daily talks with Bob in our living room with the tape recorder rolling. Kerry, Emmett, and I have been friends since meeting in high school drama class and later attending Carnegie Mellon University, a fine drama school in Pittsburgh. Our week in my house brought back memories of teenage years when we spent summers together from morning till night. As mentioned earlier, the three of us have remained in close touch and have shared all kinds of spiritual teachings and self-development courses. Like so many contemporary spiritual seekers around the globe with a profound misunderstanding of the nature of liberation, we spent countless hours pining for the day when "we" could gain "the great enlightenment" and experience freedom. We contemplated the futility of our dualistic lives and had no clue that it is impossible to avoid presence awareness. We had no idea that ultimate freedom is who we are—like it or not, know it or not.

For five straight mornings, Kerry, Emmett, Bob, and I sat in my living room discussing our favorite subject. Occasionally, Dell, Vashti, Barbara, or my friend Martin Timmons would join in. At the start of the week, we treated Bob with utmost respect and deference. By the end of the week, we continued treating him well but teased him at every turn. And he, of course, teased back. We told every spiritual joke we knew, and at meals Kerry constantly commented on Bob's strong "preference" for food. Bob "blessed" me with a spiritual name: Shree Braha-sab—a source of mirth that lasted for several weeks. The crowning shot, however, occurred in one of the restaurants we frequented. After lunch, Bob noticed a crooked wall hanging and asked Kerry to straighten it out. Kerry thus inferred that Sailor Bob Adamson—disciple of the great sage

Nisargadatta Maharaj— had told him, nay *ordered* him, to "go out and make the crooked straight!" We concluded that Sailor Bob had "authorized" Kerry to speak, and that it was a divine proclamation which could not be rescinded. Thus, it was a festive week—one that none of us will ever forget.

In truth, Bob did encourage us to teach. He suggested that after he left I form a group with some of the locals who had come to his talks and invite newcomers who might be interested. He advised Kerry to do the same in Connecticut. His obvious interest in our teaching was intriguing to us because, aside from his love of food, it was the only apparent desire we ever saw in Bob. Because of his remarkably free nature, it stood out. But the fact that Bob appears to be devoid of preferences does not mean he doesn't have them. It's just that he rarely gets "hooked" by anything. Moods, preferences, and judgments come and go, but they do so with great speed. They're not "his," as he would say, so who's to take delivery of them? But he seemed to want us to spread non-duality. Whether he wanted this for us—to help stabilize our understanding—or for the benefit of others, I don't know. Some months after he left, I asked what motivated *him* to speak, and he said, "I really can't tell you, James. It's just what's happening." When I asked whether it was because he felt for those who lacked the knowledge, he said, "No. Not really. It's just like if you see people walking down a street and know they're heading for a roadblock, you warn them to take a detour." This surprised me. He had spent thirty years helping others in such a profound way and was so simple in his answer. In the three months since he had left, I personally had sent at least fifteen e-mails expressing my profound gratitude for what he had done for me. And he had occasionally enjoyed telling me stories about others who "got the understanding real good." He is most certainly aware of the incredible contribution he has made. Thus, I assume the answer regarding his motivation has to do with seeing life as perfect—no matter which way it goes. And with his lack of vested interest in anything other than "what is."

Bob's interest in our teaching slightly startled me because I had told him on the first morning we spoke that I would not be teaching. This was, however, before my sense of separation and perpetual concerns over past and future had abated. For some reason, probably stemming from our phone conversations, I sensed that Bob would want us to teach—assuming we grasped his message. On the first or second day of their visit, Barb mentioned privately how pleased she thought Bob would be if Kerry and I got the understanding and then carried on the teaching. I gave this very little thought, however, because I was at this time trying to get the understanding myself! I was not thinking about anyone else. Further, Sailor Bob or no Sailor Bob, I would not be pushed into teaching before I felt I had something real to give. In retrospect, it is easy see why Bob expected us to grasp his message. At the time, however, I was not sure of my ability to necessarily grasp anything. I had been on "the path" for thirty years and was still seeking.

The day I realized clearly that Bob was interested in my teaching was the afternoon when Kerry made his joke about being authorized to speak. This occurred in our living room, some time after the restaurant wall-hanging event. Kerry announced the joke, and we all laughed heartily, after which I left the room joking (but half seriously), "Great! Then I won't have to teach." Upon reaching my destination—the utility room—I saw Bob following me, at which time I turned around to hear him say with puzzlement, "What's this about not speaking?" It's true that Bob wears a hearing aid and sometimes asks people to repeat themselves. But the moment he asked for clarification I knew something was up. I was, therefore, a bit startled. Even as non-dual understanding was settling in more and more by the day, I felt it could be quite some time before I'd be feeling comfortable teaching others.

In some sects of Buddhism, those who gain the understanding are instructed to wait a full ten years before speaking publicly. This is, in one sense, wise. If more teachers waited, perhaps their teachings would be clearer and more effective. Or perhaps fewer teachers would fall prey to temptations. But looking back, if I had waited ten years to speak, what would have happened to someone like Jana Lee? Jana's life has been radically altered by the non-dual understanding she gained some months after Bob's departure. She is a friend of Emmett's and had been on "the path" for twenty or thirty years. Emmett had told Jana about non-duality and advised her to visit the Sunday talks I was holding. She was on vacation right then and wanted to spend some time hearing the teaching. So I invited her to Longboat Key, where she stayed for two and a half days, "getting" non-duality better than any of my other students. Within days of her departure, I was surprised to begin receiving e-mails of profound gratitude (which are still coming) that are amazingly similar to the ones I am constantly sending Sailor Bob. The same phenomenon has happened to Kerry, who has had two students who grasped non-duality so strongly their lives are forever altered.

Contrary to what many think, Sailor Bob was never "authorized" by Nisargadatta. When people ask him if he was, he always says the same thing: "No. But it wouldn't have mattered one way or the other. Once I understood non-duality, no one could've stopped me." It is a viewpoint with which I wholeheartedly resonate. The book you are reading was begun less than one week after Bob left Florida and had nothing to do with Bob's desire that I teach. By the time Bob left, I was waking up in the middle of the night and rushing to the computer to put non-dual insights in print to share with others. When non-duality is seen, it is a bug that bites strong and hard. When non-duality, or "no thing," is recognized, it seeks itself everywhere—much like the flame of one candle lighting others, as Bob so aptly puts it. Thus, there are different viewpoints about who should teach and when they should begin.

*

Kerry Arrives

On Friday night, Kerry arrived and we immediately sat down with Bob and Barb for a talk. Although Kerry had learned of non-duality only a year or so earlier, he had understood it remarkably quickly and immediately became consumed by it. He read many books in a short span of time and resonated powerfully with Ramesh Balsekar, Nisargadatta's translator and close disciple. Ramesh is now eighty-nine years old and has written over twenty-five books on the subject. He has also spoken to thousands of students during his daily talks in his Bombay apartment. Before we had ever learned of Sailor Bob, Kerry was constantly talking about Ramesh's books and the insights he was gaining from them.

The more Kerry had raved about Ramesh's books, the more I had wondered why he didn't go see him. Actually, I felt I knew the answer. It simply wasn't in Kerry's nature to jump on a plane and fly to India to see a guru. Nevertheless, right after one of our long philosophical phone discussions, I sent him an e-mail saying, "I think you need to go see Ramesh." The message was sent innocently, inspired by my knowing how much Kerry loved Ramesh's teachings. Not in my wildest imagination did I expect him to follow the advice—even though it was given in earnest. Mind you, I had been to India twice in the 80s myself and had seen many others travel to the Far East for knowledge. Knowing Kerry, however, it seemed like a long shot. He had gone to Europe eight or ten times for spiritual courses, but India clearly wasn't his style. Or, it never had been—until now.

Kerry went to see Ramesh and was powerfully moved. So much so that several months later he flew back, bringing his fifteen-year-old son with him. All teachers have their own methods, naturally, and Ramesh's were different from Sailor Bob's. Ramesh's main focus was on the issue of non-doership, which Kerry grasped in a visceral way. I watched as he gained relief from certain psychological issues that had plagued him for a lifetime. Non-doership did not affect me much at the time, and I watched with interest as Kerry's understanding became deeper than my own in many wonderful ways. When Sailor Bob's book came along, however, Kerry, like me, was struck like a thunderbolt. Bob's teaching, simple as it is, is so direct, pure, and profoundly uncompromising.

I do not mean to compare spiritual teachers, particularly in print. Aside from the fact that each teacher has his or her own forte, the world is nothing if not diverse. Every teacher attracts the appropriate students for his or her particular teaching style. Furthermore, what is medicine for one is poison to another. In my view, Sailor Bob's teachings are remarkable in the truest sense of the word. They are remarkable for many reasons: His refusal to hold out promises of a better future—a future that simply doesn't exist. Right here, right now is perfect just as is. Period. His absolute clarity about the illusory nature of creation, and his exclusive attention on that which is real and permanent. His willingness to teach others and send them on their way without fanfare, guru worship, financial rewards, and so on. And his utter simplicity, humility, and lack of self-interest.

The greatest gift of Bob's teaching, however, is his unwillingness to include anything dualistic. He avoids the usual traps and pitfalls others fall into. Many teachers unwittingly bring in duality by holding themselves up as special—for having transcended ordinary experience and attained "enlightenment," a *dualistic* distinction to begin with. The more these teachers allow themselves to be worshiped and adored, the more they nourish duality in their students. Some teachers hold out the concept of a "final understanding," which would be fine except that the concept becomes a dangling carrot that keeps others seeking forever. As long as one believes there is a special experience to attain, one will never allow oneself to simply be. And it is in the being—not the craving or doing—where one realizes one's true nature.

One of the facets of Bob's teaching that touches me most is his absolute indifference toward spiritual or mystical experiences, miracles, people who can perform miracles, the "final understanding," or people who are said to possess the "final understanding." When Bob says there is no difference between a Buddha and an ordinary person, he means it. When he says that no one—not Christ, Buddha, Shankara, Lao-tzu, or Ramana—has ever gone beyond "no thing," he is positively correct. And, most importantly, within minutes Bob (and any of his students) can show anyone with the slightest openness that it is impossible to locate an independent self center within ourselves. When that is seen, it becomes clear that we are in fact the same space, or consciousness, or "no thing," as Christ, Buddha, Ramana, or any other saint, sage, or seer. Thus, we are understanding the same truths they did.

Perhaps the biggest illusion most longtime seekers possess is the notion that included in awakening are special powers, miracles, twenty-four-hour-a-day bliss and ecstasy, and so on. And the notion that there is some kind of "final understanding," which brings on these so-called God-like attributes. To believe these ideas is to misunderstand non-duality and/or to disbelieve what sages and seers have told us down through the ages. If all creation is, in essence, oneness, or consciousness, or, as scientists demonstrate, space/light, then *everything* in manifest creation is a miracle! A blade of grass is a miracle. A wall is a miracle. A pumpkin is a miracle. And this is not to mention science, art, literature, aviation, medicine, and so on.

It is certainly possible that some who have taught spiritual subjects have displayed superhuman traits or enjoyed phenomenal meditative states. But never have these teachers, the genuine ones at least, taught that these abilities were important. They have always spoken of such experiences as side effects that vary from person to person. Moreover, many seekers fail to realize that miracles and phenomenal meditative states are accomplished far more readily by persons from Eastern cultures. It is likely that genetics and cultural upbringing play a large part in these happenings. Cultural factors are almost certainly the (apparent) reason why Hindus have visions of Krishna and Shiva, while Westerners more readily report seeing Christ and Mother Mary, or experiencing the stigmata. Further, many Easterners have allegedly developed *siddhis*, or supernatural powers, without possessing any real spiritual understanding. Thus, miracles are not necessarily connected to the end of separation and suffering, or the experience of wholeness. Because there has been so much erroneous teaching regarding miracles and liberation over the centuries, and particularly in the last several decades, seekers are now at a tremendous disadvantage.

Those who desire liberation in order to enjoy miracles or pervasive bliss are completely missing the point. If people approach non-dual teachings but are unwilling to give the understanding a chance to sink in because miracles and trance-like meditative states are not part of the promise, they are just delaying their own ultimate freedom. This is not to say such people must change or do something different. Whatever happens is certainly perfect. It is just what is. And, in any case, no one actually needs to awaken. The dream is fine whichever way it goes because, after all, it is a dream!

On the other hand, for those who can no longer bear the persistent sense of separateness and the disturbing concerns over past and future, perhaps it is time to seriously reconsider the need and/or benefit of miracles, bliss, and superhuman abilities. For those who have wanted liberation for the better part of a lifetime and have done their due diligence of meditating religiously and attending spiritual courses and flying here and there to see all kinds of gurus for years on end, perhaps it is time to re-evaluate the meaning of liberation. Perhaps it is time to reconsider why one embraced spiritual life in the first place—usually because all outer experiences were seen as blatantly transitory and unfulfilling. Finally, perhaps it is time to go back and read all the scriptures and other books on enlightenment to see how they relate to the non-dual understanding.

Mind you, the habit of believing in miracles and bliss as part of ultimate freedom has been part of my existence for so long that for several months after Bob left I found myself wondering about my own experience. The more I thought about it, the more I realized that Bob's teachings left me with "nothing" instead of something. And because there were no miracles or constant bliss, the question of my liberation kept arising. Whenever this occurred, I followed Bob's teachings of investigating the only truth I know. I cannot say that I am not—I cannot say I don't exist. Then, as I look inward to perceive my existence, what do I find? I find that there is no James—there is no self center. And that is when I realize, viscerally, that I am free.

Why am I free simply because I cannot find a self center within? Because instead of being the someone or something that I believed I was for over fifty years, I now immediately see that I am "no thing." And that "no thing," which is the ground of being upon which all experience occurs, is eternal, unbounded, and unlimited. The "no thing" that I am cannot be cut by the sword, drowned by water, dried by wind, or burned by fire, as Krishna so eloquently said in the *Bhagavad Gita*. The "absolute" or "unmanifest" that I so dearly craved during the seemingly endless search of several decades is clearly who I am. But, for all those years, it could not be seen for so many misunderstandings and false concepts. The biggest misunderstanding was related to bliss, ecstasy, miracles, special powers, and all of the rest of the spiritual materialism that unfortunately passes for freedom these days.

For those who still desire miracles, incidentally, they are, of course, possible. Anything is possible because the purpose of the mind is to divide. And the more the mind divides, the more interesting phenomena people will create. Indeed, the desire for powers and special abilities captured my attention so deeply that one day in our living room I asked Bob why he did not want them. He quickly shot back, "Why? So this illusory person can impress other illusory people?" I found his answer interesting but told him I wanted powers. He then said, in his typical free-floating way, "Well, if you want them, they can be developed. Anything is possible." Interestingly, however, unless one is using mystical techniques to consciously develop powers and abilities, they stand more chance of occurring when the desire for them is relinquished.

Although I have not found myself walking on water, levitating, or creating ethereal bodies, life has become more effortless than ever. Daily efforts and desires seem to fulfill themselves with very little resistance. And when for some reason expectations and desires cannot be met, instead of the usual frustration and angst, there is, generally, acceptance. There is an understanding that things are exactly as they should be. Aside from the psychological relief this brings, it also somehow allows many of the thwarted desires to suddenly reverse and go my way. I have also noticed that when desires meet with failure and are then relinquished, events often turn out better than if the desires had been fulfilled. This is an interesting phenomenon and a miraculous way to live, compared to my past. To say this is different from my previous existence would be a vast understatement.

Interestingly, some five or six weeks after Sailor Bob left I was able to give up my twenty-year astrology practice. This was something I had wanted to do for a long time, but couldn't because of financial needs and a family to support. Hindu/Vedic astrology was a wonderful profession, but after some years I enjoyed writing about it more than interpreting people's birthcharts. I had felt ready to move on for years but, in addition to feeling constrained by finances, I had no clear direction of what to do next. So, one day in early October, I decided to quit and see what would happen next. I had enough accumulated investments to live for a while, but not for long. Within a month or so, I happened upon an investment that quickly produced several years of my normal salary. When I told Bob of how effortlessly my desires were being fulfilled and how odd this was compared to my past, he explained that when a person stops resisting every little occurrence and "gets out of the way," intelligence energy has a chance to organize things naturally. He calls it "effortless living."

Contrary to the teachings of some twentieth-century gurus, everyone who gains liberation—or grasps non-duality—does not immediately fulfill all desires and enjoy wonderful worldly circumstances. Although one's approach to, and experience of, life must almost certainly become dramatically easier and more graceful, anything is possible regarding events and circumstances. Lots of sages have endured all kinds of difficulties, even after their so-called awakenings. Indeed, Sailor Bob encountered some very rough years, health-wise and financially, after being with Nisargadatta. Fortunately, as he tells it, underneath it all was a distinct sense of well-being.

At any rate, below begins the six or seven days of intimate conversations that Kerry joined in on. Kerry has an excellent understanding of non-duality. He also has a remarkable intellect and a wealth of knowledge in meditation and Hindu/Vedic spiritual teachings. His insights are valuable, and the questions he brought Bob made for very stimulating talks.

*

Kerry, Bob, Barb, and James
Friday Night, July 23

There's No "Me" to Get Enlightened

Kerry: Ramesh distinguishes between an intellectual understanding and a leap to total understanding. Something that is sudden and irreversible, self-verifying and self-validating. He describes the suddenness like this: There are so many steps to the top. You're climbing step, step, step, without knowing when you've reached the last step. Then suddenly, you've reached that last step, and you realize that there are no more steps. You've only climbed one last step, and yet there's a suddenness about it because you realize it's the last step. Of course, this is all conceptual.

This leaves people who feel they haven't had that experience thinking they have a good intellectual understanding of the knowledge, but not a total understanding. And that the total understanding lies somewhere in the future. This is a big departure between the way you teach and the way he teaches.

Bob: I go back to what the ancients say. Existence is non-dual. There's no person that can climb any steps and get anywhere. There's no final step. In the immediacy of right now is the knowingness, or the presence awareness. That's all there is. It's beyond, or prior to, the mind. It's prior to any labeling.

There's no entity to get anything. The idea of an entity is when a thought arises.

Kerry: The entity is the thought.

Bob: Right. And the thought has no independent nature. Where's it going to go? What's intellectual and what's not? There's no label necessary. What it amounts to is this: what you're seeking, you already are. The idea of a seeker or a search is nothing more than an idea or a concept.

Kerry: So, the idea of a sudden shift is irrelevant. Some people come to you and hear the teaching, and they come back week after week or month after month, and so on. Then, there are people who come to you and get the understanding and never need to see you again. This implies there was a moment when they said, "Aha, I got it."

Bob: There's just a seeing. The very idea that there was a moment is false. In omnipresence, what moment could there have been?

Kerry: Only the ever-present moment.

Bob: Presence is only a label also. There is a seeing, but in fact there has always been a seeing. It's just that it was ignored. In the seeing, as it's recognized or cognized, you know there was never a time when you were not.

James: The distinction "enlightenment" becomes irrelevant. There is no enlightenment.

Bob: And the seeking that seemed to go on for all those years becomes irrelevant.

James: I think what Kerry is asking about is this: within the world of illusion, there's this great enlightenment that happens. But you don't acknowledge that, do you?

Bob: The great thing that happens is illusion also. It happens in the world of illusion.

James: The term "enlightenment" is ridiculous. As soon as someone uses the term, I just hate it.

Kerry: I cringe when I say it, and I cringe when I hear it.

James: There just is no such thing. It's the essence of absurdity. People think there's a "me" who's going to get enlightened. When you explain that liberation is when you *lose* the "me," they think, "Wow, I can't wait until I lose the 'me.' I'm going to love that." What a joke. And that's exactly what I went through!

Kerry: I was speaking with a woman on the phone the other day, and she asked me, "Do you have the understanding?" I couldn't say no, and I couldn't say yes. What I found myself saying was, "I'm not looking for answers anymore. I'm no longer seeking."

Bob: You could say, "There is understanding."

Kerry: I did say something like that, but I also said that the understanding doesn't feel personal. It has nothing to do with "me."

Bob: It can't have, or it wouldn't be the understanding!

James: There were many times when seekers asked Ramana Maharshi questions, and he would just sit totally silent without answering. They would then repeat the question several more times, and he still wouldn't answer. Then, the next day, he would address their inquiry in some way. But, essentially, certain questions were properly answered only by silence.

Bob: There's no teaching and no one to be taught. There's just a natural resonance. Innately, we already know. When it's spoken and heard—not with the mind, but with the heart—it resonates. Not the physical heart, but the heart as a symbol of the core of your being. The core of your being is waiting to resonate with this teaching. From then on, it's like lighting a candle from another candle. The flame is recognizing itself, and there's a subtle rejoicing. This is conceptual also, but there's a subtle rejoicing with the energy and stirring with what is called "the search." But there's something here that is not the mind or the intellect that already knows this.

Kerry: It's a place where there are no questions. The cognizing emptiness is something I resonate with. There's a sense that there is just nothingness.

Bob: There's no self center within you. There's no independent nature to your "I am" thought. When you see the falseness of your reference point, you realize there's nothing but space, or emptiness, inside.

Kerry: Yes. I see. It's interesting; I don't have a smooth life, and it's become very clear that even after understanding, nothing changes. My moods and thoughts are still here, but now I'm aware that they're taking place on this non-changing awareness. That term "space-like awareness" is a great description of it.

Bob: Like I said, there are still emotional ups and downs. Take the "e" off "emotion" and you have "motion." Like waves on the ocean—they're still water.

Kerry: So, what about this idea of a sudden awakening and the sanctification from the guru who acknowledges that the disciple has "made it"? For example, Ramesh has authorized a few people to speak. These are people he has authorized. In due respect, he doesn't use the word "enlightenment" and doesn't like it. He uses the phrase "total understanding."

Bob: Kerry, let me ask you this: Do you have the understanding?

Kerry: Yes.

Bob: Well, could I "authorize" you to speak?

Kerry: I don't think you could stop me from speaking.

Bob: So, what's all this about someone authorizing someone else to speak?

Kerry: Well, one thing Ramesh says to people sometimes is, "If the talking happens, talk. But don't go hanging out a shingle saying you're speaking." Because that would be a personal agenda. In Advaita circles, there's a subtle message that you're not supposed to want to speak. So everyone has a story about how they got dragged into speaking. What nonsense. These people want to talk, or they wouldn't be talking. Also, within the *satsang* [spiritual gathering/talk] environment, there's an assumption that those who ask questions don't understand. So, many people sit back at lectures and won't open their mouths. They don't want to reveal that anything is missing. They want to feel like they have the understanding.

Barb: The ego is still in the way.

Kerry: Understanding can be there. Questions can be there. Anything can be there. Contractions can be there. There can be a forgetting. For me, that no longer negates anything. I no longer think, "Oh. A question has arisen. Therefore, I don't have the understanding."

Bob: Whatever can be remembered or forgotten is not you, anyway.

Kerry: I've realized that it doesn't matter what comes up. What comes up doesn't define what's here. It's just what's coming up. It could be anything.

Bob: That's right. It becomes all-inclusive. Whatever comes up is appearance. Have a look—who is it happening to? It's happening to me. And who is this "me?" It's a false reference point.

No Destiny, No Free Will

Kerry: What about the concept of destiny, Bob? I understand that there is no destiny or free will. They're just concepts.

Bob: They're labels.

Kerry: But there is an apparent destiny and an apparent free will.

Bob: There can be an apparent anything. All appearances and any possibilities are possible.

James: Well, after something has happened, would you say that what occurred was destined? Now that it's happened, wouldn't you say that was destined? We're "being lived," right? You were being lived to speak on non-duality. I was being lived to practice astrology. That's destiny.

Bob: You're talking about the appearance. You're talking about what happened in time, which is a mental concept.

James: [*Joking*] That's the problem with Bob. He only wants to talk about reality. He never want to talk about the appearance.

Bob: That's what happens even in the scriptures. They move into duality. There's nothing simpler than "one."

Kerry: It doesn't leave much to talk about.

James: How do you have satsangs?

Bob: You just talk. That's what's happening. The idea of destiny exists only from a reference point. We look at life from a viewpoint of seventy or eighty years. But if the reference point were seventy or eighty billion light years, what would our reference point be then? We think we are the end all and be all. But the reference point we're using is false. And, because everything is, in essence, oneness, all reference points in the appearance are false.

Kerry: So, the concept of destiny implies "my" destiny. And it implies that some god-like entity or force is looking out for me and creating a chain of events that is ultimately good for me.

Bob: Yes. Exactly. If you use the reference point from fifty billion light years away, then this earth is less than a speck of dust. Where would we be on that speck of dust? Or take the life of a gnat. It hatches in the morning, mates in the afternoon, and dies at night. How could it ever conceive of our life span—of sixty or seventy years?

Barb: And the term "destiny" seems to imply time. It implies a beginning and an end.

Bob: There's a saying, "No birth, no death, no time, no space, no destiny, no free will."

James: Nothing ever happened.

Bob: But the seeming happenings go on.

Barb: Even the word "limitless" is a concept. It's hard for our minds to grasp this.

Bob: We'll never grasp this with the mind. The nature of the mind is to divide. You can never grasp non-duality with something that is dualistic. It's just a movement of energy, and the boundary that we put on it is the word, the label. In the Bible, it says, "In the beginning was the word," the label. And the word was God.

Kerry: Some teachers of non-duality are a bit more compromising. They sort of emphasize the life of the apparent person they're talking to. Clearly, some students aren't ready to hear such pure non-dual teachings, and they have to go back and live their lives. So the teacher tries to give the person something to make that life easier. Instead of trying to negate everything, instead of saying, "You're just an illusion, there's nothing,

nothing, nothing," the teacher gives them something they can use. Maybe explaining in detail that the person is not the doer, and the happenings of their life are largely due to genetics and upbringing, and so on.

Bob: I would tell the person to look for the cause of their problems, which is the self center—the belief in the separate entity. That's the cause. It's only a "me" that can be fearful, depressed, sad, or whatever. Have a look at the "me" and see that it's just a idea or a concept with no substance or independent nature.

James: [*Joking*] You're killing me, Bob. I'm losing my identity here.

Bob: In losing that, you're free. You're free to be what you've always been, but were ignoring. When the cause of the problem drops off, the effects fall away. You don't have to go to a psychiatrist or anybody who's going to perpetuate it for you. These people think they'll patch you up and make you whole. It's a waste of time.

James: Are there many takers?

Bob: [*Laughing*] How can "one" be many?

Who Am I?

James: There's this technique that Ramana used to teach, where you ask, "Who am I?" People do this for years and years.

Kerry: That's because they're expecting an answer, instead of understanding that no answer is the answer!

Bob: The questioner is the question. If that question isn't being asked, there's no questioner or question. Without the questioner or the question, you're left with the immediacy of the moment.

Kerry: The question establishes a false center within the questioner. There is an assumed "I" asking the question. The very question establishes the "me" which actually doesn't exist. It's funny; the knowingness doesn't need to know anything.

Bob: It's empty.

Kerry: It doesn't need to know anything, and therefore it knows everything it needs to know! It's an all-knowing and a nothing-knowing.

Bob: It's all-knowing. It's an emptiness knowing. In knowing that, you don't have to try and conceptualize a knowingness or an emptiness. It's there naturally.

Kerry: Thoughts arise out of that knowingness. It's kind of a non-experiential experience—this knowingness that I am prior to thought.

Bob: The thoughts are not attached anywhere. They're not independent. So there's no need to fixate on them.

Kerry: But even now some hang around longer than others. But they're starting to look like black spots on a white sheet.

Bob: Some people say their thoughts are more annoying after the understanding because suddenly they're so noticeable. Nisargadatta used to say, "Now and again, an old thought pattern comes up, and then it's immediately discarded."

Kerry: Bob, I feel funny mentioning Ramesh's teachings to you. It almost seems rude to come see you and then talk about another teacher. But the reason it comes up is because there's a need to integrate what I learned from him and what I've learned from you. I respect both you and Ramesh tremendously.

Bob: Yes. The important point is that in the end you leave both of us behind. Leave Ramesh behind. Leave me behind. You have enough understanding to stand on your own two feet. I never needed Nisargadatta after I grasped what he was teaching. I went to see him once, about a year later. And I still think of him. He kicked everything out from underneath me. He kicked out all my concepts. He didn't want me to hang around after that.

James: We have to kick the guru out, too. The guru is just another concept.

Bob: You have the understanding. Now let that develop within you. Let your own understanding come through. When a little child starts walking, he might fall down after the first few steps. But then he gets up and is eventually running and jumping and so on. All we teachers can do is point you toward what has always been ignored. We've been so conditioned to look outside ourselves. That sense of separation has made us think that if we amass, accumulate, and acquire, we'll become whole and complete. But we were never separate in the first place. All the teaching can do is point you to where you never looked before. When you do look, you see that what we've believed in falls apart. The false can't stand up to investigation. And you're left with what you've always been.

James: Non-conceptual, ever-fresh, self-shining, just this and nothing else. But some people will hear this teaching and say, "Yes, but I don't have the *experience*. I don't have the *feeling* that liberation is supposed to give."

Kerry: Well, that's because it's really a stripping away of those very expectations and concepts.

Bob: They believe everything they've read about all the wonderful experiences, and they believe they have to have them. I had all kinds of experiences—visions and yogic kriyas and God knows what.

James: Can you tell us?

Kerry: No, I don't want to hear them. They annoy me, and I don't want to hear them. Because of the damage that was done by having those beliefs. James showed me the Papaji books, and he's talking about seeing Krishna and all kinds of miracles like that. I put the book right down. It makes me angry.

Bob: Yes, James showed me that book. I only glanced at it, but all the talk of miracles is rubbish. It's useless.

Kerry: Not only is it rubbish, it's damaging rubbish for the student who reads it. All it does is make the person feel further away from the understanding.

Bob: And keeps them looking for bigger and better experiences.

Kerry: And without them you think, "I don't have it. I'm not good enough."

James: Well, what you're saying is true. But at the same time, I wouldn't be sitting here if I hadn't read those books. I started Advaita with the Papaji books [*Meeting Papaji* and the three-volume Papaji biography called *Nothing Ever Happened*]. Non-dual teachings are in those books, even though they're mostly about his non-stop miracles.

Kerry: James and I studied for a while with a teacher named Andy

Rymer. He used to break down enlightenment into two stages: awakening and deliverance. Awakening was when you've realized you're not the body or the mind. Deliverance was when you become stabilized. I think that means when you're no longer constantly getting caught in the reference point—in the "me."

James: I remember being surprised at his definition of enlightenment. He said it's when you know with absolute conviction that you are not what you appear to be or what others consider you to be. That sounds like non-dual understanding. It has nothing to do with visions, powers, samadhi, lack of desires, and all that. I was surprised. But now it makes sense.

Kerry: Bob, what do you make of the stories of all the miracles the Indian gurus supposedly do? And the story of the enlightened sage who has himself walled into a cave to die because he's ready to die and "go home."

Bob: That's all in the manifestation. The essence that you are was never born and never dies. It never changes. It's no thing. And no matter who it is, no matter what great sage or seer, they can't go any further than no thing. What they're appearing on is no thing.

Kerry: I love the phrase "no thing." The clearest experience that's with me all the time—actually there's not a focus on it all the time—but as soon as you bring the focus on that "no thing," that's the reality. There's no thing in here. That's obvious. There's obviously a physical body and there's obviously a physical world. But it's all one thing, and this one thing is no thing. You can't call it an experience. It's like a lively insight or something.

Bob: One of the things that moves people into duality is the writings of these traditions. That's a trap. All the traditions say existence is oneness—it's one without a second. But then they go into duality by writing about it.

Kerry: I read somewhere that Buddha said it's one without a second and then wrote ten thousand verses on it.

Bob: Buddha said that every sentient being has been your father and your mother. That means Buddha, Christ, and all of them have been your parent. And you've been their parents.

Kerry: What did he mean by that?

Bob: The vibrating life energy has manifested as everything. In essence, everything is the same energy.

On another subject, it says in the Bible that God made man in his own image and likeness. People think that means God looks like us. But the image is the pure intelligence energy.

Kerry: The "no thing."

James: [*Joking*] You mean God doesn't look like me?

Bob: In essence, He is you.

Kerry: When you hear people's different visions or experiences of the divine, which are very real for them and sometimes lead to awakening, they always see the God that they believe in. The Christians see Mary and Jesus, and the Hindus see Krishna and Shiva. I don't think the Jews have anyone to see.

James: The burning bush.

Kerry: In the Bible, Moses says, "I am that I am." How many Biblical scholars have any idea of the real intention of that statement? Or how complete that is?

Bob: When I lecture, I say, "I'm not speaking to any body." I can't because that body's got no independent nature. If there's no life force in the body, it's a corpse. Nor am I speaking to the mind. The mind can't see or feel or hear. I'm speaking to that sense of presence that expresses through the mind as the thought "I am." That sense of presence is an awareness of presence—or a presence of awareness. They're not two. "Just this and nothing else." And that's the immediate introduction to the natural state. You are with it—that is you.

Kerry Investigates the Illusion of Death

Kerry: Let's talk about death.

Bob: It never happened. Life continually lives on life. All that was born was the thought "I am." The "me." And that's what dies. That's why the mind is constantly dividing and chattering. It doesn't want to die. It never had any life anyway. It's like a leech—clinging onto that pure intelligence energy. Believing it has some power.

Kerry: What happens when the body drops?

Bob: It's just a switch in energy. It reaches its peak, or zenith, and then disintegration starts. Enzymes break the body down, and maggots come along and feed off it. The body goes back into the earth, and then a seed sprouts from it and grows a blade of grass. Then something eats that blade of grass, and so on. Life lives off life.

James: How about when the mind realizes it's going to die?

Bob: That's the point. You can die right now—to that sense of "me." And then there's no problem possible. Then you don't care about the so-called other death that comes along.

James: Well, as long as we're alive, we never completely lose the reference point. It's never completely lost.

Bob: Reference points will seemingly be there, choices will be made, preferences will be held, but the conviction is there that there's absolutely no entity doing any of those things.

James: Does your reference point ever come up and . . .

Bob: It's not my reference point. Reference points come up. There's no doer, but doings will seemingly continually happen. But, to whom?

James: I understand no one has a reference point, but a reference point arises. For example, I may think, "Oh, somebody has done something to me." And then I remember there is no "me." At the moment of death, I expect a really big reference point would show up.

Bob: At the moment of death, there's nothing to think. You won't know when you've taken your last breath.

James: At the moment right before, though, when the train is coming right at you, I expect there would be a big reference point coming up that says, "Uh oh. I'm about to die."

Bob: Yes, that will be a thought. An imagining about what death is like.

Kerry: And that could take all kinds of different shapes, enlightened or not enlightened. It could be the nature of this body to have lots of fear.

It could be the nature of your body to not have that same fear. For example, my father was in World War II. After that, he was never afraid of anything again! And, of course, he wasn't awakened.

I know that if I were diagnosed with terminal cancer, there would be an intense reaction. My recovery time from that emotional reaction would be pretty quick. My awareness of that reaction being projected on the "no thing," on the pure awareness, would also be there. But the emotion would be pretty gripping.

Bob: You don't really know what would happen until it actually occurs.

Kerry: Of course. But my sense of it is, there would be fear. How would you react if that happened?

Bob: How would I know? You don't know anything about what will happen in the supposed future. There are many cases where in times of crisis people do things they never expected. There was a recent case of a man who was about to throw himself off a cliff. Another man there leapt forward—risking his life—and grabbed the suicidal man back. Afterwards, people asked him why he did that, because he almost fell off the cliff himself. He answered, "I don't know. I couldn't have done anything else in that moment."

Kerry: There's an interesting phrase: "Death is part of living, not dying." My understanding is that after death there's pure awareness, but there's no awareness of the awareness. The awareness is not aware of itself.

Bob: It's just purely aware—self-aware.

Kerry: But self-aware implies a center, doesn't it?

Bob: No. Like the sun which is self-shining. It doesn't need another light. The sun doesn't know light. It can't know darkness, and it can't know light. It has nothing to compare itself to. It just shines of itself. And that's what's happening to us right now. We're self-aware. We don't need anything to tell us we're aware. When that thought comes up, "I'm aware," that's just a translation of what's already happening. All thoughts do is translate, but they're so closely aligned to that awareness, or pure intelligence energy, that they've come to believe they are the power themselves. That's what has to be seen. Prior to any translation, the knowingness—or being—is there.

Kerry: So, it's like deep sleep. Awareness is there, but there's no "one" to be aware.

Bob: Right.

*

Bob, Kerry, Dell, Emmett, Martin, Barb, and James
Saturday Night, July 24

No Method Needed—Just Understanding

Dell: In Zen, there are *koans* to sort of jolt a person into the awareness. Is there anything—any method—within non-duality like that?

Bob: When you say is there a method to help "you" reach awareness, where's the "you?" There is no doer to be found anywhere. There's no self center that you can locate. So, there are no techniques or methods.

Speaking of Zen, have you read Bankei? He calls it "unborn Buddha mind." He says, "Everything is perfectly resolved in the unborn. Why exchange the unborn for thought?" Simple as that. Instead of leaving everything as is, we get stuck into the thought—trying to work out everything with thought.

Dell: Because, as you say, we label everything. So, how do we take the labels off? How do we stop labeling?

Bob: Just understand what a label is. A label is just a word or concept. The word can never be the thing. Without a label, the thing is just what it is—unmodified, uncorrected, and unaltered. When you see this room, do you have to tell yourself you're seeing it? No. There's just the seeing—in the immediacy, before the label comes up.

Emmett: Anthropologists talk about primitive tribes who have never seen photographs. When the tribespeople saw photos of themselves, they had no idea what they were looking at. They just saw a piece of paper, but couldn't make anything of the images. We recognize photos because we have been taught the distinction, or the label, called photograph.

Bob: There's another story about the scientists taking natives outside of their forest. They had never been outside the forest, and when they were brought to the edge of the forest, they couldn't fathom distance. They had never seen any long distance before and didn't know what to make of it.

Dell: If I have a desire and it gets fulfilled effortlessly, is life fulfilling itself or is it my desire?

Bob: There's actually no entity to have a desire.

Emmett: So, we're just playing out this movie and thinking we're creating everything.

Martin: The desire is an illusion.

Bob: There is no entity there with any independent nature. You couldn't have that "I" thought without pure awareness, or if consciousness weren't there. And that's all the seeming entity is. It's an "I" thought which we've added. With concepts, ideas, and images, we've built a concrete image of who and what we are. Of course, desires will happen, choices will be made, and preferences will arise. But there's no entity there to take delivery of them. The problem is that the thought comes up and says, "I choose." If we could choose our thoughts, why would anyone choose unhappiness or depression? Sometimes a thought comes up, and we don't act on it. Then another thought comes up, and we do act on it. And then we say, "I chose." But you never picked the thoughts in the first place. So, we're being lived.

Dell: So, the script for my desire is already there?

Bob: The whole lot is already there.

Dell: So, there's no predetermined life that is happening?

Bob: When you say a life that is happening, what is happening? Patterns of energy are appearing. Patterns of energy are playing around and disappearing. But has the pattern got any independent nature? Even though it appears to be, is the pattern of energy really substantial? It's like the reflection in the mirror. Does that reflection know it's in the mirror? Do any of the reflections in the mirror have a predetermined script? You can't say the reflection isn't there. But if you go to try and grab the reflection, there's nothing there. You can't say it is, and you can't say it isn't. It only appears to be.

Dell: Here's a question that will make everyone here laugh. Can you tell who's enlightened in this room?

Bob: Everyone. And there's no one here.

Martin: Can you say there's just "one" here.

Bob: It's one essence. But even to say "one" implies that something other than one could exist. That's why they say, "One without a second." Or, "not two."

Dell: If it's habit of the mind that causes our problems, then do we just need to realize that? Then it's just a recognition, not an understanding.

Bob: Recognize that the mind has no independent nature. It can't stand on its own.

Dell: So the habits of the mind are based on our conditioning. Habits are patterns and patterns are energy. So how does the pattern stop? We have to disrupt that old pattern, so we can see the new pattern of seeing everything as appearance.

Bob: In the seeing that the thoughts have no power, no independent nature, you can't believe in it anymore, can you?

Dell: We *can* believe it, because it's the energy that's been flowing since we were two years old!

Bob: Yes, but you just questioned it and have seen that the thought cannot stand on its own.

Dell: So that's disrupting it?

Bob: In seeing that it has no real substance, you can't believe in it. You might get caught in the old habits for a while, but the intelligence will come up and say, "Wait a minute. I saw the falseness of this the other day. There's nothing there." When the energy or belief doesn't go into it, it can't live. Nothing can live without energy. That's all that's happened—we've never questioned these beliefs. That's all this is about—investigation. The false can't stand up to investigation.

Dell: So that's how we disrupt the pattern?

Bob: Yes.

Dell: [*Joking*] There's your "method," guys! [*Group laughter*]

Bob: It's just like the metaphor of blue water in the sea. You know the water isn't blue. It's just like how centuries ago people thought you couldn't sail into the horizon or you'd fall off. At one time, everyone believed that. Now, you can't tell that to anyone. It still appears that way, but everyone has seen the false as false, and they aren't taken in by it. You've seen there's no self center in you. And if there's none in you, then there's no center in anyone else. So who can ever be superior to you? Who can ever be inferior? What could I ever want of yours if we are the one essence? It doesn't mean to say if someone hits you, you'll necessarily turn the other cheek. There's no way to know how you'll respond. There's no set pattern.

That intelligence energy that's functioning has brought you this far. You don't think it's going to let you down now, do you?

Emmett: The process of questioning reality and our self center is a function of our mind, isn't it?

Bob: Yes.

Emmett: That implies that the mind causes the unraveling of our false conditioning. But the mind doesn't touch reality. The mind is encompassed by reality, or the "no thing," or oneness. So, we're using the mind to question reality.

Bob: The only instrument you have is the mind. It has no independent power. It's an instrument. Thought is subtle word. Word is a vibration or pattern of energy. The mind vibrates in the pairs of opposite—good/bad, pleasure/pain, and so on. The mind is creative, of course. But it's also the limiting factor: "I'm not good enough. I'm fearful. I can't do this. I have low self-confidence," and so on. And these become a reference point. Everything becomes relative to this image of oneself. When you see through this and see there's no entity within you, you've taken away the suffering or limiting aspect. Then, the mind is left to utilize itself in a creative way.

Dell: When we do this investigation you're talking about, and we come to realize that everything in creation is just an appearance, is it an understanding or a surrendering?

Bob: In the investigation, you find out that there's no one to understand and no one to surrender. And we're talking about the timeless. So, when you say "when," what's wrong with right now? Don't you see this *right now*? In the moment? You realize you're there. You can't get away from it. Where else could you be but in the omnipresent? It's immediate. You're knowing that you are—full stop. The rest takes care of itself. Looking for the answer in the mind will take you down all kinds of different directions. The mind keeps dividing. The only way to the truth is full stop. Without a thought, there's not a damn thing wrong.

Dell: So, Barbara never decided to become a Bowen therapist. It just happened. It's life fulfilling itself.

Bob: Yes.

Kerry: Why differentiate between free will and destiny, anyway? They're both just concepts. They're just labels.

Bob: You can call it life fulfilling itself if you like, but it's really already fulfilled. Nothing ever happened. It's all only appearance.

Kerry: When Dell asked about free will or life fulfilling itself, I could just hear Nisargadatta saying, "Who wants to know?"

Martin: Bob, you've used the terms "audible emptiness" and "visual emptiness" to describe the appearance. It seems inherently paradoxical, because when you say emptiness—that is some *thing*. How can you know it exists if it's not some thing? There must be some thing that exists in order for it to have attributes.

Bob: Those attributes are appearance only. They're just intelligence energy appearing as patterns—appearing as seeing, hearing, cognizing.

Martin: I know that your life is different since you had your conversations with Nisargadatta. But now that you know, for example, that the table is only an appearance, does it change your *experience* of the table? Does it change your perception?

Bob: No. I still see everything as it is—still seeing everything the same—but knowing full well that it's only appearing to be so.

Martin: So, your perceptions aren't transformed by that awareness? The world isn't transformed by that understanding?

Bob: Well, there's no longer any belief in an entity that can do anything. There's no longer any belief in these things being separate entities. They're appearance only. There's just that one knowingness.

Martin: Is the quality of your experience different? Is it more vivid? When you see objects, do you see them as, say, their utility, or do you actually see them as patterns?

Bob: See, what you're really asking is "how do I relate to things." But there has to be an entity to relate everything to. In fact, there's just seeing, hearing, and actual functioning. So it's just a matter of seeing everything as it is.

A Change in Understanding, Not Perception

Martin: So, is your experience of perception before and after seeing Nisargadatta quite different, or is it the same?

Bob: It's all the same. Before enlightenment, chop wood, carry water. After enlightenment, chop wood, carry water. On the other hand, before getting the understanding there were chores that *I* had to do. And I would think, "It's Joe's turn to chop the wood, not mine," and all sorts of commotion would go on. There was plenty of psychological suffering that went on because everything was being applied to "me." Afterwards, everything simply became what is. There is no entity here to take delivery of anything. Of course, there were habit patterns that came up for a while, and the seeming entity came up again. But once it had been seen through, it could never get the same intensity again. Now, there is a certainty and confidence that there is no entity here that has any substance or independent nature. The functioning goes on just the same. The feelings and emotions are there. But the fixation on them doesn't hang around.

There's no big bang or flash of light, though I've had plenty of experiences during the so-called search. The experience is never It. It's just a knowingness that is there.

James: This reminds me of when I stub my toe. My first thought is always, "Who put that damn chair there?" I want to blame someone for making this thing happen to me. It's indicative of the reference point—that there's a "me" this happened to. As opposed to seeing just what happened and realizing it's just what is. There's no difference in perception, but there's a big difference in the reaction. The chair and the toe haven't changed. The reaction to the event has changed.

Martin: The reason I ask about your perception is because I've had my own experience—with meditation and all—of seeing the unity in manifestation. And then the individuality of each object is lessened. It's just appearance. Appearance equals being, and it's okay. In normal everyday reality, the separateness of objects is essential. We don't see them as different shapes and forms of one energy. We don't see the commonality.

Bob: No, you don't go around saying, "Everything is energy, everything is energy." You're seeing life as it is, and there is an acting accordingly. The functioning goes on quite effortlessly. I call this "effortless living." You may see this body/mind taking a very active part at times, but there's no doer there.

James: Martin, it sounds to me like you're looking for a change of perception, when all that really happens is a new understanding, which then affects how your life is lived or how your life is experienced.

Kerry: It's like seeing the magician's trick of making the tiger disappear. You see it over and over again, and the tiger disappears every time. But suddenly the magician tells you how the trick is done. You're still seeing the tiger—you're still seeing the trick—but you no longer see the tiger disappear because you know where it really is. So, is that a perceptual change? No. But because of the understanding you now have, those words—perception and understanding—could blur together. But in reality, it's understanding. It's not a change of perception.

Martin: I think this may be a difference in our semantics. It's hard for me to see how, if I'm no longer caught up in the illusion of the tiger disappearing, there wouldn't be a change of perception.

Bob: Martin, you won't find the answer in the mind.

James: For thirty years I was waiting for some damn experience. I read all these books that said if you meditate long enough and well enough, you will have this very special experience. That's not at all what's happening here. I'm getting a new understanding, and the understanding is transforming my life. In all those books I read, people said that when they found liberation or awakening or whatever you want to call it, they realized they had always been free and awake. So that couldn't be a change in experience. It's a change in understanding, which then may alter one's experience. In other words, the person was awake when his or her experience was lousy and is awake when the experience is wonderful. Understanding is the only difference.

Martin: Unless there's a personal transformation, unless a person really embodies the understanding and lives it, then it's worthless. You can have an academic understanding and repeat what Bob says and agree with it, and yet not really understand it. . . . If it doesn't transform you when you walk out the door, in terms of your actions, then it's worthless. A lot of academia is worthless for that reason. It's just information. That's why I'm asking about perception and experience. For example, with drugs there is a sense of expansiveness, colors become more vivid, the emotions become more intense, and so on.

James: If you suddenly understand how the disappearing tiger trick is done, how could your experience not be different?

Martin: Of course. I agree.

James: Everything Bob is saying here is showing the illusory nature of our self center, as well as everything in creation.

Martin: What I'm asking is, in what sense is it different?

Bob: The difference is that psychological suffering ceases. The entity that suffers is that imagined self center. It's not that emotions don't continue to arise. But where that suffering with anxiety and fear and anger builds up and snowballs and becomes overwhelming, now it disappears almost immediately because you're not fixated on those emotions. There's no entity that can fixate on them. There's no entity that can be transformed. All there is, is the natural functioning. As far as perceptions go, everything seems much the same as it always was. There's no personal involvement with them because there is no person as such.

Martin: Thank you. That's what I was asking.

Labeling Dissipates Energy

Dell: I find that *trying* to understand causes tension. If I drop all the effort and just let things be, then it all falls into place. The table is just the table, the snake is just the snake, and so on. Trying to figure this out just gets in the way.

Bob: You can't try or not try. All you can do is recognize your resistance. And that recognition can only arise from the point of non-resistance. If you're totally resistant, you don't know it. You can only recognize resistance from the point of non-resistance. And that comes up of its own accord. You'll notice a subtle relaxation. That'll come up more and more.

Dell: And then you reach full stop.

Martin: One of the things that prompts my questions is that it seems like when a person stops believing in the reference point, there might be new sources of energy, or there might be expansion.

Bob: There's not a new source of energy. But most of our energy throughout the day is taken up with the thinking process—to the exclusion of hearing, seeing, touching, and so on. There needs to be an overall openness where you're giving as much energy to thought as you are to the senses. The energy needs to be spread evenly, instead of constant mental chatter and worries that take away from your senses.

Martin: I would imagine that would be a more vivid experience than being constantly stuck in the mind, where you don't notice much of what is actually happening.

Bob: When people stop labeling everything, they often start seeing things very differently. Labeling is a dissipation of energy. Any fixating or attaching to something, or mental chatter, is a dissipation of energy. Energy is in conflict with energy when resistance is there. When a person says, "I don't like this," it's resistance to what is. That stops the flow of energy.

Martin: So having the understanding, or realization, that all creation is an appearance is sufficient? You don't concern yourself with whether the appearance is really real? You accept that it's appearance and real at the same time?

Bob: It's real in essence, but not in appearance. It's the one essence appearing as many. The problem is that people take the appearance as a reflection but can't see themselves as a reflection. When you see that even we are a reflection, you realize it's like one reflection trying to know another reflection. If it weren't for the mirror [that is, the essential oneness] there wouldn't be any reflections.

Martin: So you don't damn the appearances for being appearances?

Bob: No.

Martin: In the West, or in Greek plays, there was a message that anything transient had no value. In order to have any value, there had to be an aspect of timelessness or unchangeable reality. In Christianity, there's a similar feature with the physical body being corrupt or fallen. Your message is different. You seem to be saying that we shouldn't confuse appearance with reality. But you don't damn appearance.

Bob: No, because everything becomes all-inclusive. There's a saying, "First there are mountains and rivers. Then mountains and rivers disappear. Then mountains and rivers appear again." It becomes all inclusive again.

Emmett: That's the old Donovan song: "First there is a mountain, then there is no mountain, then there is."

*

Kerry, James, Bob, Dell, Judy, and Pat
Sunday, July 25

Meditation vs. Investigation

Dell: Last night I was reading Suzuki's book *Zen Buddhism,* which I hadn't read in many years. In light of non-duality, the book makes so much more sense.

Bob: Yes, that's very common for people who get this knowledge. All of a sudden, books they've read before come alive.

Judy: Can a person's energy start to function on a higher level where one's experience and the things we create become more beautiful or more subtle and grand?

Bob: First, it's not "your" energy. It's one universal energy that's expressing as the creation. And it manifests in all diversity—in all the opposites. So the energy can and will express in higher or lower ways, as you call it. But it's all the same energy. You will be attracted to whatever you need to be attracted to. This isn't one chaotic mess. It may seem that way sometimes, from our limited view. But from fifteen billion light years away, it would seem quite orderly. Overall, life is functioning perfectly.

Dell: Bob, do you meditate?

Bob: There's no one to meditate and nothing to meditate on. Therefore, I can't be out of meditation. It's a natural meditation that goes on effortlessly and spontaneously. There's never any distraction.

Dell: When I do self-inquiry, is that meditation?

Bob: It's investigation.

Dell: What's the difference between meditation and investigation?

Bob: Meditation is trying to still the mind. In self-inquiry, you're investigating with the mind to find out that there is no mind—to find out that there is no self center or person.

Dell: In your process with Nisargadatta, were you involved in self-inquiry or "transmission" from Nisargadatta?

Bob: There was no process. Even though I didn't know it then, there was no "me" present. There was a revelation—through the pointing out that Nisargadatta did—that I was able to see. In the immediacy of the moment, I saw that there was no entity here. There was no body or mind here that I could refer to that had any actuality, any substance or independent nature. But, in that seeing, I didn't die or fall apart. I was just as is—the is-ness or beingness. And that beingness is constantly with you.

If I ask you about something you did as a child, you'll tell me some story. If I ask, "How do you know?" you'll say, "I know." If I say, "Did you have the same body then as you have now?" you'll say, "No, that body has changed." So the body is not you. Every cell in that body has now been replaced. If I say, "Did you have the same image about yourself then as you do now?" you'll say, "No, I certainly didn't." Since then, your image has been constantly changing. So what was it then that was you? It was the same knowingness that's there now—which everything has appeared and disappeared on. That essence, or knowingness that you are, has never been contaminated by any of the dramas or traumas that have happened to you. It's been untouched. It's the immediacy of you right now. Before you try to decipher what I'm saying, that sense of presence is constantly with you. And to the mind, it is "no thing." It's no thing you can ever grasp with a thought or a concept. You're nothing! [*Laughing*]

Pat: Are the words "knowing" and "being" the same?

Bob: Yes. The Hindus use the term "sat chit ananda"—existence consciousness bliss. Those three things are not different. They are three aspects of one thing. Existence is being. Consciousness is knowing. Bliss is loving to be. So, being, knowing, and loving to be are ever with you. That sat chit ananda is actually who you are. It's not something you have to attain or acquire. You've never been anything other than that. Nisargaddatta put it another way. He said that awareness of being is bliss. Isn't it? Don't you love to be alive?

Pat: What about the word "love"?

Bob: It depends what love you're talking about. If you're talking about the love/hate relationship, that's always in the pairs of opposites. That's a mind thing. If you're talking about the "uncaused love," that's the light of being. Love is another word for light. Whenever anybody dies—a person or an animal—the first thing that happens is the light leaves their eyes. That light is love.

Dell: That reminds me of a Hafiz poem: "Even after all this time, the sun does not say to the earth, 'You owe me.' Look what happens with a love like that. It lights up the whole sky."

Bob: He understood.

Pat: There's another one by Hafiz: "God only speaks four words: 'Come dance with me.'"

The Effect of Non-Duality on the World

Dell: As more and more people get this non-dual understanding, will it affect the world?

Bob: The world's problems are based on the belief that we are separate entities. The term "nisarga" means natural, or natural state. Dattatreya was the legendary primal guru. He wrote the *Avadhut Gita*. That's how Nisargadatta made up his name—combining those two terms. Natural means nature. Nature functions perfectly. If it's winter, nature isn't wishing it were summer. The tides come in and out at the proper time. Day follows night, and so on. There's no conflict. But our sense of separateness—that we gained at the age of one or two—brings along vulnerability and insecurity. And all the world's problems are caused by that. One nation conquers another nation in order to feel more secure and abundant.

And all our psychological suffering arises because of that sense of separation. It's only a "me" that can be anxious, fearful, depressed, unhappy, or whatever. The "me" doesn't feel complete. It feels separate. In our whole life, we've never looked inside to see the obvious—that we're not separate from nature. We are nature. We're not separate from air. Our bodies are made up of air. We're not separate from earth or water. Our bodies are made up of earth and water. Our problems all stem from feeling separate.

James: So a person who is free of the reference point essentially doesn't suffer from worldly problems because he or she doesn't feel separate. But if a person like that is right in the midst of war—in the midst of the killing—and watching it happen . . .

Bob: There would still be no sense of separation. But they might be moved to respond in some way.

James: So there would be no sense of separation, and therefore no suffering?

Bob: That's right.

Kerry: But Dell's original question is whether there are more people coming to this knowledge now.

Barb: Are you hoping that the world is getting better? [*Laughing*] It doesn't need to. It's just as it is. Lots of people say, "The world's getting more spiritual." But that's only their own assessment that it needs to be better. There is no such thing as "more spiritual."

Dell: I'm just wondering whether the world is being affected by more and more people waking up.

Bob: Our *essence* is never affected. Since you were a little child, your body's changed, and your self-image has changed. But has the "base" that everything has appeared on changed? Not at all. The thing people never look at is the wakefulness that is who we are. Has that wakefulness ever changed? That's the base that everything appears on. It never changes. Not one iota. All the events of the day happen on that wakefulness. It's your basic experience of life, and it never changes. You know that you're awake. Prior to that, you're asleep.

Dell: If there were ten million people who were awake, would the war in Iraq still be happening?

Bob: It may or it may not. We don't have to conceptualize it because it's not now.

Kerry: Once you've become absorbed in this, you go on the Internet and find other Advaitans and see all the other non-duality books, and you think it's everywhere. But Bob's book, which is probably the best book on the subject, has only sold 1,000 copies. That's not a big number.

James: [*Joking*] But just wait until Bob's United States tour.

Kerry: Well, we're going to promote that with circus animals.

James: [*Laughing*] Let's get him on *The Jerry Springer Show*. There'll be fights. "Advaita is the best way!" "Advaita is not the best way!"

Kerry: They'll have a surprise guest: "Bob slept with my daughter." [*Group laughter*]

Dell: Last night, I asked you if you could tell who in the room is enlightened, and you said, "We all are." Well, there's a section in Nisargadatta's book where a person asks, "If Ramana entered the room, would you recognize him as a liberated man?" And he answers, "Of course. As a man recognizes a man, so a *gnani* [self-realized soul] recognizes a gnani. You cannot appreciate what you have not experienced. You are what you think yourself to be, but you cannot think yourself to be what you have not experienced."

Bob: Well, you might not know you're unbounded and free, but I know that you are. You couldn't be anything else. If you've got that ignorant belief that you're not, then energy goes into that belief and makes it so. You can't be anything other than That, whether you know it or not. As it says in the Vedas, "From Brahma down to a clump of grass . . ." Even the clump of grass is That. And if I keep telling you this, maybe you'll hear it!

James: The terms "enlightenment" or "awakening" have no meaning if everyone is in the same state. Some are suffering horribly, and some are living in freedom—but in essence we're all the same. So the term "enlightenment" is a joke. Of course, it's not too funny if you think it's real, and you're chasing it.

Bob: It's how we think about it. Shakespeare said, "Nothing is either good or bad, but thinking makes it so." Christ spoke of the reality when he said, "Which of you by taking thought can add one cubit to his stature?" You can think all you like, but it has no real effect.

Dell: One problem is that I'm so analytical. My left brain gets so immersed in this knowledge, and I find that I can't comprehend it. And then I say, "Stop. Enough!"

Bob: Listen to what you're saying. "I am so analytical." You're putting that label on yourself, and energy goes into that. Then it's, "My damned left brain." Has your left brain got any power without the life essence in it? And *who* is analytical? Has that thought, "I am analytical," got any power or independent nature?

Dell: It's all based on my upbringing and my conditioning.

Bob: What conditioning is there right now if you're not thinking about it?

Dell: None.

Bob: That gets rid of all your conditioning in one instant. Why take it up again? As Bankei says, "Everything is perfectly resolved in the unborn mind. Why exchange the unborn for thought?" On that unborn, seemingly come thoughts, which are believed to be real. Thoughts come and go, but the unborn—or pure essence on which everything appears—never changes. It's constantly with you. You haven't exchanged it for the transient—thoughts. You stay in the unborn, in the reality. Reality is that which never changes. The whole manifestation around you is constantly changing.

Who you are is the "no thing." And, nothing can be added to that or taken away from it. That "no thing" contains everything. Something can't come from nothing. So you don't need to take notice of the manifestation.

Pat: Do Advaitans use the term "God"?

Bob: The problem with the word "God" is that everyone has a different meaning for it. And whatever concept you have about God can get you lost in that concept. I prefer to say intelligence energy.

Must Desires Be Given Up?

Dell: Nisargadatta says, "All desires must be given up. Because by desiring, you take the shape of your desires. When no desires remain, you revert back to your natural state." Now, those desires all come from the mind. And the mind gets us into trouble. Well, what about biological desires? Food, sex, and all that. These aren't mind-based; they're biological.

Bob: You have to eat to live. The next urge is to reproduce. These are natural urges. But when they dominate the mind, they become a problem. Nisargadatta says desire is the fixation of the mind on an idea. Look at dogs. Sex isn't a big deal for the dog. It's not even interested until the female goes into heat and sends out the scent. Then it becomes an urge. But once the female is out of heat, the dog goes back to hunting or whatever. With humans, we get into sex and become compulsive about it. Then it becomes dominant because the mind fixates on it.

James: I'm not sure I understand this. What's wrong with fixating on something, as long as we stay out of the reference point?

Bob: Who's fixating on it? Me, me, me.

James: Let's say there are two people having sex three times a day. One of them is fixating on it, and the other isn't. The one who's fixating on it shouldn't be doing that. And the other person is fine. Where's the problem?

Bob: There's no value in shoulds or shouldn'ts. But if the person is fixating on it, then it's becoming a problem and getting in the way of other aspects of life.

James: As long as it's not a problem, the frequency is irrelevant.

Bob: That's right.

James: This is interesting because there are natural urges and desires, and there's no problem with those. But a few months ago when I said I was suffering due to desire, you said, "Desire is a fixation in the mind. Just drop the fixation." So, there's a natural desire, which is no problem. But then, that desire can become a fixation, which is a problem. This is an important issue for me because when I want something very badly, non-duality suddenly goes out the window. I don't care that the world is an illusion—*I want what I want!*

Kerry: Why are we getting into the concept that there's a "me" that could be fixated on something? Fixating is happening. The dropping of the fixating eventually happens. What's the problem?

James: You're absolutely right. There's only an appearance of a fixation. Once the realization comes that it's an appearance—and that there's no "me" to be fixated on something—the problem starts decreasing.

Kerry: Bob, a gnani could a have desire just like anybody else. But if it doesn't get fulfilled, he or she drops it before it affects the emotions in any serious way. But that seems to imply that if you find yourself with strong desires, then you don't have non-dual understanding. So some desires could be there, some desires could be stronger than others, but the transparency is there—even though the desire may be strong enough to keep you working on its fulfillment. What am I missing?

Bob: Who's calling it a desire? Is it a desire, or is it just an urge to do something? You'll either fulfill the urge or you won't, but either way you can abide with it. When there's a "me" that's desiring, then it becomes overwhelming. And as soon as you label it a desire, you're loading it down with every other desire you've ever had. Just like anger or fear or whatever. If it's just what is in the moment, you'll act on it or you won't. It's only a "me" that can have fear and anger and all. Those are the labels we put on these things, and that's what causes the suffering. The emotions are just what is. When we label them and dwell on them, we start suffering.

As soon as something comes up, you might say, "This is fear." How do you know it's fear? Because we've had this feeling before, and we labeled it fear. Well, as soon as you call it fear, you're not seeing it fresh and new. You're seeing it with the past label, and all those other fears you've had come into that moment. You're remembering all those past fears, and then it becomes worse than ever. And then you resist it, and it grows and grows. We move away from it—we don't want to be with it. In the labeling, we move away from it, and we're not with it as it is. If we're just being with it, we experience it fresh and new, and it's either acted on or it's not. The label becomes a reference point. Then you're relating to a name.

Kerry: Without the labeling, you can't say a desire is one thing or the other. It becomes a problem when you say, "I shouldn't have this desire," or "This desire's too strong," or "I'm going to memorize this concept from Nisargadatta and drop this desire. . . ." As long as it's spontaneous and no involvement with it, there's nothing to be said about it.

Bob: Right. You just fulfill the desire, or you don't.

Kerry: And each desire is a separate arising of an individual thought. Maybe there's one and the next thought is, "Well, that's not practical." And you drop it. Or maybe it's "I want this. I want this. I want this." But they can be all new individual arisings, without involvement.

Bob: Yes, they all are. But when you relate them to a reference point, a "me," you're judging them from past events and experiences. That's what the "me" is made up of—past events and experiences and conditioning. And everything is judged from there as good, bad, pleasant, painful, I want it, or I don't want it. I've had this before, I want more of it, and so on.

Kerry: What complicates this for the spiritual seeker is that now, not only is there a desire, but there's this overlay to the desire saying, "I shouldn't be having the desire. Because I have the desire, I'm not enlightened." So the person has taken what was some involvement and referenced it back to the "me". . . . And now you have a double whammy!

Dell: The guilt comes in.

Bob: Most spiritual teachings say we must get rid of desire and fear. So as soon as we *label* these feelings, we think we shouldn't be having them. Then the guilt comes in. The problem is in the labeling or the fixating.

James: So that's why so many so-called enlightened sages say that life doesn't change after awakening. They still have good and bad feelings. I never understood that. On one hand they write about their non-stop bliss and peace, and then in the same breath they say they have good and bad feelings and emotions like anyone else. This means they are no different from anyone, but they don't go crazy labeling and fixating on everything. They simply accept whatever comes along. I think I used to believe what they said about bliss and miracles and effortless living, but never took them seriously when they said they still have ups and downs and bad feelings just like any ordinary person.

Dell: There's no difference between a Buddha and anyone else.

Kerry: Every time we open our mouth we're talking concepts. But certain things you [Bob] or other sages say are spoken from experience—like "there's no self center here, the 'me' is just a mental creation," and so on. But when sages talk about things in the appearance, they're not speaking from any cognizing or experience. They're speaking from their own concepts.

Bob: As soon as you open your mouth, you're conceptualizing.

Kerry: There's a tendency for seekers to think that when gurus speak, everything they say is truth. But this can't be true.

James: That used to drive me crazy when I was in spiritual movements. You have six different gurus all saying their method is the best and fastest technique to liberation. Each one is just promoting ideas and the traditions he or she has accepted. But the disciples are sure that anything that leaves their guru's lips is the word of God. Like everything they speak is truth. How ridiculous.

Bob: That's right.

*

Bob, Kerry, James, Dell, and Emmett
Monday, July 26

Why Gurus Give Techniques

Kerry: Looking back, did you feel a sense of growth when you were with Muktananda?

Bob: There was always that idea that I was going somewhere and was going to get something. The carrot in front of the horse's nose.

Kerry: The sense of a "path." One thing that's a mystery to me is what these spiritual teachers do. I assume that someone like Muktananda had the understanding. Why do teachers let disciples have these illusions—about techniques and a path, and "if I do this, this, and this, I'll reach the ultimate goal"?

Bob: I'll tell you why. You know about kundalini? The energy that rises up the spine?

Kerry: Yes.

Bob: Well, Muktananda was able to give that experience to people by touching them. And then he would give people mantras and techniques to cause the kundalini. But his basic message was, "Kneel to yourself. Bow to yourself. Honor and worship your own being. God dwells within you as you." Full stop.

Kerry: Aha!

Bob: And he would often get up and tell the parable about the man who went to India searching for enlightenment. The seeker goes to one ashram, and the guru tells him, "Thou art That." So the seeker says, "Yes, I've heard that before." But it doesn't mean anything to him. It's not satisfying. So he goes to the next ashram, and the guru says, "I can give you the Truth, but you'll have to serve me for twelve years." So the seeker agrees, and he spends the next twelve years cleaning up cow dung on the farm. After the time is up, the guru gives him the Truth. He says to the seeker, "Thou art That."

All of Muktananda's disciples laughed at the story, not realizing that that was exactly what *they* were doing. He told them, "God dwells within you as you. You don't see that? Okay, come and chant the mantra, enjoy the kundalini, meditate, eat this way, do this and that." And they do that. Some do more than twelve years. They go on for thirty or forty years or more. After seeing Nisargadatta, I was fortunate enough to see that.

Kerry: So many people who come to you have been on spiritual paths and are now ready to hear what you're saying. But they still have vestiges of the concepts of old paths. And they wonder, "Wait a minute. I don't have to *do* anything to get this. Where's the technique? Where's the effort? How can this be Truth?" I think parables like the one you just gave are powerful for longtime seekers. It reminds me of the story of Buddha. Buddha struggled for years to get awakening and finally gave up. And when he gave up, that's when he got it.

One issue I think is important is this idea of awakening and deliverance. People have experienced a sense of getting the understanding, but then they suddenly get caught in the mind again, and they get confused. They think they've lost it. Doubts come up.

Bob: Clouds will always arise in the sky. But the sun is continually there. It never changes. If the sun weren't there, the clouds couldn't come up.

Kerry: I love that metaphor. Without that sun, we couldn't enjoy the thunderclouds. And I enjoy those thunderclouds. [*Joking*] I really enjoy it when I'm miserable. They're some of my best times. [*Group laughter*]

Emmett Grapples with the Mind

Emmett: Since the creation doesn't exist, how do we talk about anything?

Bob: Talking is happening.

Emmett: But as you say, it isn't really.

Bob: That's right. It's just an appearance. Its essence is intelligence energy.

Emmett: And the nature of this intelligence is to manifest this illusory existence.

Bob: Right. The manifestation has no substance or independent nature. It vibrates into different patterns. Just like the ripples and waves appear on the ocean—but they're still only water.

Emmett: I'm trying to understand all this with the mind—and the mind doesn't even exist!

Bob: The mind is just an appearance, and it's trying to find the answer to the appearance.

Kerry: [*Joking*] You're just a toaster trying to understand electricity.

Bob: [*Laughing*] Good one, Kerry. I may borrow that sometime. It's sometimes hard to see the illusory nature of creation, and then let go of it. But when you do let go, you find that you don't fall apart or disappear.

Emmett: You and Nisargadatta speak about this experience of reality, as if we could let everything go right now and just "get it." You speak as if it's so easy, like "This could happen right now. Just let go. It's so easy and natural." But you can remember a time when you were like us—when you didn't get it. One thing that seems to be consistently written about in scriptures is the idea of blissful experience and waves of ecstasy. It's repeated so consistently in so much spiritual literature. But you talk about those experiences like they're not worth much—they're just experiences like any other. My feeling is that if you could have non-dual understanding *and* have bliss all the time, it would be much preferred!

Bob: Any ecstatic state is an experience. Any experience will come and go. Nobody can be in that state all the time. It would burn them out in no time. You can have glimpses of it. But that's not what you're looking for. Hindus use the term "sat chit ananda"—existence consciousness bliss. The bliss feature is "loving to be."

Emmett: You definitely appear to be very joyful. But you're also very casual about everything. Nisargadatta also seems casual, even *dry*. There's no appearance of joy in his writings.

Kerry: What I heard is that bliss is the absence of desiring or expecting anything.

Bob: That's right. With Nisargadatta, there's a lack of concern. That's the casualness. But there's a natural compassion that arises also. You don't become bland and ignore everything. Nisargadatta used to say, "There's nothing wrong anymore." Also, he used to say, " My emptiness is full." There are many statements he makes that can be interpreted as blissful. It may seem dry and casual, but the essence is vitality and the love of being.

Emmett: That's evident in you, as well as in Nisargadatta's talks—especially your compassion. You keep getting the same questions from people over and over. And you have infinite patience and never seem to judge anyone. When I read *I Am That,* I kept wondering how Nisargadatta could bear listening to so many people challenging him all the time.

Kerry: Actually, Nisargadatta had somewhat of an intense or angry nature. Compassion was there but impatience was too. He used to ask people, "How can you ask the same question again? You've been here for six days."

James: On the Nisargadatta video, *Awaken to the Eternal*, Stephen Wolinsky tells the story of how Nisargadatta told him at the start, "You should be able to get this in seven days. Can you stay here that long?" Well, on the seventh day, Wolinsky asked some question, and Nisargadatta got intense and shot back, "You've been here long enough. You should know that by now." And he told him to leave. On the train home, Wolinsky realized that was his seventh day there. I guess he understood pretty well. He wrote a nice book, *I Am That I Am.*

Bob: I can assure you that before this understanding, there was no compassion here. I was very agitated.

Emmett: You were talking about the idea of letting go, about how we could get the understanding right here, right now.

Bob: Here's a joke about letting go. There was once a man who fell off a cliff and grabbed onto a branch or rock as he was falling. He was hanging on for dear life, and he starts yelling, "Help, help. Is there anybody up there?" Suddenly he hears the booming voice of God answer, "Yes. I'm here." So the man says, "What do I do?" And God says slowly,

"Let go." The man thinks for a minute and says, "Is there anybody *else* up there?" [*Group laughter*]

James: My favorite joke is the one that Wayne Liquorman tells in his book *Acceptance of What Is*. It takes place in a Jewish temple.

In temples, they always have a janitor who's not Jewish to do chores that we Jews can't do on Saturday. Well, one day the janitor walks into the temple, and he sees one of the rabbis prostrating on the floor in front of the Torah, the Holy Scripture. And the rabbi is repeating over and over, "Oh God, I am nothing. I am nothing." The janitor becomes intrigued with this. Then, as he's watching, another rabbi comes in and falls to his knees and says the same thing, "Oh God, I am nothing. I am nothing." So now the janitor is very moved and decides to try it too. So he prostrates himself and starts repeating, "Oh God, I am nothing. I am nothing." All of a sudden, one of the rabbis says to the other, "Look who thinks he's nothing!" [*Laughter*]

Need to Search for Years?

Emmett: Bob, you talk about this knowledge like anyone can get it. But the people who get it have generally been seeking for years and years and years.

Bob: That's right. I spent sixteen years searching for it. And I can tell you with certainty that what you're seeking, you already are. And you can full stop right now and see it.

Emmett: You say that, but how do you know a person can do that without first traveling on the path? Without all the experience leading up to it?

Bob: Drop all that rubbish, and you'll see it's obvious and evident that you are That. When you go along with that story—about the path and the techniques and all—you simply haven't paused long enough to see that it's evident.

Emmett: So we haven't paused or experienced long enough. We have to dwell on that reality, if we are to go by the evidence of people's experiences.

Bob: Now you're back into time again. You're not pausing. You're not full stopping. Knowing is immediate. You know that you are. You cannot negate that under any circumstances. Full stop. But that's too subtle for the mind. Immediately, people will say "but" or "why" or "how ." But you cannot negate the beingness that is here right now. Just let that sink in.

Emmett: There appears to be a barrier to that understanding happening—until the mind has been made soft enough to allow that in. That process seems to be necessary.

Bob: Who or what is going to do that? If what you're seeking you already are, who or what is going to remove that obstacle?

Emmett: [*Joking*] The illusory mind is going to do it.

Kerry: There are people who get the understanding quite suddenly, without having spent years seeking it. What's interesting is that whether the person strived for it or just stumbled into it, the conclusion is the same. They all say, "I had nothing to do with it." The path was apparent, but there was no one on that path. The thought, "You can recognize the understanding immediately," fits the awakened person's understanding *after the fact*. There was no seeker and no path. There was only an apparent seeker and an apparent path. That's why so many of these people laugh so hard when they see it. The joke is that they should have gotten it immediately. What was all the seeking and drama about?

It's pretty sad news, actually. It's like you're sitting with the *Encyclopedia Britannica*, and the reality is you're the binding! So of course there's confusion. You think you have to read the whole book, and the answer's not there because you're the binding, not the book.

Bob, how many people went to see Nisargadatta every day? Five or ten?

Bob: When I was there, it was about that many. Later on, after lots of Westerners heard about him, he started to have more visitors. But not too many. The room wouldn't hold more than twenty or twenty-five people, completely packed.

Kerry: It must have been hot as hell.

Bob: It was. He had one fan going, and it was blowing all the incense and the cigarette smoke around. He usually had eight or ten sticks of incense going all the time. And there were bugs crawling out of the wall.

Kerry: There's a charming story that Ramesh loves to tell about a sadhu who had no money and came to see Nisargadatta. The sadhu was so poor that when he traveled by train to Bombay, he would get on with no ticket and then get thrown off at the next station. Then he would get on and get thrown off again and would do this over and over until he reached Bombay.

Well, he happened to be a pundit of some kind, and when he was at Nisargadatta's, he occasionally did prayers or chanting for people, who paid him a few rupees each time. When he was ready to leave, he had saved about twenty rupees and wanted to give it to Nisargadatta. So Nisargadatta accepted it with great gratitude. The next day—the day the sadhu was going to leave—Nisargadatta gave him brand new clothes and two hundred rupees. Nisargadatta completely accepted the gift and then gave back more. It's an interesting story.

*

Bob, James, Kerry, Emmett, and Dell
July 27

Samadhi Comes and Goes

Emmett: Bob, there are mystics and saints in the past who said they experienced samadhi and claim that the experience is significant. What would you say to them?

Bob: I would say good luck to them. That's their experience. But none of them has ever gone beyond "no thing." They could have a million experiences of all kinds. But ultimately, where do they finish up? No thing.

Kerry: The samadhi issue is an interesting hang-up. It's so prevalent. For so many, it becomes an objective criteria for whether a person's enlightened or not. You know, "Can you go into samadhi?" "Can you close your eyes and go into this swoon that's like suspended animation, where you can meditate without food or water for days?" To me, that thought has been an obstacle. I can't do that. So how do I integrate that into the great enlightenment? I like hearing Bob's answer because it's one of those things on that list we've all developed of what great saints have been capable of doing.

Emmett: Well, it also distinguishes a different reality. A reality for those in that natural state.

Bob: Investigate the definition of reality. It's that which never changes. Samadhi comes and goes. Therefore, it can't be real. It's an appearance on reality. In *essence* it is reality, because it's made of the same underlying consciousness that is the basis of everything. But, as appearance, it's not reality. It comes and goes.

Kerry: You don't have to be self-realized to achieve samadhi. Also, you could go into samadhi for a month, and you still come out exactly where you went in. Because it is a suspended state. So, if you're in a certain place in your understanding when you go in, you come out in the same place. One way I heard it described is that if you haven't had lunch, and you go into samadhi for a month, then when you come out, you'll be asking, "Where's lunch?" It's basically useless. And there are warnings in some writings saying not to get involved in it because it's very charming, but it doesn't really help your evolution.

Emmett: In the *Yoga Vasishta* [an ancient Hindu scripture], there are repeated stories about sages who go into samadhi for thousands of years and come out, "Hello, how's everybody. . . ." [*Laughing*]

Bob: That's the beauty of that scripture. There are all kinds of experiences described, but it's always coming back to non-duality. In spite of these wonderful stories—people living for thousands of years and going to the end of the world—the message of the book is clear. Creation is an illusion, and oneness is all there is.

Emmett: That's true.

Bob: It's a beautiful book.

James: In the Papaji book *Nothing Ever Happened*, Papaji talks about his past lives. I know a lot of Advaitans don't believe in past lives, but he does. He said he had a vision of all his past lives and that he died in samadhi in his last life. What happened was that he went into that state and was motionless for many days. So his disciples thought he was dead. According to his vision, there was one disciple who said they should cut open his skull to see if he was dead! So they did that and killed him.

So people can go into samadhi and still not be enlightened. Because if he had been enlightened, he wouldn't have reincarnated again. At least that's what the Hindus teach—you keep reincarnating until you attain final liberation.

Are There Past Lives?

Dell: Why did Papaji believe in past lives?

Bob: That's his tradition. Like, if a Christian has a vision, it'll be of Christ. A Hindu will see Krishna or Shiva; a Muslim will see Mohammed; a Buddhist will see Buddha.

James: Many sages say that when you die, you see whatever you believe. If you believe in heaven and hell, you go to wherever you believe you should. There's a fascinating teaching in the *Srimad Bhagavatam*—the scripture that contains the *Bhagavad Gita*. There are two families at war. One of the families clearly represents the good guys and the other family are the bad guys. Well, at the end of the story the good guys go to hell and the bad guys go to heaven. The implication is that when the good guys—who were always struggling to be good—died, they felt guilty about whatever bad things they had done. So they believed they deserved to suffer, and they went to hell. And the bad guys never gave their bad actions a second thought. They felt they deserved to go to heaven. That blew my mind when I heard it. I was sure I'd be going to hell because I've always felt so much guilt about things I've done.

Bob: In the Dzogchen scriptures, they tell you there's no reincarnation. But then they go out looking for some child who is supposed to be the reincarnation of some famous lama who just died.

Kerry: Didn't Buddha say there are no souls, and therefore there is no transmigration of souls?

Bob: Yes.

Kerry: I used to be a devout believer in reincarnation. And I got disabused of that belief when I realized it's difficult to integrate the understanding of having never been born with the concept of reincarnation. Once it's understood that the personality is merely a string of thoughts, images, and impressions with no independent nature, what is there to reincarnate?

Bob: Exactly. And reincarnation implies time—something that happens in the future. Time is only a mental concept. So reincarnation is also a mental concept. There is no past unless you think about it. There's no future unless you think about it.

Kerry: So what we're saying is that yesterday, when we all sat here talking (and which I have on tape), didn't happen?

Bob: It happened. But it was *now* when it happened. And it's *now* when you're recalling it. And it'll be *now* when you're imagining anything in the future.

James Makes the Case for Reincarnation

James: Bob, whatever happens occurs only in the world of appearance. It seems to me that reincarnation may indeed occur, but only in the world of appearance. So, when you say there's no reincarnation, that's only from a particular point of view. It happens to be the ultimate point of view, but so what? From the ultimate viewpoint, not a damn thing has ever happened. From the world of appearance—where we live—I think reincarnation does exist.

Bob: Well, from the viewpoint of appearance, everything is reincarnation. The whole manifestation is appearing and disappearing and reappearing. It's all transient.

James: Yes, but in the world of appearance, reincarnation is significant. It's significant because people are born with certain talents, abilities, and problems that must come from somewhere. Otherwise, life is a crap shoot. Why is one person born with some natural aptitude and another person not? It shows up at birth—a talent that can be developed shows up in the horoscope. [Note: I am not referring here to the horoscope as seen in newspapers and magazines. I am referring to astrology as it has been practiced professionally for thousands of years and is based on the exact time, place, and date of birth.]

Bob: It's the way the energy gets patterned. Energy can pattern in any shape or form.

Kerry: Some Advaitans believe that all memories and impressions go into a "pool" where energies or patterns are taken from. This explains how someone could be born with a certain talent but not be a reincarnation of a whole person. Something is simply grabbed out of a pool of consciousness or a pool of memory. This also explains why sometimes little children can know things about a village or a house they've never seen before.

Bob: Child prodigies may be tapping into energies that already exist in consciousness.

Dell: Tapping into a pattern of energy.

Bob: There's no actual "one" doing the tapping in. It's just a particular pattern expressing through a mind/body.

James: So, you're saying that when a person experiences past-life regression, he or she is basically deluded? They're just tapping into some experience someone else had?

Consider this: Some people asked Nisargadatta why certain seekers could work toward enlightenment their whole lives—for forty or fifty years or more—and never get it. And he answered that they may have latent desires. *Latent* desires—it's an interesting statement. He doesn't say they have desires that are unfulfilled or repressed. He says they have *latent* desires. These are desires that are yet to be born—in seekers who are already in old age.

Bob: Yes, but who has the desires? It comes back to that. There's a belief in an entity that never ever existed.

James: I understand what you're saying. Let me put it this way. From the point of view you're taking, I agree with you. From the ultimate viewpoint, there's no reincarnation. But from that viewpoint, there's no manifestation either! Will you agree with me that within the world of appearance, reincarnation is certainly possible? And by reincarnation, I mean, for example, some apparent human being in one life treats his son badly, so in his next life he is treated badly by his father. In the world of appearance, can you see that possibility?

Bob: That's what appearance is—it's all appearance and possibility. In essence, everything is the same thing.

James: In essence, we're not here is what you're saying.

Bob: That's what *is* here—the essence itself. Without that essence, the appearance couldn't be.

Emmett: The essence is here. None of the appearance is here. And within that world of appearance, reincarnation is just another possibility. It could exist in the world of appearance. It's just another drama, another plot line.

Bob: How does that sound to you?

James: It sounds like in the appearance there can be reincarnation.

Emmett: Yes, but in the end, if I can't participate in my former lives, it doesn't matter one way or another.

James: Some people are participating in a way—through past-life regression. Some people say they gain some apparent relief or growth through that process. And I've seen people have that experience in my astrology readings.

Kerry: Yes, but reality is in the Now, and everything you're talking about is in the past or future. It's imagination. It's in the mind, which is the only place time can exist. So, is karma real? As long as you believe it is. Is reincarnation real? Yes, as real as heaven and hell. As long as you believe in it, it has seeming reality to that apparent person. But it's no more real than the appearance itself. This is why it says in scriptures that when you enter the final door [that is, liberation], throw out even the scriptures. Don't take any concepts with you. You can't carry them through the door. They're all appearance. And the appearance is not the thing. The "essence" has none of that stuff stuck on it. So it doesn't matter what you believe in—including reincarnation.

Bob: Exactly. That's good what you just said. And it's good what James said. Get into it yourselves. It's not me alone who knows this. You all ultimately know it—even if it comes out in little bits at a time. Different knowledge is coming out. Get into it.

James: [*Joking*] Dell's holding back. He hasn't said anything.

Dell: What I'm getting is that we have all the past lives within us. We are part of the whole, and each wave that comes from each individual encompasses every past life that has ever appeared. In essence, we're every past life. I have every past life within me, but I'm only picking up or expressing whatever frequency this Dell appearance can pick up.

Bob: That's what Buddha supposedly said: "Every sentient being has been your parents." And, as sentient beings, you also have been the parents of all the other sentient beings—including the Buddhas and all the other sages. It's all one essence expressing in all sorts of different shapes and forms.

Kerry: Bob, you're so generous as a teacher. You're telling us, "Hey, you all have this. It's not just me." I've never heard another teacher say that. They're more inclined to say, "No. Joe has it. The rest of you here don't have it. One other guy five years ago got it—and that was me." [*Group laughter*]

Bob: If I'm expounding non-duality—"You are That"—how can I deny or negate anyone? I'd be talking rubbish. [*Joking*] "You haven't got it. But I have!"

Kerry: From the tone of Nisargadatta's book, it doesn't seem like he took your approach, though.

Bob: He took the more traditional approach. He got it from his guru in the traditional way. So he taught in a similar way. He wasn't exposed to Westerners until he was much older. He wasn't well known until his book came out.

Kerry: It's interesting that many teachers will say, "I'm no better than you," but there's no emphasis on that fact. It's also fascinating that in so many traditional Eastern spiritual movements the same knowledge you're teaching us is there. But there's no emphasis on it. The emphasis is on mantras and techniques and behavior and all kinds of other stuff. And the emphasis is everything.

Bob: That's right.

Emmett Seeks a Time Frame for Getting It

Emmett: When you were with Nisargadatta, there was a certain point when you "got it." Is that accurate?

Bob: He pointed out that I am not the body or the mind. And I saw that. But can you say there was certain "point" when that happened? That puts you back into time. From the appearance point of view, I could say it was when I first saw him. I'd opened up enough to hear what he said. But if you put the implication of time on when I got it, you're back in time. And then you start conceptualizing it and thinking, "I've got to do this, this, and this, so I can get there." When I understood what he was saying, I realized there was never a time when I was not That. Old habits didn't drop off immediately, of course. But after seeing the falseness of something, you can never believe in it again. They could never get the same intensity again. When the old thoughts came up, they would quickly be seen as rubbish, and I would drop them. I would let go of them. No fixation or attachment to them.

And there was no resistance to them, or "I shouldn't be like this. I have to be in a certain state." There was no image of how I should be. No trying to change, alter, or modify thoughts or habits. That would be trying to change "what is" with a thought. When these habit patterns come up, they're just what is. The only way you try to change anything is by thinking about it. If it's left in its natural state, with no resistance, it leaves on its own. There's no cloud that's ever attached to the sky. Thoughts are not attached anywhere in you.

Emmett: We're here listening to you every day, trying to get this ability to see the falseness all the time. But it keeps coming back. Of course, we will always be aware of the falseness and then returning to the essence. But, is there a time when . . .

Bob: NO TIME! You're trying to manufacture a time . . .

Emmett: Is there ever a quantum "drop" or "loss" of the tendency to be stuck in time and stuck in the appearance. Or is it incremental, incremental, incremental?

Bob: NOW HEAR THIS! What's wrong with right now unless you think about it?

Emmett: Nothing. And the fact is, we keep thinking about it!

Bob: In that brief second of no thinking—that is the thing you are looking for. In that moment where nothing is wrong—or right—it is just as it is.

Emmett: And we . . .

Bob: And the "and" gets you back into it again! In the pausing, without thought, everything is just as it is. It's only in the labels that there can be good/bad, right/wrong, or whatever. Without that, everything is just what is. You're spontaneously knowing that you are.

Emmett: But we are in such a state of vulnerability to the appearances that can take us right out of that awareness. Does there come a time when the appearances can't grab you anymore—when you are like concrete in that reality, so you can't be pulled out anymore?

Bob: You gained that sense of separation at the age of two when you were taught you are an individual. You have to question that belief in the "me." As long as you believe in that "me," you will be vulnerable and insecure.

Emmett: But was there ever a sudden grasping of this that made it complete, once and for all?

Bob: In seeing that there is no individual entity, *who* can it be gradual or sudden for? It just is. And it was always so.

Dell: Nisargadatta said that he did self-inquiry for three years, and then he finally got it.

Bob: I can put a time on it too, but I'm telling you there is no time. Nisargadatta said to stay with the "I am." That "I am" is a translation of that sense of presence. Right now, you're aware of being present. Turn that around—there is a presence of awareness. They're not two. And that is the immediacy of all of us. If that weren't here, we couldn't have any appearance whatsoever. The appearance has no independent nature. It relies on the presence. In staying with the "I am," you can't help but see this.

James: As I understand it, awakening shows up differently in different people. For some it's gradual and for some it's sudden. A lot of the books we read make us think it has to be sudden because that's how it happened for that person. Like, for example, Eckard Tolle [author of *The Power of Now*]. But remember that Nisargadatta was often asking individuals whether their understanding came suddenly or gradually.

Bob: That's true.

Who Cares About Death?

Kerry: Let's talk about death. We hear these sages say, "I don't care if I die in the next five minutes." What's the experience that makes them say that?

Bob: It's just the ego—the "I" thought or false self center—that was born. And that's constantly in fear of dying. Because people haven't recognized the functioning prior to thought—the seeing, hearing, touching, smelling, and tasting that's happening spontaneously—they fear death. People think that mind is all there is, and that it's real. When they see that mind is just a bunch of concepts appearing on the essence, and that who you are is that essence, and that you as essence were never born, then the fear is over. And you can't say there will be a time you will cease to be. You can only *imagine* some conceptualizing going away. So it's all mental stuff. You are no thing that was ever born. What's to fear? Who's to fear it?

Kerry: But there's still a big change when death comes. Right now we know we exist. So awareness is aware of itself. Death is awareness *unaware* of itself. It's existence, but it doesn't know it exists.

Bob: That's right. It's just pure being.

Kerry: The funny thing is that if we weren't actually living the better part of our lives in the natural state—even though we don't realize it—we would be in a panic, fearing death every moment of every day. It's only the fact that the core of our experience is the non-changing natural state that lets us walk around with an innate sense of immortality. That's probably why people don't take care of their health and why we do so many seemingly stupid things. How often does it happen that a person has a heart attack and suddenly becomes health conscious? Death has always been imminent, but suddenly the person is faced with it.

Bob: That innate sense of immortality you were talking about becomes more evident when you see that the "me" is false. When you investigate death and see there's no actual self center there to die, immortality becomes more apparent.

Emmett: I've heard that when Ramana Maharshi got cancer, he allowed the doctors to give him some major treatment. And I wonder why he bothered to try and save his mind/body.

Bob: Why not? I don't care much about death, but why do I take vitamins?

Emmett: Exactly. That's what I'm asking. What motivates someone once they're realized?

Bob: The same thing that motivates you all the time. The pure intelligence energy.

James: You're being lived.

Bob: Exactly.

Emmett: Well, I've read stories about enlightened sages who sat around and let bugs crawl all over their bodies. If they don't care about that, why care about death?

Kerry: I could be wrong, who knows, but those stories never struck me as being true. So many stories are made up.

James: There's a story in the Papaji book about a yogi in the woods who's living with an open sore, and there are bugs or worms eating it! When Papaji asked if he wanted him to clean it up, the man said, "They're having their lunch. Let them be." Or something like that. The stories sound weird, but they could be true. Aside from the fact that there are infinite possibilities within the appearance, there are billions of people on earth, and everyone has some quirk or another. Anyway, letting bugs crawl on the body without swiping them away is just a bit more strange than doing nothing about cancer, like Nisargadatta did. He never tried to heal it, and he sat up giving talks in pain until the day he died. Hell, I can't even fathom how a yogi can live alone in a cave for fifty years. To me, that's bizarre. There are infinite possibilities.

Bob: They did give Nisargadatta some oxygen toward the end.

Kerry: There's a story of a famous sage that Ramesh talks about. The sage confused people who have preconceived notions about death. When he was dying, he was in tremendous pain and was screaming for his mother. People wondered how someone who was enlightened could be screaming like that. Well, the body cries out.

As far as the yogi with the bugs, it may not have been anything cosmic. He may have just been tired of constantly swatting them away. Who knows?

Bob: You don't know. And these stories get embellished all the time. People add to them to make them sound incredible. "Oh yes, I saw the saint and blah blah blah."

Kerry: [*Joking*] Do you remember when Sailor Bob came to America, and he ate the equivalent of ten meals at once? [*Group laughter*]

James: And he tapped me on the forehead, and I had visions.

Kerry: And when he was alone, I saw him float to the cottage! And he took on everyone's karma.

Bob: Aha. I have to raise my price now!

Kerry: What's interesting, though, is that the only way a guru can actually take away anyone's karma is to give him or her the understanding. Karma only exists in the world of appearance. There has to be a doer for karma to exist. And there are no doers because no one has a self center. So when a person gets the understanding and sees the illusory nature of creation, that's when he or she can be relieved of karma.

James: That's true. But I don't think we have to deny the existence of all miracles. I don't know why Advaitans are generally so skeptical of extraordinary happenings.

Kerry: There's a brilliant point that Leo Hartong makes through his book title. He doesn't call it *Awakening in the Dream*. He calls it *Awakening to the Dream*. We are still in the dream until we die. As Bob helps us see through the dream, he actually is relieving us of karma. That's what I think is really meant by "the guru taking on someone's karma." But it's been so misinterpreted that people think it has to do with some great, fantastical experience.

James: Yes, but that doesn't mean there haven't been times when gurus did do something extraordinary for a person or a disciple. Look at the stories of Christ healing the blind or the miracles Papaji did for people. Are those all necessarily false accounts?

Kerry: Not necessarily.

Dell: How about the story of the Zen sage [Chuang Tzu] who dreamed he was a butterfly? The next day he wondered, "Am I a person who dreamed I was a butterfly, or am I a butterfly now dreaming I'm a man?" [*Group laughter*]

*

Bob, Kerry, Emmett, and James
July 28

Emmett Enjoys a Full Stop

Emmett: We read stories of angels and gods and all. What about that?

Bob: When you talk about seeking and becoming, and gods and angels, and all that, it's a mind trip. The purpose of the mind is to divide. It never stops dividing. And that which is duality can never understand non-duality. So the answer will never be found in the mind. And the only way out of the mind is full stop.

Emmett: But full stop doesn't occur on the basis of our mind, or on anything really.

Bob: You can just stop right now.

Emmett: *Who* can?

Bob: No one. But the stopping happens. In the very seeing of that, pause without a thought.

Emmett: My mind will pause, but . . .

Bob: Repeat "I am," "I am," "I am," "I am," quickly.

Emmett: I am, I am, I am, I am, I . . .

Bob: STOP! [*Long pause*] Was there a thought there in that stopping?

Emmett: No.

Bob: Did you fall apart?

Emmett: No.

Bob: Still seeing and hearing? Still aware in that pause?

Emmett: Yes.

Bob: That was beyond the mind, in that instant. The pure knowing was there. That's what people talk about and struggle for—to go beyond the mind. In that pause, you were there. That's pure intelligence.

Emmett: Who took the action to stop. Who initiated the stop?

Bob: There was a stopping. You're trying to find the answer in the mind. There was a cessation—a pause. That's all. Who's thinking? Who's seeing? Who's breathing? Who's beating your heart? [*Laughing*]

Emmett: When you made me stop, I saw intelligence energy.

Bob: What was it that stopped?

Emmett: Thought.

Bob: So thought can stop and begin. But that which thought appears on didn't stop. And you didn't disappear. Prior to the mind is our seeing. You were beyond the mind in that moment. The knowingness, or intelligence, was still there. That is what the mind appears and disappears on. And you see from that that the mind's only a translator. It has no power or independent nature. The answer to life will never be found in the mind. Eventually you have to think, "Maybe I'm looking in the wrong direction."

Emmett: Isn't it the mind we're using in this investigation?

Bob: Yes. You use the mind to see that the stopping is needed! [*Group laughter*]

James: It's paradoxical.

Kerry: We're using the mind to find out that we can't use the mind.

James: Nisargadatta said, "You have to think yourself out of this problem. There's no other way." And that's exactly what we're doing. I was startled when I heard that.

Emmett: At some point, the mind breaks. . . .

Bob: Emmett, you're looking for the answer. You don't need the answer.

Kerry: Before understanding non-duality, if a question arose, and I wanted to express something, a stream of thoughts would occur. Now, if there's a question, my mind shuts down, so an answer can arise out of silence. Does that make sense?

Bob: Yes. It has to be translated into a thought—by the mind. The thought "I am" is a translation of the knowing that you are—that sense of presence or presence of awareness. The thought "I am" is a translation. It can never be the reality. Without the thought, the knowingness is still there. You don't need a label for it.

Emmett: That was the experience—the knowingness, or emptiness—that I had when you stopped me from repeating "I am, I am, I am."

Bob: It left you in your natural state. That's it. [*Laughing*]

Kerry: [*To the tape recorder*] Make a note: Bob's laughing heartily. [*Group laughter*]

Silence Overwhelms Sound

James: In the last week or so, I've been getting more and more quiet inside.

Kerry: It seems like the quiet goes on at the same time the mind is chattering.

James: Yes.

Bob: Where are those Tibetan singing bowls of yours, James?

James: I'll get them.

Bob: [*Bob smacks the singing bowl, which rings loudly for seven or eight seconds*] Notice how the silence overwhelmed the sound? No matter how much noise there is, the silence is much greater.

Emmett: That's so dramatic!

Bob: The same with movement. Get a bowl of water and stir it a lot. And then stop stirring it. The stillness will overwhelm it.

Kerry: That same silence happens when I go to the floor of the NYMEX [New York Mercantile Exchange]. It's so intense there, it's hard to describe. There are thousands of people on "the floor," packed in like sardines. And they're screaming at the top of their lungs. The silence dominates because the noise and the frenetic activity is so intense, it amplifies the silence. It's very tangible. It's hard to put it into words, but the noise is on the background of silence.

Bob: People search and search for years, looking for silence and stillness, not realizing it's the changeless background that everything appears on. That's what this teaching is about. It brings your attention to things we've never investigated before.

Kerry: That reminds me of that great book title, *The Open Secret*. It's amazing because the answer to life is hidden in plain sight. Hey, that would make a great book title: *Hidden In Plain Sight*.

Emmett: When you had me say "I am, I am, I am," it left me in the pure knowingness, which is where I want to be. And that is there all the time, even when activity or thought is happening. By seeing it in that one experience, I'll be able to always recognize that. My understanding can never be the same again.

Bob: That's right. And so you see, nobody can ever teach you or give you anything. No one can do anything at all for you. When your attention is drawn to something, that's all you need. It happens right here, right now, where you are—not with anyone else.

Kerry: That's beautiful.

Bob: So kick the gurus out. I've just suicided myself! [*Laughing*]

Kerry: Isn't that the meaning of that famous phrase, "If you see Buddha on the road, kill him"?

Bob: Yes.

Kerry: You can't stand on your own two feet until you destroy the concept of the guru.

James: This issue about the silence taking place in the midst of noise, or as the background of noise, is interesting. Yesterday afternoon, we were in a store buying Julian a toy, and they had this loud, abrasive music on. I asked the cashier if she had to listen to that all day long, and she said yes. I told her that in the morning it wouldn't bother me, but by the end of the day I'd want to slit my wrists. By the end of yesterday, my nervous system was vibrating.

Kerry: You want the answer? I'll give you the definitive answer. You had a five-year-old with you! All bets are off when you're taking care of a five-year-old. [*Group laughter*]

James: Well, that's right. That's exactly what I'm talking about. Being frazzled by a five-year-old—often.

Emmett: That's a question of the nervous system.

James: That's actually my point. Some gurus say we must purify the nervous system, and then nothing whatsoever can make us frazzled.

Bob: The answer is: Go ahead and try that. Go ahead and purify the nervous system.

James: I did that crap for thirty years.

Bob: That's what I'm saying!

Kerry: I just described an experience of silence on the loud, crowded floor the NYMEX. That's still just an experience owing to my nervous system. Nisargadatta described an experience of being "one with a flower." When I read it, I thought, "Oh, I don't have that. Something's wrong here." But that's just an experience owing to his nervous system. Some people have musical talent; some people don't. Some people are good at math; some aren't.

Bob: That's right. And even when you were frazzled by the music, James, it still only happened on the background of silence. The silence was still your background whether you were aware of it or not.

James: Exactly, but my experience was of being frazzled. I don't like that.

Bob: *Who* doesn't like it? The image you have about yourself—the self center or reference point—is saying, "This is frazzled. I've had this experience before, and I don't like it." But what is it if that reference point is not there? If it's not hitting that mental picture that you have of yourself?

James: Then, it's just a happening.

Bob: As a happening, when it's not hitting that reference point, it's just a flow of energy. That's all. Look at it this way. You're frazzled—well, just be that.

James: Be frazzled?

Bob: Yes. Be frazzled. Then, is it "frazzled?"

James: No. It's just what is.

Bob: You've got nothing to compare it to. If you're angry, be the anger. What is it then? Is it anger? Fear? Be the fear. Don't muck around with it separating. Be completely that. Just as it is.

James: With no label.

Bob: You don't need a label. If you're pissed off, be pissed off. Full stop. What is it then—if you're totally pissed off? It's not a mind trip then. It's just what is. "What is" means unaltered, unmodified, uncorrected. Warts and all. Just as it is. [*Group laughter*]

Seekers vs. Non-Seekers: Who's More Screwed Up?

Kerry: When you say that, it makes me realize that seekers are often more screwed up than non-seekers. Because they're always self-examining. "What does this mean? Why did I have that reaction?" And so on. You get another observer, another layer of observation. It takes place for the seeker.

Bob: Seeking is the problem.

Kerry: There are people who don't self-examine, who don't seek. They would laugh at this conversation and wouldn't spend three minutes listening to this stuff. They do what they do and don't care. They're better off than the poor seeker who's constantly self-examining. And yet it's the seekers who reach the understanding we're now discussing.

Bob: The self centers of those people who don't self-examine are not getting them into trouble in certain instances. But they're also certainly experiencing a reference point about lots of other issues. With seekers, they have become overwhelmed by suffering from their self center, and feel they want to do something about it. Most of us who start seeking have had some traumatic experience that sets us on the path.

Kerry: Enlightened dissatisfaction. But some people suffer and start seeking, while others suffer and never seek.

Bob: It's like the Bible parable: Some seeds that fall on the ground sprout a little, some a lot, and some not at all. In the scriptures, they tell you that you have to give up the ego. You have to be selfless. But none of them directly tell you that there is no self there. It's just a fiction.

Kerry: It's interesting, though. Seekers, in self-examining, could appear to be weak when compared to non-seekers who are so sure of what they're doing. Someone who's strong, by society's standards, doesn't do a lot of questioning about themselves. If they're challenged, they stand their ground. They appear strong. When seekers are challenged, they may look inward. They're vulnerable. What does that imply? It implies that their self center isn't that strong a reference point. It's kind of loose. So, the person appears to be weak. Maybe they run to a psychiatrist because they're getting beaten up by these people with stronger self centers, who actually don't have a clue. The non-seekers are telling them how it is, when they don't really have a clue. They're going this way and that way. The so-called weak ego, which it could be argued is actually very strong, begins to self-examine. And yet, all examination has to eventually drop away.

Emmett: The willingness to be vulnerable is a willingness to possibly self-destruct. It's a willingness to say, "Maybe I'm not right." That self-destruction is what we're talking about. That ego has to be destroyed.

Bob: It doesn't have to be destroyed. It's a fiction. There's no self center there.

The knowing that you are translates through the mind as the thought "I am." You can't do much with "I am," so you add onto that "I am." You say, "I am this, I am that, I'm great at this, I'm bad at this," and so on. You add to that "I am" and form a mental picture or image of what you believe yourself to be. That seemingly concretizes—and becomes a reference point. But when you investigate it, you see it's only a group of ideas and images or concepts which have no substance. And above all, they are not independent. You couldn't have any of them without awareness. So the ego is a fiction. There's nothing there.

Emmett: That's right. And unless you investigate it, you don't see that. So there has to be a willingness to investigate—to self-destruct or have that fabric be totally unwoven.

Bob: Now you're starting to bring "willingness" in. Then we have to ask, "Who's going to bring this willingness?"

James: You have to stop believing in the self center—the false reference point. That's what Emmett's calling "destruction of the ego."

"This Can't Be It"

Kerry: When most people read or hear about non-duality, they don't walk away feeling like they got it.

Bob: "Well," they say, "I see that, *but* . . . " or "What if . . .?" And the big one is "Well, if I'm 'nothing,' how will I live my life?" And they're immediately back in the trap of duality again. And if a habit pattern comes up again, they'll say, "This one's a strong one." In fact, it's got no power at all unless a belief goes into it.

James: I think that what's behind that "Well, I get it, *but* . . ." is this feeling of "This is it? This can't be it. I don't feel great. I don't feel bliss." First of all, there are all these teachers saying how fantastic it's going to be when we get there—as if there's a person to be there when it happens. It's the height of absurdity. We're all looking for *some-thing*—not "nothing." When "nothing" happens, it's anticlimactic. It's like, *"So what? What's the big deal?"*

Bob: When you say, "So what?" you've subtly moved back into it. See how subtle it is? "I don't feel great . . ." You're back in the mind.

James: Yes.

Bob: This is it. Full stop. Just as it is.

James: You give the person the experience of what is. You go through that process of "I am, I am, I am, STOP." And the person pauses and stops labeling for a few seconds, and they see "what is." They see that which is beyond thought or prior to the mind. And that's not great; it's not fantastic. It's just what is. It doesn't match their pictures of the great enlightenment that all these gurus and sages write about. So, the person walks away from it.

Bob: Exactly. They go straight back into the mind.

James: Straight back. I've seen it with some people who have come to hear you.

Kerry: It occurs to me that the great experiences may have some truth to them, but first the person has to stop seeking so hard. The silence doesn't sing the first moment you pause thought and experience what's prior to the mind. That comes from relaxing into it.

Bob: We're used to gross sensations. And that's what they're looking for. But the beauty or enjoyment is in the subtlety and simplicity.

James: There can also be a problem when someone feels they "got it." If the person gets it, the next step the mind takes is to say, "I'm enlightened, I'm liberated, I'm awake." That can be difficult. There can be resistance to that. You start thinking, "I'm not good enough for that. Could I possibly be liberated?" There are a million reasons not to take it on and stay with it. And there's only one reason to say, "This is it."

Kerry: If you get rid of that word "enlightenment" and just say, "I understand," then you don't trigger those reactions.

James: Yes, but you know the world we live in. We've already been conditioned by all these spiritual teachers and movements.

Bob: Get rid of the idea that "I got it." Go back to the fact that "I am" is it—not that thought—but what the thought represents. That sense of awareness, or presence, is it.

James: Also, you think, "I'm awake now, but I was awake years ago when I was suffering. What is this?"

Bob: The suffering or the not suffering couldn't have taken place without the underlying wakefulness. That's the eternal constant.

James: Exactly.

Bob: That's "understanding."

James: Yes, and that was my first question when I called you months ago. When I asked, "What role does the intellect play in liberation?" what I meant was, "Is enlightenment just an understanding? Could it really be just that?" It was shocking to me after hearing all about samadhi and purifying the nervous system and all that. It was bizarre. So much misconception.

Kerry: I think there's an element that has to come into this for many people. And that's faith in the teaching. Because the understanding is so subtle and isn't initially supported by dramatic experience. Look at Nisargadatta's process. He said, "My teacher told me I am the Divine Awareness. I am the Eternal. And I believed him. And I abided in That." And he stayed with the "I am" for three years. I'd bet that for the first six months or a year there was nothing flashy about his experience.

James: That's why there are millions of people going to these gurus who give out techniques and all sorts of things to do. And tell disciples, "It's going to be great in the future." Non-duality is too simple for people, until they're ready. I've noticed one common denominator to many people who are willing to say, "I got it." They go searching, and they decide, "I'm not returning to my life until I find the answer." When people like that hear truth—truth that's genuine and authentic—they take it. These are the ones who are committed. The ones who said they refuse to return to life without it.

Bob: And the answer was totally different than what they thought they were looking for!

James: That's right. But they were so serious that when they heard truth, they took it.

Kerry: That's earnestness. Nisargadatta was always telling people to be earnest.

Bob: You were talking about purifying the nervous system. What nervous system is there if there's no vitality in this body?

James: The nervous system is just another concept.

Kerry: There was a very interesting exercise Ramesh talked about when I saw him. He says to analyze any action you take in the course of the day and see if it's really *your* action. For example, half a minute ago I made a decision to say what I said. Well, Bob said something prior that brought up my thought to say what I did.

Emmett is sitting here with us because James called him up and said,

"Sailor Bob's coming here." James couldn't have invited Bob to come here if Meryl hadn't told him to get Bob's book. So there is no action we can take that's really independent. All kinds of things have to happen for the next action to occur. Nothing is self-generated. It's all integrated into the totality. There's genetics, there's our upbringing, and everything.

Bob: And that can go right back to the stars—to the astrology that James practices.

James: Absolutely. The horoscope shows so much of what's going to happen in a person's life.

There is no need of a way out! Don't you see that a way out is also part of the dream? All you have to do is see the dream as dream. . . . Wherever it leads you, it will be a dream. The very idea of going beyond the dream is illusory. Why go anywhere? Just realize that you are dreaming a dream you call the world and stop looking for ways out. The dream is not your problem. Your problem is that you like one part of your dream and not another. Love all, or none of it, and stop complaining. When you have seen the dream as a dream, you have done all that needs be done.

—Nisargadatta Maharaj, *I Am That*

CHAPTER FIVE

Never the Same Again

*

From the age of twenty, when I learned about meditation and enlightenment, there was one pervasive current of thought running through my brain. It began when I awoke and was there until I slept. And the intensity never lessened. It was, of course, the desire that my sense of separateness and incompleteness would one day be replaced by the peace or so-called bliss of enlightenment. By my late forties, my thinking remained unchanged except that expectations of success had seriously diminished. Shortly after Bob arrived, however, my worn-out concepts of, and desires for, liberation were replaced by the conclusion, *I will never be the same again.* Indeed, that thought became somewhat of a mantra for the five weeks of Bob's visit. And I heard similar reactions from others who spent more than two or three days hearing Bob's non-duality teachings.

Amazingly, this was unrelated to experience. It had only to do with understanding. During Bob's visit, there was no transmission of bliss, no trance-like state of meditation, and no tapping on the forehead. There was simply a reaction to following Bob's instruction to investigate the belief in the "me" we have all lived with since childhood. It was a reaction to seeing clearly that the past and future are nothing more than mental images. If past and future are illusory, then so is our entire existence. If past and future never happened, what exactly did? It was a reaction to looking within and, instead of experiencing an independent entity, finding emptiness or "no thing." And it was a realization that since "no thing" has been with me ever since birth—while absolutely everything else about me has changed—then emptiness or "no thing" must be who I am. That being the case, who I really am is, and has always been, whole and complete. That being the case, who I really am is omniscient, omnipresent, and omnipotent.

For ten years during my thirties, I had taken the Werner Erhard EST seminars. Werner is not an Advaitan, but he's a brilliant teacher. Many times I had heard him state emphatically, "This is it. This is how life turned out. Stop expecting it to be different." He also said, "Life has no meaning. Get used to it. Life has no meaning—and it has no meaning that it has no meaning!" For years, I wondered what it would be like to be able to really comprehend such statements. Somehow, Sailor Bob had a similar message, said in different words. But he said them in a way I could grasp. And it was all simple and painless. It was as if we were little children entranced by the beautiful blue ocean, and Bob handed us empty buckets and said, "Go fetch me some blue water from the sea, and watch what happens." It was exciting beyond description.

The effects of this understanding have ranged from changes so simple and normal they are barely worth mentioning to a radical shift in life. While "The Bobs," as we sometimes called them, were here and visitors were streaming through our house, I was so busy—and so excited—there was no way to fully appreciate the changes that were occurring. A few weeks after they left, however, I noticed a blatant "before and after" effect. Life before Sailor Bob and life after. The most revealing experience, initially, occurred every time I awoke from sleep. Before Bob, my first thoughts upon awakening were directly connected to feeling separate, limited, and incomplete. And they were always accompanied by some corresponding desire that when fulfilled would supposedly set the problem right. There was often a sense of impending doom and a probing of what could possibly go wrong. This was naturally followed by a strategy of how to control any problem or potential predicament. Even in the best of times, there was always something missing and always something needed. The kicker was that no matter which desire might get fulfilled, the feeling of separateness and incompleteness never abated. Not even close. I could never get enough of what would not bring peace. Still, desires persisted. If, as they say, the definition of insanity is doing the same action and expecting different results, I should have been placed in an insane asylum decades ago.

After Bob's teaching, waking from sleep is radically different. Instead of feeling something is lacking and needs fixing, there is a sense of wholeness and completion. There is nothing missing, no sense of "becoming," and no worries about the future. There is finally a sense of belonging. Instead of a bunch of niggling, needy thoughts and desires demanding attention, there is simply life as is—presence awareness, moment by moment. The experience is so normal and undramatic it is barely worth mentioning. But it is so contrary to my previous life it is still surprising—and it is a relief beyond description.

In the months since my sense of separation has disappeared, I have also felt frequent moments of concentrated well-being. These are, I believe, what many would call bliss. But bliss, in my view, is a poor description for what is actually a sense of intense, *natural* well-being. While this may seem moot, the word "bliss" generally conjures up great ecstasy or the kind of miraculous peak experiences that sometimes take place during periods of extended meditation. The occasional sense of concentrated well-being, on the other hand, is something normal and natural that spontaneously arises from time to time, completely uncaused. This peace or joy, or whatever one wishes to label it, bubbles up strictly in the *absence* of distractions. It occurs on its own, with no particular rhyme or reason and is clearly related to being, or "no thing." What it is unrelated to is any particular action, belief, desire, occurrence, or other worldly phenomenon. Thus it is, as Bob says, "uncaused." While I cannot speak for others, I can say that in my experience the intensity of this well-being makes it unlikely to persist for long periods of time. There is a somewhat dominating presence to it, which overwhelms the normal focus and attention that one needs for daily living. I have even occasionally commented to my wife that if I weren't such an active person, the brief episodes I enjoy might last longer. Ultimately, I suspect the bliss that seekers have read about and consider the long-awaited prize is, to a large extent, a mind-created phantom. I am not saying that the bliss experiences many liberated people speak about don't exist. Nor am I asserting that some people haven't felt a state of bliss, or extreme well-being, for a year or two. In manifest creation, anything is possible. Indeed, in my late twenties I experienced a state of heightened awareness that lasted nearly two years and was brought on (in the world of appearance) by the impact of a devastating divorce. Based on the periods of extreme well-being I have felt lately, however, I suspect that unless one lives a very settled life with little activity, such occurrences are brief and transitory. At least, that has been my experience.

One of the most interesting effects of understanding non-duality is how quickly problems, worries, and upsets pass. When apparently bad things happen, intelligence energy comes up to meet the challenge. When disturbing thoughts begin to express, they try to cause their usual trouble but have nowhere to stick. First, they meet with the knowledge that there is no James. Then, they struggle against the realization that past and future are unreal. Then, they bang up against the awareness that who I really am is eternal and immortal. Problems generally become non-issues. This is, of course, the polar opposite to life before non-duality. At that point, there was no conceivable way to win. Life, enjoyable as it was in many ways, was essentially a vicious circle of solving problems—the solving of which made no lasting or significant difference. Death was always around the corner. The worldly pleasures of money, power, fame, love, and whatever else one can name were never enough. They could never fill the gap that was created the instant in which individuality was believed. And even if there were peaceful times, who could possibly know what problem or tragedy was lurking around the corner—in a future that was considered real?

By the time I noticed the changes that had taken place, a few weeks after Bob and Barb left, I found it fascinating that I could not pinpoint when they had happened. I knew early on I would never be the same because my perceptions and beliefs were clearly altered. But it was only after all the excitement and activity abated that I realized the change in my experience. The fact that I did not know when my sense of separation had dropped away was both remarkable and a verification that time does not exist. The present moment is all there is. At any rate, events happened as they did. Any explanations I can offer are both false—because there are no real causes in the transitory world of appearance in which we live—and after the fact. In the world of concepts and appearances, however, there are two things worth noting. One was my fervent desire to grasp non-duality. This intensity allowed for a certain courage and willingness to ask anything and everything I needed, and to press Bob, if necessary. The other was Bob's extraordinary ability to convey the understanding. I am referring not to his intellect, but to his tendency to focus almost exclusively on oneness—on the reality of existence—and to acknowledge the illusory appearance we live in only when appropriate and useful. In this, he was certainly masterful.

The conversation you are about read is a highlight of what I have just described. It is an example of my intensity and drive meeting Bob's ability to stay rooted in reality and teach only that. The talk took place the same night as the conversation that ended Chapter Four and centered around why it appears to take time—which clearly does not exist—for people to grasp non-duality. I felt that somehow people should grasp non-duality immediately, instead of having to mull it over or process it for months or years.

The words you are about to read do not convey the full extent of "fireworks" that were happening. But they were certainly evident in person. My question, I am sure, would have been answered with infinitely more patience had it come a week earlier. But Bob knew exactly where I was in my apparent process and had no intention of letting me off the hook. In fact, he said as much within the talk. For my part, I was comfortable with Bob as soon as he arrived. But, by the time of this talk, the comfort level had grown, and I was pulling out all the stops. I was pressing him to the limit. Voices grew loud, and there were times when we were actually interrupting each other in order to press our case—a slightly embarrassing fact as I listened to the tape. In retrospect, it seems that perhaps the question I was asking was not what it appeared. In retrospect, perhaps I was testing something in myself, in the teaching, or in Sailor Bob. But that is appearance only, in any case.

The conversation is a wonderful example of the necessity to finally—once and for all—drop the mind. As Bob so often states, the purpose of the mind is to divide. Until one does a full stop, there will be question upon question upon question, and never a truly helpful answer. The answer to life will never be found in the mind. The answer lies in being. And more specifically, in *being without labeling.* When the mind finally stops—whether briefly or for a long period—oneness is the only possible experience. While Bob was here, there was no way for me to grasp the significance of this fact. In my house was one of the best living examples of non-duality, and I wanted to take full advantage of the fact. I had no desire to sit in silence with him. So I asked anything and everything. And Bob, being the great teacher he is, did his part to "kick everything out from under me." It was therefore not until a few weeks after Bob left that I noticed my mind becoming very still. It was then that I began to understand what he meant by "living without labeling." And it was then that I began to have glimpses of what Nisargadatta meant in the following interchange from *I Am That*:

> **Question:** You are giving a certain date to your realization. . . . What happened?
>
> **Nisargadatta:** The mind ceased producing events. The ancient and ceaseless search stopped—I wanted nothing, expected nothing—accepted nothing as my own. There was no "me" to strive for. Even the bare "I am" faded away. The other thing I noticed was that I lost all my habitual certainties. Earlier I was so sure of so many things, now I am sure of nothing. But I feel I have lost nothing by not knowing, because all my knowledge was false. My not knowing was in itself knowledge of the fact that all knowledge is ignorance, that "I do not know" is the only true statement the mind can make.

In the following conversation, one of the funniest of the summer, I was questioning while Bob was mercilessly "kicking everything out from under me." The fact that we were both jovial and that there was so much laughter did not by any means diminish the intensity of what was happening. It was an important experience.

*

Kerry, Bob, Barb, Dell, and James
Friday Night, July 23

"I" is a label

Barb: I had an incident once that is similar to the process Bob uses to show people the pure awareness that's prior to mind.

Dell: You mean the one where he has us say, "I am, I am, I am," STOP?

Barb: Yes. I was about eighteen or twenty years old, cuddling with my boyfriend on a hillside. There was a river at the bottom of the hill. It was lovely.

Bob: [*Joking*] I hope that's all you were doing. [*Group laughter*]

Barb: It doesn't matter because . . .

Dell: [*Joking*] It doesn't matter because it's just a label.

Kerry: It matters because it's happening right now! [*Group laughter*]

Barb: Anyway, we were enjoying ourselves, and I heard a sound and a paper ruffling. And suddenly I saw a big snake. I don't remember a thing after that except being at the bottom of the hill. Of course, my boyfriend came down and asked what's wrong. I told him I saw a snake. But I couldn't remember anything except the snake and then being down at the bottom of the hill. I didn't remember running. I didn't remember anything. I was there, and I didn't know how I got there. It was a perfect example of spontaneous action without labeling.

Kerry: I have a friend a named Gregg Goode, who's had the understanding for many years and has a non-duality website [www.heartofnow.com]. He was telling me about the amazing implications of the fact that every thought and experience we have is out of sync with the happening.

Bob: Exactly.

Kerry: Because the whole thing is after the fact. We're never in the present moment, experientially. We can't be. It's all interpreting what already happened.

James: That's why there's no ultimate satisfaction in living this illusory life. Everything's about labeling and interpreting. That's why everyone's chasing the silence beyond—or prior to—the thought. Life as labeling isn't satisfying.

Kerry: Krishnamurti said, "As soon as you say something's beautiful, it's over."

Bob: Our very reference point is a label. It's a dead image we're referring to. The reference point is invalid because it's based on the past. "I," "me," and the rest of it are just words. Where do those words come from? They're not fresh and new. They're old labels.

Dell Relaxes into Emptiness

Dell: Nisargadatta and lots of spiritual teachers talk about the idea of witnessing life. And they make a big deal about it. Well, once this so-called entity is beyond the witness . . .

Bob: Hang on. No entity can be beyond. The entity is a witness, too. You have to see the falseness of the entity. That's the main thing. If you see the falseness of the entity, is there any witness? Is there anything beyond the witness?

Dell: No.

Bob: What are you?

Dell: No thing.

Bob: Just presence awareness. No thing. So, have you stopped knowing? For you to be able to say "no thing," the intelligence energy must be there. That is what you are: "no thing," in which witnessing and every other thing is appearing and disappearing on. If you are "no thing," and you're still hearing, thinking, seeing, and so on, it must be the emptiness, or "no thing" that is causing or allowing that. That's where the activity is coming from—from that knowing capacity that's in that emptiness.

Dell: So, how does the personality that we have . . .

Bob: *Who* has it? The characteristics of the personality are just patterns of energy that are appearing on that "no thingness," which is emptiness. So, if it's emptiness, who's having them? They're just appearances, like a cloud in the sky. Is a cloud attached to anything? Of course not. Once you start creating an entity and getting involved in mind stuff, you keep going down the wrong track. The nature of the mind is to divide. And it can only divide in the pairs of opposites. It'll go on forever. Whatever you think about will be a division. And division is dualism—it's duality. Non-dual, as we've just explained, is empty. In that emptiness, can there be a center? Can there be a circumference in space?

Dell: No.

Bob: Just relax into that emptiness right now. No center. No circumference. Have you fallen apart or disappeared?

Dell: No.

Bob: Just pure awareness—emptiness with no center and no place. Even your body is appearing on that emptiness.

Dell: Is it possible for a person with no spiritual knowledge to be living this reality—this non-duality—without having a clue about it?

Kerry: He's asking, "Can a person be enlightened and not know it?"

Dell: I didn't want to use that word.

Kerry: We all hate the word, but it communicates it.

Bob: The whole world is like that. Everyone's enlightened and doesn't know it. [*Laughing*] But, seriously, yes, that is possible. If they've been like that their whole life, with nothing to compare it to, how would they know it?

Kerry: There's a French man named Steve Jourdain who was realized and thought that everyone was having the same experience he was. In fact, he was having a completely different experience than others. And then certain things happened that made him realize he was different.

Barb: It's easy to adopt a feeling of being special. In fact, we're all actually the same. Many so-called spiritual people think, "We're special because we've got this knowledge." There's no difference in anyone—no matter what people are doing. Seekers are only doing what they're doing because they're being lived to do that. And some of them don't want to ever stop being a seeker because they'll find out that they're nothing special.

Dell: They'll lose their labels.

Barb: Exactly.

Why Does It Appear to Take Time to Get It? (or, James and Bob Turn Up the Volume)

Bob: What's Braha-sab doing? Any questions there? Ask your questions.

James: The ability to let life be, the ability to let experiences be, without resisting or pushing anything away, comes simply from the understanding that there is no individual? Correct?

Bob: Yes. That's the natural state. Look at a little child. It's not locked into any trouble before reasoning has started. The interference is based on the idea of a separate identity.

Dell: The emotions and feelings, or likes and dislikes, are based on your personality and upbringing. They'll come up, but they won't take hold.

Bob: They're just part of the functioning. We've had these reactions so much in life—so habitually and so often—that so many events can trigger them. Something brings on bad memories, and suddenly tears are there almost instantly. With so much repetition of these things, we've hypnotized ourselves. Just like a stage hypnotist. He puts people under a spell and has them do all kinds of tricks. And he gives them a post-hypnotic suggestion so that after their spell, all he has to do is snap his fingers, and they're back in the spell again. So, we've hypnotized ourselves into these reactions through constant repetition, without checking and looking to see who it's happening to. We've never turned inwards and had a look. As soon as we do, we see that these ideas and beliefs we have about ourselves have no validity whatsoever.

James: Will the repetition of looking within to see *who* it's happening to become a de-conditioning process? Instead of resisting any unwanted feeling or experience, we'll ask ourselves, "Who is this happening to?"

Bob: There's no de-conditioning process. It's immediate. The recognition of resistance to anything comes up spontaneously in that intelligence energy. There's nothing to do. You can't be non-resistance. You can recognize resistance from the point of non-resistance. In that moment of recognition, you're out of it.

James: Within the world of appearance—the world that we live in—it looks like a process. You told us that after you got what Nisargadatta was teaching, you left his flat, and then within minutes you were back in the mind again. Five or ten years later, it was easier to be non-resistant and to avoid getting caught in the reference point.

Bob: See, this is what consistently happens when people ask, "What happened for you?" I tell them the story, and they think it has to be the exact same way. They don't see what I've been saying beforehand. It's always the same, "Oh, he had it in a flash. And this one had it this way. And this was a process. And he did this for years and years." And they don't recognize what I'm telling you now. This is about knowing you are present and aware immediately—just as is. You can go into the story of how it happened to someone else. Or, "the process was this way or that way." And, "there was an entity there doing this, and I've got to do the same." But I keep pointing out that you're already knowing that you are. This is something you can't negate.

James: Well, actually, that's what my question is about. It *should* be immediate. But, somehow, it's not. It appears to happen in time for many people. Since there's really no such thing as time, why does it appear to take time for a person to get the immediate recognition? You seem to have the immediate recognition, and I don't. I feel the same way you felt when you left Nisargadatta's flat and went straight back into the mind and into reactions and all that. Now that I have the understanding, it seems like that should be the full stop. Not two or three or five years later.

Bob: What does the word "seems" mean? It means "appears to be." So, you're taking the appearance to be real. It's appearance only.

James: Right. There is no such thing as time. Therefore, now that I have this understanding . . .

Bob: *Whose* thought? *Whose* understanding? And what's this "now"? You split up all those things. Even "now" is a concept of time. Even the word "presence" is a concept of time.

James: [*Laughing*] I can't ask the question. I don't know how to ask. . . .

Bob: Right. And in that stopping, where does it leave you?

James: In the present.

Bob: Instead of staying in that and realizing there was nothing to say and nothing to do, you said, "I can't ask the question."

This is getting deep now. Have a look at what you're saying. You'll never work it out in the mind. Never.

James: This goes back to what we were talking about today. The way people say "I got it, *but* . . ."

Bob: You see that?

James: Yes.

Bob: Why do it? [*Laughing*]

James: Why do it? Because . . .

Bob: Because. A cause! [*Laughing*]

James: What?

Bob: *Because* means "cause." Cause and effect. *Who's* the cause? [*More laughing*] Drop it. You're trying to find a way out of it again with another question. Just sit in that emptiness for a moment.

James: I can't. I need to ask this from a different point of view. [*Laughing*] My reference point is going crazy here. I understand reality. Or, I have some understanding of reality. I am presence awareness.

Bob: What's the definition of reality? [*Laughing*] You're not going to get away with this, James.

James: That which is eternal. That which never changes.

Bob: Can the changeful understand reality? Can the changeful understand the changeless?

James: No.

Bob: Who's the "I" that understands reality? That's the changeful trying to grasp the changeless. Full stop again.

James: But I want to talk about the appearance—I want to talk about where I live for a minute. [*Group laughter*]

Bob: Well, what are you here for? To talk about the appearance or understand reality?

James: I want to understand. . . .

Bob: [*Mocking*] "'I' want to understand." Is there understanding right now?

James: [*Joking*] Bob's resisting me! [*Group laughter*]

Bob: Is there understanding there right now? Are you knowing that you are?

James: Yes.

Bob: Isn't that understanding?

James: Yes.

Bob: Then what do you want to know? You're trying to understand the content? There'll be a million questions there. But just stay with "That." When I kick everything out from under you, just stay with that emptiness. I can kick everything out from underneath you—all the time. But can you fall out of that knowingness?

James: No. But how is this helping with my question?

Bob: [*Sarcastic*] All right. Go on, ask your question. I'll chop it off. [*Group laughter*] It'll keep you in this forever. Go on, ask your question.

James: What I'm asking is this: There's no such thing as time—it's just a mental concept. There's only the present moment. Understanding is happening that the reference point is false. Since that understanding is happening right now . . . [*Pause*] If something upsetting were to happen, there would most likely be a recognition of resistance.

Bob: You're asking a hypothetical question about something that might happen in the future, and it's taking you away from the understanding right now.

James: Yes, I get that. We're not allowed to talk about that?

Bob: Look, you can talk about that as much as you like, but if it's taking you away from right now, and right now is where reality is . . . [*Pause*] If something should occur in the future, when will it be happening? It'll be happening *right now*, and you'll have the tools to handle it right now because you're used to being with the Now. Why are you hypothesizing, "What I'm going to do in the future"? You're right into concepts again.

James: I know that.

Bob: [*Laughing*] Why bother asking the question?

James: I want to know why a person who gets the understanding . . . [*Laughing*]

Kerry: This is great!

James: I want to know why—since there is no time—why it's not instantaneous.

Bob: It is immediate!

James: Bear with me for a minute. Two days from now, if something upsetting comes up, there will be a reaction . . .

Bob: Do you understand that there is no time? That the present is all there is?

James: Yes.

Bob: [*Loudly*] WHY THE HECK ARE YOU TALKING ABOUT TWO DAYS FROM NOW?

James: BECAUSE I LIVE IN THE WORLD OF APPEARANCE.

Bob: Two days from now is time. What is time?

James: Illusion.

Bob: Right. A mental concept. So you're conceptualizing about some future that's non-existent.

James: Well, you know how I'm able to predict those car bombings in Iraq every day? [*Group laughter*] Here's another prediction: Today's Wednesday. I predict we're all going to be here in this room talking again on Thursday. Even though there's no time, watch me be accurate.

Bob: Yes, but it'll be *now* when it happens. [*Group laughter*]

James: All right. I think I see it.

Bob: Well, don't "think" it. Know it.

James: My question's absurd because there never will be a future.

Bob: Right. And drop the question, and what's left?

James: Wait, wait, wait. I got an idea. [*More laughter*] How about this? I'm feeling slightly embarrassed. Everyone's laughing, and I'm thinking, "Everyone's laughing at me." So there's some resistance here. It's very, very slight, but good enough that I can bring it up as an example. Okay. I'm feeling some resistance. Oh, but now resistance is over.

Bob: You recognize that?

James: Yes.

Bob: As soon as you recognize it, you're out of it.

James: Okay. It took five seconds for the embarrassment to leave. Oh, now I'm embarrassed again. Bob looked at me a certain way and laughed. Oh, this time it only took three seconds for the embarrassment to go away. That was interesting. I got upset before, and it took five seconds to disappear. Then, I got upset later and only took two seconds. Why did it take five seconds, and then only take two seconds—since there is no such thing as time. Why am I . . .

Bob: WAIT A MINUTE.

James: WAIT. WHY AM I . . .

Bob: NO. YOU WAIT.

James: Non-resistance seems to be getting better or faster. Something is getting better.

Bob: You agree there's no such thing as time, and you're going into time constantly. So it must be a belief in time that has to go.

James: Yes. I see your point. Okay.

Bob: You see the point.

James: Yes.

Bob: Where are you right now?

James: The present.

Bob: [*Laughing*] Simple, isn't it?

Conceptualizing Is Okay When You Know You Are the Reality

Bob: Now, while all this talk about time was going on, did you ever move away from presence awareness?

James: No. I was always in the present. But my reference point was all over the place.

Bob: Well, what are you? The reference point or the reality?

James: Reality.

Bob: Right. Well, know that constantly. And then you can conceptualize all you like about it. It becomes all-inclusive again.

James: Wait a minute. You're not going to stop me if I conceptualize again?

Barb: Get Bob to make a promise for the future!

Bob: Realize that the changeless background is what you really are. Then, whatever appears on it is understood to be appearance. It's no big deal. There's no personal involvement about the Iraq bombings, for example.

James: Was there personal involvement in the last ten minutes when I was asking all these questions?

Bob: Yes. There was somebody who wanted to know.

James: [*Laughing*] WELL, HOW CAN I ASK QUESTIONS? If I conceptualize again, you're going to say there's somebody who wants to know!

Bob: Yes. But then—if you understand that there's no "me" there . . .

James: If I know I'm the eternal, how can I conceptualize?

Bob: The same ways clouds appear in the sky.

James: Isn't that what just happened? I was in the presence awareness, even though I was conceptualizing. I may not have known it but . . .

Bob: Did you know that? Was that knowingness there? Or was there involvement—with the embarrassment?

James: There was a big "me" going on. But that was an illusion. You knew that I am That. So what's the difference?

Bob: Of course I do. But did you?

James: No. I didn't know that. But that doesn't matter.

Barb: As long as Bob knows it! [*Laughing*]

James: How could I ever be anything but That?

Bob: That's right.

James: You knew I was That, as I was talking.

Kerry: All I know, James, is that you've helped to make a really good talk on tape. That'll be a great dialogue for people to hear.

James: [*Joking*] Well, I'm going to nail Bob. I'm going to get him at some point. He thinks he's like Ronald Reagan. Nothing sticks to him. [*Group laughter*]

Kerry: He loves it. He looked about twenty years younger during that interchange.

Bob: You can't nail me. I'm "no thing." [*Laughter*]

Kerry: You're not here.

James: I'm going to nail the appearance.

Bob: You can have the appearance. Take it!

James: We'll get Bob. We'll find a reference point in him.

Dell: Bob, did you wrestle with Nisargadatta with this stuff?

Bob: He'd get me up front and kick everything out from under me. "No, no, no, no."

James: Good thing he didn't speak English. You had the interpreter as a buffer.

Bob: And my reference point would get pinched. "Augh, augh, augh."

Barb: We took our friends to see him, and that's what happened.

Bob: Just the same as James was doing. [*Laughing*]

Kerry: What's fascinating is that all of that "back and forth wrestling" that you [Bob] had with Nisargadatta happened after you had the understanding. Because you got the understanding in the first few days you were with him. But then the fine tuning took place.

Bob: Well, that's the same here with James.

James: Same thing.

Kerry: That's what I call the "small rocks." You really worked hard to defend the "small rocks." [*Laughing*]

Barb: I went over to India with a friend and her daughter. And Bob took them to see Nisargadatta. They weren't very impressed, and that was apparently because Bob and Nisargadatta were yelling at each other like what just occurred. My friends thought everything was supposed to be peace and light. They had a concept that enlightenment is peace and light. So they weren't impressed by Nisargadatta. They weren't interested.

Kerry: They probably didn't think that enlightenment smoked cigarettes like Nisargadatta does. There was a time, if I had gone to see

Nisargadatta and seen him smoking, when I would have walked out.

Barb: And, James, if those words about embarrassment were true, at least you had the courage to ask your questions.

James: Well, it was just an example.

Dell: He was playing.

James: No, I wasn't playing. I was looking for an example, and when everyone was laughing, there was a tinge of some embarrassment. It was tiny, but it was something I could point to that was happening right in the present.

Kerry: James, the difference between you and Bob—versus Bob when he was yelling at Nisargadatta—was that you have less of a reference point going on. Bob was really fighting with him. He was attached to his position. You were discussing. But you quickly let it go.

Bob: Any more questions?

Dell: No.

Kerry: Bob, you said something earlier that I'll never forget. Fifteen billion light years away from here, it's still now. That's amazing. It really conjures an image about the ever-present Now.

Bob: You can only evaluate time from a reference point. And the earth is not a valid reference point because it's traveling around the sun.

Kerry: Time for bed. I'm tired.

Dell: That's part of why I was laughing.

Kerry: Oh, it was the engagement. The passion going back and forth was scintillating.

Dell: Actually, I was laughing more at Bob than James. The expounding was so intense. For me, it was like a spike going down deeper and deeper into railroad tracks.

*

Vignette
The Next Morning

Questions Can Keep Us in Duality

James: The problem I had last night was that asking anything about the future is totally negating the knowledge of non-duality.

Bob: It's subtly moving you away from presence.

James: It's negating any understanding. [*To Kerry and Emmett*] Why didn't you guys give me a smack?

Bob: You've just seen it.

James: When that reference point was in action, I really wanted an answer. "I want to know. I want to know."

Bob: If I'd have given you an answer, it might have appeased your reference point for a few moments, but then another question would have come. And another, and another.

James: I'd be back into duality, living as if there's a "me."

Bob: Yes, and that's what we do all the time. It's pointless asking questions. Where are you going to go from there? When there's no question, there's no questioner. You can only fall back into emptiness. In the "no question" and "no questioner," you still are.

James: I see. By the way, I have another joke.

Emmett: Let's hear it.

James: There was once a man who traveled all over India in search of enlightenment. He searched for years and years and years. Finally, he found an ashram where the guru said, "I can give you liberation, but it's not easy. It's a long, hard process." At which point, the seeker said he would do anything to reach the goal. So the guru told the man he would have to go into a room and meditate day and night, and food would be brought to him. That way, he would never have to leave the room. And he had to stay in silence the whole time, until the end of the year when the monks would come and check up on him. Then, he would be allowed to say two words.

Bob: Two words?

James: Yes. Two words. So one year goes by, and the seeker has been meditating and praying, and he's been in complete silence the whole time. The monks come into his room and ask, "So, how's it going? How's everything?" The seeker gets a pained look on his face and says, "Bed's hard!" The monks answer, "Oh, great, great. Just keep meditating. You're doing fine. You'll get there." Then, another long year passes, and the monks come to see him again. "How's everything—how's your progress?" they ask. Again he gets a pained look on his face. This time he says, "Food's awful!" The monks reply, "Oh great, great. That's fine. Just keep meditating." Then, a third year goes by, and they come to check up on him again. The monks ask, "So, how's it going?" The seeker says, "I quit." They answer, "It's about time. You've been complaining since you got here!" [*Group laughter*]

Bob: That's great. I'll have to tell that in Australia.

*

Bob, Kerry, Emmett, James, and Anne
July 29, Morning

The following conversation mainly involved Bob and a local woman named Anne Feely. While Kerry, Emmett, and I had breakfast in another room, Anne spoke privately with Bob. After thirty or forty minutes, the rest of us joined in. What follows are excerpts from that morning.

Life Lives on Life

Anne: It seems that if I were to get to the place where I thought life was unreal, I'd be laughing all the time—like an idiot. I don't think I'd be able to operate in this illusion appropriately. I'd be saying, "This is all a game."

Bob: But, if the "I" is false now, has it ever been real? So, who has operated in the illusion up till now? You were being lived throughout all the dramas and traumas and everything. Whatever you did in the past, did you think "you" did that?

Anne: I did. But I don't anymore. Parts of my life were horrible. Does this mean that if I hadn't had the belief in a "me," I wouldn't have had the bad experience?

Bob: Probably not. But life took you through that, and now you've turned around and are looking at this non-duality.

Anne: Yes, I know that about myself.

Bob: Doesn't that imply that there's an intelligence or higher power that's looked after you?

Anne: Then why are some people tragically dying in their story, or their horror?

Bob: There's a tree outside that has thousands of seeds on it. When they all fall to the ground, how many of them will germinate and become trees?

Anne: So, what about the ones that don't germinate?

Bob: They go back into life. Life lives on life. Those seeds will fall on the ground and rot and then become fertilizer, so something else can grow. And then after that grows, something will come along and eat it, and so it goes. Life lives on life. It doesn't know death. It can't know death.

James: How many microbes did you kill when you washed your face today? Thousands? Millions? We think our life is valuable, but from a bigger perspective all life is the same. It's all valuable. So the problem comes from the reference point.

Anne: Why do Advaitans use the term "pointers?"

Bob: There's a pointing toward your true nature. I can't do anything for you. Nobody else can do anything for you. Innately, you already know this reality because it's your true nature. Instead of looking "out there" for the solution, you start looking at what's being pointed to. Once you see the truth, the old habit patterns start falling off.

Anne: So you're on this earth having this experience but are aware that it's not real?

Bob: Yes. Just like when you go to the ocean and see blue water that isn't really blue. It's the same thing. As the Bible says, "Know the truth and the truth will set you free."

Doing Good When You're Not the Doer

Anne: In this becoming free, do you then start doing good for humanity?

Bob: *You* can't do anything. You never could and never will. But a natural compassion will arise. And then whatever happens will happen.

Kerry: After getting this understanding, it may be that doing more good happens. But it may not. That has to do with your nature. There are people who are do-gooders who don't have the understanding. And there are people who have the understanding and don't give a damn about what's happening in, for example, Africa. There's a great story about the seals being clubbed to death. The great sage J. Krishnamurti saw the news story about it on TV and turned it off because he didn't want to see the brutality. Brigitte Bardot saw the news story and started a movement that brought the killing to an end. Krishnamurti was the so-called realized soul, but it wasn't his place to be moved by that. I only bring this up so you don't have an expectation that unless you suddenly become a selfless servant, your understanding is incomplete.

Anne: A person wouldn't become evil, would they?

Bob: Not if it's not in your makeup. Were you evil before the understanding?

Kerry: Good and evil is a reference point—a human construct. Talk to your dog about good and evil.

Anne: Is it helpful to be in the company of people who are awake?

Bob: It can be helpful in keeping you in the reality for a while. But you take this understanding wherever you go. Initially, you may go out and the ninety-nine percent of the world who don't understand this may drag you back. But after a while, if you keep coming back to this understanding, instead of them dragging you back, you'll start dragging them in. That's when you can stand on your own two feet. Keep reading the book [Bob's], and more and more insights will come up for you.

Anne: When we die . . .

Bob: It's only the "me" that dies. You can die to the "me" right now, and then your worries of death are over. It was the "me"—the sense of separation—that was born. It's only the "me" that dies.

Anne: Are more people awakening these days?

Bob: Maybe so. With mass communication and the Internet, the knowledge is more accessible. And it's your natural state. Why shouldn't people awaken to it?

Anne: I know. So why aren't more people doing it?

Bob: [*Laughing*] Worry about the others later. Get it yourself first.

James: Nobody's doing anything, Anne. And it's not you doing the awakening or pursuing awakening. Awakening is pulling you. I was on the path for thirty years, thinking I was doing it. It was just happening, and then I attributed it to me. "Oh, I decided to meditate. I decided to do this and that. The other person decided to become a Christian; the other person decided to become an alcoholic." And everyone thinks it's them who did all this. In fact, we're being lived. Things happen, and then we say, "That's me. I decided to become an astrologer. I decided to write books." Well, there is no "me."

Look at Kerry. For the past five days, he's been coming up with these witty statements and metaphors. How does he do it? Well, it's not "him" doing it. The thoughts arise in his head and come out of his mouth. The same thing happens when I write. I'm not doing the writing. I sit down, look at the computer, and thoughts come up. It's not really "me."

Kerry: [*Joking*] James, I was being polite. It *was* me making those witty statements! Actually, it's easy to let go of your accomplishments and say they're not yours. The challenge is to realize you were never responsible for any negative thing you ever did. You never committed a sin. You couldn't have.

Anne: I was hoping you could just hit me on the side of the head and give this understanding to me.

Kerry: [*Laughing*] What the heck do you think he's been doing? He's been hitting you on the head for the last half hour.

James: Your head's in the lion's mouth now.

Bob: You've come to the end of the road here.

*

Bob, Kerry, Emmett, James, and Barb
July 29, Evening

God and the Devil, Heaven and Hell: All Mind Stuff

Kerry: Bob, this is such a rare opportunity for us—being able to spend day and night with you. We all have this background image of the guru on the dais who, to our knowledge, has never used a toilet in fifty years. In your talks, you try to let everybody know that you're just like us. Those are great words, but we're still hearing this great wisdom coming out of your mouth.

Emmett: It's true. We've always been looking for someone who's perfect.

Kerry: We wouldn't listen to a teacher unless we felt he was somehow more than us. What would be the point? So we automatically put the teacher on a high platform.

Bob: That's why I say to everyone, "In the immediacy, what you're seeking, you already are." Instead of stopping and seeing that, people go into the old habits that "there has to be something more; this is too simple." But you couldn't be anything else. If the ancients were telling the truth that existence is omnipresent, omniscient, and omnipotent, then there's no room for anything else. Everything must be That. The idea that "if I do this or that, I'll get somewhere" is impossible. You're That, right now.

Kerry: [*Joking*] No, that can't be it, Bob. You're holding back. [*To the tape recorder*] Make a note. Bob is holding back. We can tell by the look on his face. [*Group laughter*]

Why was the concept of God and heaven and hell created? One theory is that heaven was created because of the mortality that comes with the sense of separation—the "me." So we had to create some story we can believe in, that the "me" will survive after death. So now we have the motivation for heaven. But if there's no hell, then everybody goes to heaven. And that isn't convincing. So we have to work to get there. And reincarnation is the same thing. It's still a story of the survival of that "me," of that ego. That's our biggest motivation, our biggest fear. The death of the "me."

Emmett: In the last year, I've realized that reincarnation isn't very comforting anyway. Because even if it exists, I won't remember my former lifetime. So even if I come back, I'll be another person entirely. I don't remember who I was before and what good things and bad things happened to me. So it's completely irrelevant. I'm dealing with my life as it is now. I can envision the possibility that the illusion we live in might include reincarnation and karma and all that. It's conceivable, the same way that God as an originator or creator is possible.

Kerry: I went from a *firm* belief in reincarnation to a *firm* belief that it's complete nonsense. And now I recognize that we just don't know. And any firm belief is a reference point. As you said, it's a moot point. It doesn't matter whether it exists or not.

Bob: But you see, that all takes place in time. It's all about becoming. And there is no becoming. Non-duality is all about being. You can't negate your being. After the sense of separation comes upon us, we're geared to look "out there" to become whole. Because we feel separate. It's all about acquiring and amassing. And then we get the wealth or material security, and what happens? We still feel incomplete. Then we imagine maybe there's a God out there who will make me whole if I do such and such. And with God comes the idea of resurrection. It's all mind stuff—never about Essence. Then you have God and the devil, heaven and hell. It's all mind stuff. It's all about becoming.

Emmett: But you don't constantly refer to the fact that life is an illusion, and this conversation isn't happening, do you? In other words, this conversation is no less an illusion than reincarnation and gods and deities.

Bob: That's right.

Emmett: It's all one.

Bob: We're having a conversation now, and there's no one here to have that conversation. We're just vibrations, or patterns of energy. What you have to realize is that with mind stuff—God and angels and the devil and all—it just continues. The mind keeps dividing. There's always more and more and more. It's duality. There's no end to it.

Kerry: About a year ago, there were times when I'd become moved by some passage in a book on non-duality. And I'd put the book down and just relax into being—without labeling anything—for several minutes. Sometimes I'd sit there looking around the room for thirty or forty minutes. Occasionally, thoughts would come, but basically the senses were stopped, or completely in the background. This was before I heard the concept of "being without labeling." I told Ramesh about these occurrences, and he called them "free samples." And this happens now when I'm just resting, not doing anything. It seems to be brought on by a lack of resistance or something. Or by an acceptance of what is. It's a very settled feeling. And then there's a sense of what the sages are talking about.

Bob: It's an empty seeing. You can't get away from it, you can't fall out of it. There's no point of getting a concept of silence or stillness or emptiness. Just know that it's there. Not even that it's there, but just an empty knowing. An audible emptiness, a visual emptiness.

Kerry: There's a change happening. Before, there was a feeling coming from the concept. Now, the concept is coming from the feeling.

Bob: That's a translation of the experience. You don't even need that translation. If it comes up, it comes up. You might find yourself talking, and as soon as you stop talking, silence, or emptiness, is there.

Kerry: That's what happens. It's happened a lot this week because of these talks.

No "Me" to Get Upset

James: Bob, you talk about investigating the falseness of the "me" every time a mental upset occurs. I find myself doing that, and it's powerful.

But sometimes the upset is so intense that it still takes a while for it to dissipate.

Bob: Once the mind gets into something, it's hard to stop it. But are you just saying, "There is no 'me,'" or are you actually investigating? Seeing it—not the saying of it. Saying it is just the concept.

James: First I may say, "There's no 'me'; there's no James." But there's no change. Then I actually start looking to find a "me." I ask, "Who is this happening to?"

Bob: Can you find anyone?

James: No. There's no one here. It becomes clear that there's no one inside.

Bob: That's right. It becomes clear there's no entity there. And you see it again and again and again. You keep seeing it again and again for short moments of time. There's no use trying to remember the concept that there's no "me." You have to investigate each time some upset occurs. The investigation will come up more and more frequently. And then it'll come up of its own accord. The same as you know two and two is four.

James: That's happening now. I ask, "Why is this upsetting me?" And then I look to see if there is a "me," and of course there's not.

Bob: Don't even ask, "Why is this upsetting me?" That's giving the "me" a seeming reality. If there is no "me," who is getting upset? There will be no upsetting if there is no idea of a "me."

James: Can I say, "Upsetting is happening?"

Bob: There won't be if there's no "me" to get upset. Just look at the happening and investigate and see there is no "me" for it to happen to.

James: So when something is happening that doesn't feel good . . .

Bob: That's just what is—unaltered, unmodified, and uncorrected. It's a happening. If there's no reference point, where can the upsetting lodge? It will play around for a while and then dissipate. It has to, unless you keep referring it to a "me."

It's time to let go of the "me." It never existed. You're nothing; you're emptiness. You're seeing that. You're convinced of it.

James: I sometime have a concept that I shouldn't get upset.

Bob: *You* never got upset. If there's no "me," what was it that ever got upset? Patterns of energy appear, patterns of energy disappear. What was it that ever did anything? Once you know there's no "me," there's no need to even investigate. It's immediate.

Expecting Perfection

Barb: I have a question for the three of you. You all did TM for so many years. What were you expecting to be the result?

James: First, it was all about bliss and miracles and special power. I eventually reached a point where all I wanted was an end to resistance. I wanted to be able to just accept any experience that came along, without grief or suffering.

Emmett: I had a concept that enlightenment meant perfection—purity.

Kerry: It's hard to even remember. I had a very vague idea of bliss and a total lack of suffering. A total loss of fear. Immortality. I don't really know what kept me going because I wasn't terribly focused on those things. It was all vague. In fact, we didn't think these things through. Even a little examination would have told us that the rapture we imagined enlightenment to be couldn't possibly last long, or we wouldn't be able to function. We could have figured out the practical aspects of enlightenment if we had put our minds to it.

Emmett: We didn't though.

Kerry: No, we didn't.

Bob: If you had, you would have seen that you were already perfect.

Barb: Because of my religion, I had an idea I was supposed to be perfect.

Emmett: Everything is based on the notion of an individual "me." Christ is the image we're given.

Bob: Christ never actually fit the image they present. He was supposed to be perfect in non-violence. Yet he belted the heck out of the money lenders. He got angry; he rebuked people. But over the years they make him out to be their image of perfection.

Emmett: Right. Any negative things about him must be some mystery that we mortal humans can't understand.

Kerry: Plus whatever things were covered up. Who knows what truths were distorted over two thousand years? God is the positive pole. God is the good, and evil is the opposite. Non-duality tells you that everything is God. Good and evil are only human perspectives.

Bob: Good and evil are dualism. In fact, they're not two. It's all one. That's the simplicity of it. It doesn't get more simple than one without a second. Or no thing.

Kerry: Here's another thing we made up: Omnipresent, omnipotent, and omniscience. What did they mean? All powerful. Able to move mountains. All present. Able to know everything at any time. Able to see everything all over the world. When you distill it down, these terms are presence awareness. They're none of the things we thought they were.

Bob: The other way attributes the terms to an entity. We call it "God" and put a bigger and better label on it. All it really means is all presence, all power, and all knowing. Nothing other than That.

*

Bob, Anne, Vashti, James, Kerry, Emmett, and Dell
July 30

The Mind in Conflict with the Mind

Bob: Presence awareness, or awareness of presence, is who you are. Full stop.

Anne: But I still have ego thoughts.

Bob: *Who* does? When you say that, you're referring it to that "I" thought, which was added to the events and circumstances to form a mental picture. So, when you say, "I still have ego thoughts," the "I" is a thought itself. So thought believes it's having thoughts, and that's a conflict. It wants to get rid of thoughts because it doesn't like them, or it wants different thoughts. So it's mind in conflict with the mind. You'll never get anywhere with that, except suffering.

Anne: Any question I ask will basically be a "cloud" on presence awareness.

Bob: That's right.

Emmett: When I first heard this knowledge, I thought that clouds [thoughts] were bad. As if we should be getting rid of them.

Bob: People think they have to get rid of the mind. Mind isn't the enemy. It's a wonderful tool when used properly.

Emmett: From the absolute perspective, there is no preference of a human being's awareness over a dog's awareness.

Bob: No.

Emmett: Religion has taught us that we're better than animals. That we're a higher form of evolution and are therefore superior. That's all mind stuff. The dog is living the presence awareness as much as we are. Religion gives us a reference point to hold all the other reference points together.

James: When I told one friend that every time he washed his face he was killing thousands of microbes, he said that humans are the highest form of evolution, so that fact is irrelevant! [*Group laughter*]

Kerry: In most cases, a well-cared-for dog is happier than its owner. All a dog needs is food, shelter, and some loving. Look at our list of needs: love, money, power, recognition, and on and on and on. It never stops.

Choices Will be Made, But by No One

Anne: Bob, I have intense political leanings. So now I'll just be seeing them as thoughts?

Bob: You might take an active part in them. But *who's* doing them? Is there a "you" there doing them? That's just how the functioning happened.

Anne: But it seems like I'm making a choice.

Bob: Choices will be made; preferences will be held; reference points will come up. But there's no entity they could ever happen to. We've merely believed there's an entity here. Has the "I" got any ability to choose? The "I" is just a thought. It has no power or independent nature.

It's powerless. It wouldn't even exist without the presence of awareness. Thoughts are just patterns of energy. You are the livingness itself. Nothing can ever be taken away from intelligence energy. It's perfection itself. The rest is all appearance.

Anne: I want to say that I have to think about all this. [*Group laughter*]

Bob: [*Laughing*] You won't find the answer in the mind.

Anne: No.

Kerry: I can certainly see how someone's nature could be political. At the same time it's really important to realize that the pairs of opposites are integral to each other. You can't have evil without good. They define each other. They're different ends of the same stick, and you can't have a one-ended stick. So where is the railing against evil, in a sense? You lose some of the steam to say, "This shouldn't be. We should eliminate that." You can't eliminate anything. So the understanding of non-duality took a lot of the steam out of my feelings about anything.

James: And yet, so much of the fun of creation is the ability to stop a war or cure polio or fix some apparent problem. It's just fun. It's not significant, but it's fun.

Kerry: Exactly. I have no interest in politics, but someone else could have the understanding and still have a political nature.

Barb: Back in Australia, there was a man in a phone booth having a talk with Bob about non-duality. And when he heard what Bob was saying, he said, "If there's no meaning to anything, and everything is an illusion, I won't do anything." And Bob said, "Try staying in that phone booth for the next thirty years." [*Group laughter*]

Bob: Thinking can cause so many problems. If you look at herds of animals, you'll see that when a lion chases a herd and finally catches one, the herd runs on for a while and then stops. It gets back to grazing or whatever and forgets the past. If that happened to us, we'd be looking back all the time wondering, "Is he still there? Is he coming after us?" All the head stuff would be going on, instead of getting on with life.

Dell: Whenever I catch a cockroach in my house, I pray for it and then kill it. [*Group laughter*] One day, I caught one, and I threw it outside so it could live. In a second or two, a lizard came out and ate it!

Bob: It was good for the lizard, but bad for the cockroach. When you're in India, you find yourself giving money to one beggar and telling another to get lost. Why? That's just what happened.

Anne: Yesterday, Dell said that he got upset about something, and he recognized that the problem may have had something to do with his upbringing. The event triggered something that reminded him of his past. With that recognition, are future upsets less likely to happen?

Bob: Sure. You might catch yourself quicker.

Anne: If my intensity about a problem isn't too much, or if I find it amusing, then I see it as a game, and it doesn't matter.

Barb: The knowledge of non-duality makes life so much easier. It's easy to stop worrying about future problems that may never come to fruition anyway.

Kerry: Sometimes things come up that are just aspects of totality. For example, sometimes when I get angry, it's just an emotion happening. It doesn't feel like it's mine—it's just a happening that everyone with me experiences together.

Advaita Is Not a Prescription for Getting Better

Bob: Braha-sab's pretty quiet this morning?

James: [*Joking*] I'm not taking delivery of anything today. [*Group laughter*]

Dell: Lost your reference point?

James: Oh, I'm sure that'll come up soon.

Bob: Did you ever have one?

James: The "imagined" reference point will come up.

Bob: [*Laughing*] That's better.

James: Anne, regarding politics, I was telling someone about non-duality, and she was getting into it quite well. I was explaining that there's no blame or guilt for anyone because there's no doer. It's all an imagined "I." Well, it was all fine until I said, "We don't even have to blame George Bush for the war. The thoughts are arising in his head, and he's following them." The conversation came to a dead halt. [*Group laughter*] That ended the Advaita talk.

Emmett: Everyone has their limits!

Kerry: Most people do. For my wife, it's child abusers. We can talk about non-doership for an hour, but if I mention child abusers, it's all over.

Anne: So, my need to make somebody wrong can come up?

James: Anything can come up. Everybody has their own conditioning and personality traits. Based on your personality and conditioning, certain thoughts arise. With the knowledge of non-duality, however, you start to realize that those thoughts aren't you. They're just patterns of energy.

I think if you're looking to make Advaita a "prescription" to make life better, it's not a great idea. This isn't about getting better. It's about accepting life as it is, and seeing through the illusion. If you use this as a way to make life better, then you're still in the mode of chasing pleasure and avoiding pain. And there's no end to that. There's just no end. Also, if you make Advaita a prescription, there'll be limits. You'll say, "Everything is fine unless I get 'gripped,'" or "Everything is fine unless I have a bad experience." Well, everybody's going to reach some point where there'll be some huge problem. If you understand non-duality, it won't matter how big or small an upset or problem is. You'll start investigating *who* the problem is happening to. But you don't do it as a prescription. If you do it like that, you're screwed. What I'm saying is you have to allow for anything and everything. Because creation is duality, so *anything* is possible. Somebody could come in here and start shooting us all with a machine gun.

Emmett: [*Joking*] Not us!

James: If you make a prescription out of this, you become susceptible to the "Oh God, I didn't really get it" syndrome. You'll say, "I felt good for a few weeks, and now I feel bad. Oh, I didn't really get it." Well, why would you be looking to feel good? You can only feel good and happy and wonderful because there's also the possibility of feeling sad and lousy. There has to be room for everything. You can't feel good unless you're also going to feel bad sometimes. And you can feel really fucking bad. That's okay. When you feel really fucking bad, just remember at some point to say, "I'm feeling bad. *Who's* feeling bad?" Or, "I'm feeling bad. All right, I'm going to feel bad." Just feel bad—until it dissipates. But don't resist it.

Anne: We could get lost in it.

James: Yes, but what's wrong with getting lost in it? In the creation, we're all here getting lost. Some people are finding answers. Some people are staying lost. Some are getting lost and getting answers and getting lost again. Life goes on; anything is possible.

There, that's my diatribe. Bob was looking at me for being so quiet.

Bob: That was very good.

Anne: Thank you. I needed that.

Barb: That was good. [*Laughing*] James had been holding back.

James: I had to say something before Bob put me on the spot. I saw him staring at me.

Dell: Now we have to edit the tape because you said the "f" word twice.

Bob : That makes the tape! Leave it there. [*Laughing*]

Kerry: Absolutely. These are Americans here.

Barb: That's interesting. I was so absorbed in what you were saying—and I really don't like that word—and I didn't notice you saying one of them.

Bob: [*Joking*] You're not listening, Barbara.

Barb: I was listening to the substance, not the frills.

James: The "f" word is just another boundary. We have so many boundaries.

Everything Happens by Itself

Anne: So, when I'm planning . . .

Bob: Plans will be made, but there's no plan maker.

Barb: Make all the plans you like, but don't get attached to them.

Anne: I see.

Emmett: Bob, where do we draw motivation from?

Bob: Do you need any motivation to beat your heart or grow your hair? Well, that extends to thought. Thoughts arise, and we think we are the thinker. Everything happens by itself.

Barb: Everything is just a happening. Some people are seeking enlightenment, and some aren't. But that's just what's happening. Nothing is actually better than anything else.

Anne: Well, I've become very good at looking at so-called negative thoughts and catching them. But that was "me" catching them. Today, what you're teaching is different. There's no judgment of positive and negative about the thoughts.

Bob: Just what is.

Kerry: When you were having thoughts originally, they were from a particular reference point. Then, when you started catching the so-called negative ones, you had a second reference point. So, were you better off with two reference points? Who's to say? But when non-dual understanding happens, it isn't an additional reference point. An Advaitan friend of mine tells the story of when he was little and found out there was no Santa Claus. He saw his parents putting presents under the tree. When that happened, his belief in Santa Claus was destroyed, but it wasn't replaced with another reference point. He didn't have to keep reminding himself there was no Santa Claus. When the first concept was gone, it left an absence of concepts related to Santa Claus. Is that right, Bob?

Bob: Yes, that's pretty good.

Kerry: Pretty good? Uh oh, that was a "B minus"?

Bob : *Who* wants to know? [*Group laughter*]

Kerry: [*Joking*] The snideness of the guru. Snideness is happening.

Bob: More concepts! [*Group laughter*]

Expecting Bliss and Miracles

Anne: I thought that when I got this knowledge, something spectacular would happen. I would be able to read minds or something.

Bob: And where did those concepts come from—from reading?

Anne: Yes.

Vashti: I thought I would be able to live on the scent of rose petals. Ever since the age of thirteen, when I read *Autobiography of a Yogi* [by Paramahansa Yogananda], there was always a thought in my mind that that was possible for me.

Bob: Yes, but was *he* living on the scent of roses? He's talking about somebody else. Was he able to do the things he's saying others can do?

Kerry: He died of a heart attack in the middle of dinner.

Dell: According to his disciples, that was a planned transformation.

Emmett: These miracles are all taking place in the realm of illusion. Not necessarily deceptive illusion. There are all kinds of laws of nature within existence. We can't say these things aren't possible. But miracles are just another experience. It's a moot point. It would be the false self enjoying the ego experience. The person might think, "Wow, people will know I live on the scent of roses." Or, "I lived without food," or whatever. That's all ego stuff.

Bob: It's all appearances and possibilities. The appearance is just how it appears to be. In essence, it's still the one reality.

Emmett: I was just seeing the possibility of somebody who had believed in all that stuff for so long feeling like a chump for being deceived. But it's not a deception. It's just another level of awareness.

Bob: That feeling of deception or being a chump is just another mental image. That has to go also. You always were the one reality anyway.

Emmett: Innocent deception doesn't sting as much for me. If I thought that all the gurus were frauds and con men, that would draw a lot of energy out of me.

Kerry: The expectation that you had, Anne, of the miracles and powers are the same for almost everyone who comes to these talks. Maybe there's one in one hundred who doesn't have them.

Anne: Well, after reading Bob's book and then talking with him, I walked out of here yesterday feeling like I got it. But then all day I was thinking, "This can't be it. Where's the bliss?" It's not a negative thing, but I had a story about what would happen once I got the understanding.

Bob: That story has become your reference point. You're referring your experiences to the belief of what you expect to happen. Everything is judged from that reference point. So you have to investigate that reference point and see it's false. It's just a bunch of thoughts that have no real substance, no power, and no independent nature.

Anne: As a child, I wondered why there were so few so-called chosen, awakened people.

Bob: No one is chosen because there are no actual entities. There are just a bunch of energy patterns appearing as people.

Living with the Five Senses Wide Open

Emmett: Bob, we've all heard the expression "Before enlightenment, chop wood, carry water. After enlightenment, chop wood, carry water." But something changes about the way you chop the wood and carry the water, right?

Bob: Before enlightenment, life is all about the "me." "*I* have to chop the wood today, and I don't want to. It's a hard job." Or "Why should I have to chop this wood? It's the other guy's turn to do it." And so on. Afterwards, it all just gets done. It's a happening. No one takes delivery of anything. No one is concerned with it. All the mental commentary is gone.

Vashti: Bob, you've spoken about how when a person gets out of the way, the five senses can assume their proper place. You said that with the five senses wide open, they function more equally and fully. So, if a person is chopping wood and carrying water with the five senses wide open, then the experience of that activity would be different or richer.

Bob: Activity would be effortless. Your attention would be on the whole thing. There would be equal attention in all the five senses. The hearing, seeing, tasting, smelling, and touching would have equal proportion.

What people do is they put so much attention in the mental function—past, present, and future concerns, and so on—instead of attention being evenly divided. If the senses were functioning evenly, there would never be a problem. Imagine looking through a keyhole. You can't see too much. But if you knock the whole door and wall out, you can see the whole view of what you're dealing with.

Vashti: So your emotions wouldn't be all tossed around. You wouldn't be thinking, "Oh, wow. I feel good chopping wood today. I hope I feel like this tomorrow."

Bob: No. Everything is just as it is in the moment. If it's good, it's good. Let tomorrow take care of itself. You're still with the hearing, tasting, smelling, touching, and seeing. You don't go into the thinking part—anticipating and imagining a future. And you're not going back into memory. All your energy is overall. The Buddhists have a saying "Be utterly awake, with the five senses wide open." And they say, "Be utterly open, with unfixated awareness." You don't fixate on anything.

Vashti: Would you say this kind of attention is more like that of a child? Is the unfixated awareness what a child would use if he or she were chopping wood?

Bob: Yes. The little child is in the natural state until reasoning brings on the sense of separation. And that separation brings on every "ism"—capitalism, idealism, atheism, communism, and all that. They all are brought about by the idea of "me" and other. If there's no "me" and no other, then everything is just what is.

Vashti: So if a child and an adult both had the five senses wide open, the result would only be different in the sense that the adult would get more done?

Bob: Yes, the adult has greater capacity.

*

Later That Night
Meryl and Jack Arrive

Meryl Baratz was the friend who first told me about Sailor Bob's teachings. She advised me to order Bob's book, even though it could then only be purchased from Australia. Years earlier, Meryl had told her friend Jack Smith about Advaita, and he became quite interested. Eventually, he came across Bob's book and told Meryl about it. Meryl and Jack arrived in Sarasota midday on Friday, in anticipation of the first weekend public talk which started the next day. Thus, I invited them to an intimate gathering with Bob, Barb, Dell, and myself Friday night. After some greetings and small talk, Meryl and Jack were somewhat quiet and deferential. So Bob gave a non-duality lecture and asked for their questions and doubts.

Despite having read many books on the subject, Meryl and Jack found themselves in the same position of so many other students. They understood the teachings, but felt they were getting it intellectually—not experientially. Below are excerpts from the meeting, in which Bob addresses that critical issue. The talk was almost certainly one of the best of the summer. It had a powerful impact on both Jack and Meryl, who by the end of the weekend saw their search come to an end. As Jack eloquently expressed it to Meryl on their drive home, "Case closed."

Seeing Through the Mind

Meryl: The mind just keeps going. It doesn't stop.

Bob: The mind will always keep going. Many seekers think the mind has to stop. As long as you have a body, the mind is going to function in the pairs of opposites. But in seeing through the mind, you're not bound by it. If I told you to go to the ocean and get me some blue water, what would you say?

Meryl: It's impossible.

Bob: That's right. You see the blue water, but you're not taken in by it. You've seen through it. It's the same with this. You're not taken in anymore by the concepts within the mind. They still arise, just like the ocean water is still blue. But you know the truth now. Like the Bible says, "Know the truth and the truth will set you free." You're free of the imagined bondage of the self. That's all this is really about.

Jack: No one can tell the truth because any time you say something, there's a positive and negative aspect.

Bob: As soon as we open our mouths, we're conceptualizing. But we use concepts to point to the truth. That's all we can do. I can't teach you anything. I can only point.

Jack: In the final analysis, whenever we speak, it's a belief system.

Bob: A belief system becomes a reference point. A belief is never the thing. So we have an invalid reference point again. It's not worth anything. What you are is timeless, spaceless, bodiless, mindless, birthless, deathless, pure presence awareness, just this and nothing else.

Jack: But that's another belief.

Bob: It's a concept.

Jack: That's the problem. No matter how far back we go, it's a belief. We can't know anything beyond the phenomenal world.

Bob: No, and you don't need to. The fact is that we can't negate our knowingness right now. That's the only fact we know. And there is no time other than right now, unless we're conceptualizing. We can't say there was a time when we were not, because we would have to conceptualize to do that. And we can't say there will be a time when we don't exist—unless we conceptualize.

Jack: Okay. Case closed. [*Long pause*]

I Get It—Intellectually

Jack: But we still have to go on living our lives.

Bob: Not *you*—Jack. You're being lived. The idea of a "me" is false. You can't find a self center anywhere inside.

Jack: Even so, when you get diagnosed with cancer, you get scared again. Because you're going to die.

Bob: Well, then you can understand why people who understand non-duality lose the fear of death. They know that this body can fall apart without touching them. Just like a wave on the ocean is just water. We're just like the ocean—ever changing, but never changing.

Jack: But we can't be convinced of this.

Bob: Oh yes, you can. That conviction comes. That's the beauty of it. Once you see clearly and that conviction comes, then nobody can ever toss you out of it. Who can move you away from nothing? All the saints and saviors have never gone beyond no thing. And I know for certain that I am that no thing. Don't you?

Jack: Therein lies the crux of the matter. Intellectually, I have to say yes.

Bob: Don't you see that all our problems come from labeling something. Why put that label "intellectual" on it? If you haven't got that label, then you know. The same as we create a difference by calling ourselves human beings and God the supreme being. But if you understand the words "supreme" and "human" as labels, and you take those labels off, can you separate the beingness? [*Pointing to glass*] This is being a glass, this is being a table, that's being Meryl, that's being Jack, this is being Bob. Take away the labels glass, table, Meryl, Jack, and Bob, and what's left? Being. Being means "is-ing." When you hear this, you resonate with it because innately you know it. That's why you've been on this searching track. Non-duality is your natural state, but it's been glossed over by your acquired mind—by your reasoning. It's like the sun, which is always in the sky but is sometimes hidden by clouds. When you hear this knowledge, it's like the sun breaking through the clouds. You've been waiting to hear this for so long. As Ramesh Balsekar says, "You've got your head in the tiger's mouth." And as Nisargadatta said, "This is like putting a match in a bale of cotton." Once the match starts to smolder, you can't put it out. It'll burn until the whole bale is gone.

Jack: I wonder when I'm going to go on fire.

James: Bob, I just understood something. I've heard you say a hundred times that when people say, "I get it *intellectually*," they should get rid of the word "intellectually." Well, if a person sees the blue ocean and then finds out it's not really blue, they don't say, "Well, I know the ocean isn't blue *intellectually*."

If you know it, you know it. Or, if you're outside in the dark, and you realize the thing you thought was a snake is really a rope, you don't say, "Well, I finally realized intellectually that it was only a rope." If you know it, you know it. It's the same with the reference point. If you know that the reference point is false, there's no reason to say, "I know it intellectually." If you realize there is no "me," then you know it.

The Mind Searches with "Yes, Buts . . ."

Bob: People always have this hierarchy: "Someone knows it, but I don't." That's what we've been conditioned to believe: "Somebody's got it, and somebody doesn't." Everybody and everything is That. If what the ancients told us is true—that existence is one without a second—how can you not be That? Why believe that you aren't That? Start from the fact that you already are That. And then all you have to do is find out what's stopping you from seeing that. What concept are you holding that's in the way?

Meryl: It's just a story we make up.

Bob: That's right. You can make up whatever stories you like. But you don't believe fairy tales. You can enjoy them, but you don't believe them.

Jack: So, in the final analysis this is all the conditioning. The "yes, buts . . ." are the conditioning over the "I am."

Bob: Like clouds in the sky.

Jack: Yes, those are the clouds.

Bob: If you ask yourself, "What conditioning is there if I don't think about it?" and you pause without thinking, there's no conditioning in that instant. But what people do is try to analyze the conditioning. It becomes like peeling the skin off an onion. Take a layer off, and there's another one underneath. You can do that forever and never reach the end of your conditioning because another "but" will come up. That's why you'll never find the answer in the mind. It's the nature of the mind to divide. We go down one path with the mind and think we've got to the end of that, but we're never satisfied. The mind will branch off and go into another path and continue to divide within that path. The mind has worked out all kinds of things. But the answer to life will never be found there. Using the mind for realization is just looking in the wrong direction.

Meryl: We were taught that when someone becomes self-realized, he or she has a change of vision and [*laughing*] sees light all around.

Bob: That's all part of a story to create a hierarchy—the hierarchy that someone's better than someone else.

Barb: [*Joking*] You've disappointed them, Bob.

Jack: You haven't disappointed me! But I've always gone into the "yes, buts . . ." That's what you've helped me with now. Now I'm beginning to see this clearly. I see that I'm searching with the mind every time I say, "Yes, but . . ."

Bob: The answer's not in the mind. So, you full stop when the mind comes up. In full stopping, what's left? You're still aware. And that presence awareness has been uncontaminated by anything that's ever happened to you. It's the same presence awareness that has been with you for as far back as you can remember. Your body was different, your thoughts were different, and your self-image was different. What's stayed constant? That "no thingness," that cognizing emptiness, or pure awareness, has never changed. It's just like the reflections in a mirror. All kinds of reflections come into the mirror, but the mirror is never contaminated by them. You can't say the reflection isn't in the mirror, because you're seeing it. But try and grasp the reflection to see if it has any independent nature apart from the mirror. You can't. So, you can't say the reflection is, and you can't say it isn't. It's just as it is. It's appearance. It's the same with us. And if we're appearing as a reflection, fine. If the reflection's rubbed out, fine. The mirroring is still the same.

Jack: But there is fear about when "I" die. Because I'm identified with this "me."

Bob: Look at what you said, "The fear is about *when I die*." When you analyze fear, you'll see it's always a projection into the future. There's nothing to fear in the present moment. Any fear will be a projection in the future or an image in the past. It's never about "what is." We can always handle what is. If I dropped a snake at your feet right now, the appropriate response would take place. You'd run out of the room or something like that. There might be some heavy breathing or heart pounding. And after the event you'd label that fear. But in the actuality it wasn't fear. It was a natural response to keep your body alive. When we put the label on, we take on all the baggage of the past that the label carries with it. And then we move away from what is. We don't want what is, and we start resisting. And the resistance causes all kinds of problems.

Jack: I got it.

Bob: [*Laughing*] Keep it. It's yours. Don't let it go with a "but."

Jack: This is great.

Dell: Bob, you were talking about personality today. In the last three or four days, I've noticed that my usual patience is changing.

Bob: If you were attached to it, maybe it needed to change. As long as you're not trying to be any particular way. Just let the natural functioning happen.

Dell: The patience was mind-driven. It was from the ego. Now I get angry once in a while.

Bob: Does it last long?

Dell: No, not at all.

Bob: Nature always flows in the pairs of opposites, but they're never in opposition. With us, instead of letting energies come and go, we hang on to the ones we like and resist the ones we don't. By holding these resentments and emotions, we cause all kinds of problems.

Is Searching a Waste of Time?

Jack: This is like Nisargadatta saying to stay with the "I am."

Bob: He means stay in the sense of presence awareness. Have a look and you'll see you can't move out of it. You can't go into the past or the future. You can go there *in the mind*, but when you do that, it's still the present. Try to get out of the Now. It's impossible. When you realize you can't ever be out of the present, then the concern disappears.

Jack: Years ago I read that even the term "now" is not accurate.

Bob: There's no such thing as now. Now is a subtle concept of time, like past, present, and future. But I use the term to point to the momentary beingness. We have to use words—or concepts—to point to the truth.

Jack: It's a shame I had to read forty years' worth of books to find out the simplest thing.

Bob: We all say that, but back then when you were searching, it was actually now. Just like, right now it's now. When you see that now is all there is, the past disappears. I was searching for sixteen years myself. And when I saw the truth, I thought those sixteen years were wasted. But nothing was wasted. It's all just as it is. And even though you didn't know it at the time you were seeking, you were That anyway. And if all the dramas and traumas hadn't happened, I wouldn't be sitting here now talking to you. We were being lived then, just as we are now. If I were the doer, I'd be worrying about taking the next breath and beating my heart. But that's our natural state.

Jack: I have another "but" here. Other people think I'm a mental case if I tell them I'm not the doer.

Bob: Well, if you've seen that you're not the doer, and you have that conviction, then it doesn't matter what other people think. Let them stay in their apparent bondage. I spoke to a person this morning who said, "I understand all this now, but when I go out into the world again, I'll forget and get caught up again." And that does happen sometimes because ninety-nine percent of the world believe in that false self center. If you listen to them, you can get caught up again. But if you continue to investigate and see for *yourself*, you'll start dragging them in, rather than them dragging you out. You know the truth and you're free in that truth.

Jack: I see. So, how do you like it here? Have you been to America before?

Bob: Barbara has been here before, but it's my first trip. I'm having a great time. They're spoiling me.

James: He's spoiling us! I'm getting this knowledge.

Bob: [*Joking*] What's this "getting?" [*Group laughter*] What are you?

James: Non-conceptual, ever-fresh, self-shining presence awareness. Just this and nothing else.

Jack: He's got the rap.

Barb: You are nothing!

James: I am nothing. Oh, God. I am nothing.

Bob: Look who thinks he's nothing! [*Group laughter*].

You're not *getting* this. You *are* That. Is there anything other than That?

James: No.

Bob: One without a second. So, you must be That. There's no *getting* That—you *are* That.

James: A few months ago on the phone with you, I wondered how anyone could get to that point of *really* knowing they're not the "me"—not the false reference point. Now, I no longer question it. I get caught up sometimes, but then I immediately investigate and see the "me" is false. I see that there's no self center here. None at all. I don't feel that I have to get somewhere. For that, I'm eternally grateful. And, in a strange way, I don't know how I got here.

Bob: You were always there. If there's only That, you must have always been there.

Meryl: What about emotions and fears and such?

Bob: That's the natural functioning. Thoughts, feelings, and emotions are one and the same thing. You couldn't live without them. But instead of holding on to them and resisting them, we let them come and go. The main thing is to leave everything unaltered, unmodified, and uncorrected. So, if a thought comes that "I don't like this thought or feeling," you just let it be there until it passes. There's no acceptance, no rejection, no attachment, and no detachment in what is. You might have an attachment that comes up. Leave that unaltered, unmodified, and uncorrected. That gives it a chance to move on. If there's any fixation on something, it stops the flow. Any blockage of energy is conflict. Had enough?

James: We have a big day tomorrow. The public talks begin.

Barb: How many people are coming?

James: Probably ten or fifteen. But they are serious seekers. Most flew in from other states.

The great way is not difficult for those who have no preferences. When love and hate are both absent, everything becomes clear and undisguised. Make the smallest distinction, however, and heaven and earth are set infinitely apart.

—Seng T'san, *Hsin Hsin Ming*

CHAPTER SIX

The Weekend Talks

*

On Saturday, July 31, Bob gave the first of three publicized weekend talks. People traveled from around the country, while those living near Connecticut, Chicago, and Santa Cruz waited for Bob to visit their areas. Twelve to fifteen people showed up for the first two weekends. The third was unfortunately interrupted by the first of a record four hurricanes that hit Florida in 2004. Those who came were clearly earnest and sincere. They also seemed well versed in non-duality. At the same time, some were probably in the same boat I had been in two weeks earlier—waiting for a dramatic experience that would confirm that liberation, or awakening, had occurred. Some had the same fanciful expectations about liberation that today's spiritual movements convey—special powers, non-stop bliss, the ability to perform miracles, blah, blah, blah.

A few said they enjoyed periods of freedom or peace, but the experiences were transient. Others had good understanding, but wanted to know how they could stop from occasionally getting "lost" or "caught up" in attachments and desires. Most had read Bob's book or heard his CDs, which state unequivocally that the search is the problem. They had heard that "what you are seeking, you already are." But printed words were somehow not enough. So they came to see whether hearing Bob in person would help. In some cases, I believe it did.

I was touched by how many thanked me heartily for bringing Bob to the States. Some even offered donations to help with expenses. When introducing Bob, I advised participants not to leave until all their questions and doubts were answered. I conveyed my brief but profound experience that one could read Bob's books or hear his CDs as much as they liked, but there was no comparison between that and interacting with him. As far as I could tell, many grasped Bob's message. Whose search ended and whose did not, I have no clue. But everyone appeared happy and thankful for the weekends.

My favorite talk occurred on the third and final Sunday—one that was almost cancelled due to Hurricane Charley. The storm hit Florida about seventy-five miles south of Longboat Key and would certainly have affected our area had its path not been remarkably narrow. In that regard, we were very fortunate. Nevertheless, we endured several stressful days as Bob and Barb experienced their first hurricane evacuation. We spent one full day trimming trees, securing items on our property, gathering valuables, and re-arranging furniture, in case of flooding. Early the next day, we headed north to Orlando with our five-year-old child, our dog, three visitors—Emmett, Bob, and Barbara—and three cars tightly packed with luggage and belongings. Vashti, with good foresight, had made hotel reservations in Orlando early on, before they were all taken. As fate would have it, when we reached Orlando, radio announcers said the storm was headed straight toward us! So we headed to the East Coast and then drove south to Fort Lauderdale. By the end of the day we had traveled ten or twelve hours, often through heavy rain. All hotels and restaurants were closed, and our first meal other than breakfast came late at night. The only enjoyable feature was that Bob and Barb got to see some of South Florida and meet a few of my relatives. At one point, Bob commented that the event would make for an interesting part of the book I was beginning to consider writing.

The next morning, Saturday, I checked phone messages and was startled to hear that two women had traveled all the way from Arizona, dearly hoping to meet Bob. So we scheduled a talk for Sunday. The meeting was one of my favorites because of the passion evidenced by these two longtime seekers. Their hunger for liberation was palpable, and whereas so many seekers seemed quite passive, they pressed Bob beyond the norm.

What follows are excerpts from all three weekends. On Saturdays, Bob spoke for twenty or thirty minutes and then took questions. Sundays were questions and answers only. Because the discussions were so similar to the material already presented in this book, what follows are brief excerpts. The discussions were profound but the issues nearly identical to the ones Bob answered in his first two weeks. Some of the participants are named. Those whose names are unknown are labeled

"V" for visitor. Bob started each of the Saturday talks with the following message.

*

The First Weekend

Stay with the "I am-ness"

Bob: I can't teach you anything. I can't tell you anything. All I can do is point you to what you already innately know. I'm not speaking to your body. Your body's nothing without the life essence in it. And I'm not speaking to any mind. What mind is *there*, apart from consciousness or awareness? How many thoughts can you have if the life essence isn't there? So I'm speaking to that "I am" that I am. I'm speaking to that awareness of presence, or presence of awareness—that which you can't negate. The knowing that you are—just that and nothing else. So there's no "me" here speaking to you. If there is, there'll be no communication. But, if there is a speaking and a hearing . . . If there's a hearing from the heart—not the physical heart, but the essence—then there will be a "heart to heart." If there's just essence to essence, then there will be a communication because there is that oneness.

Now, any questions, doubts or arguments?

Steve: Nisargadatta said that his teacher gave him something to do, and he did it for three years and then became realized. Do you have anything like that in your teaching?

Bob: Nisargadatta said to stay with the "I am-ness." He's talking about the sense of presence—the knowing that you are.

Steve: Stay with that?

Bob: Yes, and realize that you can't get away from it, even if you try. Even if you begin thinking about past or future, you're doing that in the present. You couldn't be thinking without that presence awareness that is always with you. Sometimes there are seeming clouds in the way. But the awareness is there anyway. Just like the sun is always in the sky, even on a cloudy day when it's blocked by clouds. Knowing that, you're no longer fooled into thinking it's gone. So there's nothing you need to do.

Anne: After being with you last week, I was able to see clearly. But can a person get lost again after that?

Bob: Once you know that the sea water isn't blue, can you ever go try and find blue water?

Anne: I've done that my whole life.

Bob: But you'd never go try and get blue water from the sea now that you know it's not really blue.

Anne: So why does the question keep coming up for me?

Bob: Because the sea still *looks* blue. You say that clouds come up from time to time. Notice that they come up in the present. They come up now. Those clouds are just appearance. They're not real. So when the clouds come up, you can still rejoice in the fact that they're just appearing on nowness. Even though the cloud appears, rejoice in knowing it's still really presence awareness. Relax in that.

Anne: So there will still be reactions?

Bob: There'll be responses. They'll come up sometimes.

Anne: I'm having trouble sleeping lately.

Bob: When you say, "I'm not sleeping," you've attributed it to an entity. That causes conflict. You want to sleep, so there is resistance to not sleeping. That resistance is conflict, and it keeps you awake. You can't do anything about resistance. Because you aren't the doer. You can recognize the resistance, from the point of non-resistance. There's no doing or not doing. Just seeing, seeing, seeing.

All You Need to Know Is That the "Me" Is False

James: There's a Nisargadatta quote that I love: "Liberation is not a matter of acquisition, but a matter of faith and conviction that you have always been free, and a matter of courage to act on this conviction." The interesting part is the courage. So many seekers say, "I've seen that the 'me' is false, but I only know it intellectually." People say they know for certain the sea water is blue, but they only know the "me" is false intellectually. For some reason, it seems to take courage—or some special faith or conviction—for people to just say they know the "me" is false—period. If you know it, you know it. Just have the courage and conviction to say it.

Meryl: It's a huge loss.

James: Exactly. A huge loss. And all that really gets in the way is the picture we have of what liberation, or awakening, is supposed to look like. It's supposed to look like all heaven breaking loose. Instead, it's nothing—no thing. It doesn't match the picture. So people seek without finding until they die.

Steve: Well, that's the reason I came here—for inspiration. And to find out how to make this knowledge real. I've read all the books, but that doesn't seem to be enough.

James: What's made this real for me has been interacting with Bob for two weeks. Let me ask this: Do you know that the "me" is fake?

Steve: Yes.

James: That's all that you need to know. Now, that doesn't mean that you won't still react or get caught in the reference point. If someone says they don't like you or does something harmful, it doesn't mean you won't say, "Ouch." You probably will. But after ten or twenty seconds or two minutes, you're going to say to yourself, "Wait, who was that person talking about? There's no 'me' here in the first place. He's talking about a fake 'me.' He's talking about an appearance." In the last few weeks, many of us have been asking Bob whether there comes a time when there's a deepening. Does there come a point when we no longer get caught in the reference point ever again? And the answer is that it's irrelevant because the reference point is false whether we get caught up in it occasionally or not. As long as there's a body, there will be apparent preferences and apparent choices. But they're only appearances. There's no actual deepening—there's only an appearance of a deepening. We're all That, whether we realize it or not.

Steve: It helps me to hear that. I could be feeling guilty or bad about something for a period of time, and then it eventually goes away. That means that whatever bad thing happened isn't an indication that I don't have the understanding, and I have to start over from scratch. That's encouraging.

James: I knew Bob's teachings from his book and CDs, but it didn't make much difference really. Then he arrived and something happened. Bob pressed me. If I said I understood there was no "me" *intellectually* or "Yes, but . . . ," he would say, "Wait a minute. Do you know it or not? Yes or no?" And I had to say yes. So, at some point, you have to step up to the plate and decide whether the "me" is real or not. And then you have to live it. And that's what Nisargadatta meant, I think, when he said liberation is a matter of faith and conviction that we've always been free, and a matter of courage to act on that conviction. That's why I felt it was necessary to see Bob. I wanted to know whether he was genuine or not. Bob appears as normal and natural as anyone. But there have been a few times in the last two weeks when some issues have come up, and egos have flared, and suddenly it's been obvious that he's not acting from a reference point. That was something I definitely needed to see. That's when I could really accept the teaching and especially the statement: What you're seeking, you already are.

Bob: In seeing that, the search must stop. It's the search itself that's keeping you away from it. When you understand that simple statement James mentioned, then who's to search, and what is there to search for? There's a full stopping. Let that realization dawn on you—that you are. The search takes you back into time again. The search implies that there's something you don't have right now. There is no future. Omnipresence is all there is. Instead of looking to get something, all you have to do is see the cloud that's coming up and let it be. No need to fixate on the cloud.

*

Sunday

Focus on the Space, Not the Content

Bob: After getting the knowledge of non-duality, one of the things people often ask is, "How will I live my life?" No one can tell you how. Did you know how you were going to live your life up to now? Or did it all just unfold naturally? The highs, the lows, the good, and the bad has all unfolded the way it has. And it will continue to do so. Now, are there any questions?

Anne: When I left here last week, I felt like something changed. Well, what if my mind is just making all this up, so I can say the search is over?

Bob: You're aware of all the thoughts and concepts coming up? Aren't they the content, or the appearances, in the awareness? They are things. And you are no thing. There's no thing you can grasp and say that is you. The changeful can never be you.

Anne: So the personality can't see this. Correct?

Bob: Yes. A thing can't grasp no thing.

Anne: Why do I continue to need you to support me?

Bob: Because the focus is still going into the things. When I say to people, "Look over here. What's the first thing you see?" most say they see the wall or the light or a person. No one says space—or emptiness—even though that's the first thing that is seen. The focus immediately goes into the content, instead of what everything is appearing in. There couldn't be any content if the space weren't there. It's the same with awareness. The focus immediately goes into the content of what's happening in the awareness, instead of the awareness itself.

Now, take it back to where it's happening. How many eyes do you have? I'm asking from your present evidence—from what you're actually seeing.

Anne: None. I can't see any eyes.

Bob: That's right. There are no eyes, but there is space there. So it's an open window. How many thoughts are in that open window? Have you ever seen a thought in that space?

Anne: No.

Bob: It's always clarity and emptiness. In fact, you can't even see your head. But seeing is happening. You can't see your ears, but hearing is happening. This is cognizing emptiness.

Jack: Can you speak about your own journey and how you got to Nisargadatta? And maybe tell us what Nisargadatta was like?

Bob: I can go into all the stories, but of what value would that be?

Jack: Probably as important as anything else that people are saying.

Bob: [*Laughing*] What we do here is kick everything out from underneath you and leave you with That. If I start on the stories, that's all it is—a bunch of stories. My story might be better than someone else's. So what? And that's what goes on in so many groups and movements. Everyone talks about their experiences. "My experience is better than your experience. This happened. That happened." This keeps people from understanding we are all abiding in the natural state.

Jack: Full stop!

Bob: Full stop.

Wayne: How would you explain your compelling nature to help the suffering of others from the illusion?

Bob: Does it need any explanation? It comes up of its own accord. It's just what naturally occurred. There could be a compelling force, but why get in the story of it? That's all conceptual. Just let it be. Let it resonate.

Can One Move In and Out of the Understanding?

Cory: I seem to move in and out of the understanding. When I move into it, I tend to say, "I got it." And that immediately takes me out of it. It's like I sabotage my experience.

Bob: Can an "I" move into it or out of it? "I" is just a thought. The sense of presence is prior to the "I" thought. That's how presence translates through the mind—as "I am." So, the thought "I move into it and out of it" is an appearance in awareness. Does the awareness move in or out of itself? Start from the basic fact: You cannot negate your beingness. That knowingness, or awareness of presence, is always there.

Cory: Right. Everything else is an assumption.

Bob: So, does that knowing that you are move in and out of itself?

Cory: No.

Bob: That's right. A concept might come up . . . An "I" thought may seemingly come up and move around, but awareness itself does not move in and out. So, you're telling yourself a lie that you move in and out of awareness.

Wayne: The sage Rumi said, "Outside the ideas of right and wrong, there's a field. I'll meet you there."

*

The Second Weekend
Saturday

Pure Knowingness Is What You Are

Visitor: In the twenty-five or more years that you've been awakened, have you found any methods that can help us achieve this state?

Bob: Well, get rid of the idea that there's anything to achieve. Start with the fact that you already are That. When something comes up that seems to be a problem, investigate and see how real it actually is.

V: You seem to say that the knowingness prior to thought is better than thought. Why is it better?

Bob: First of all, there's nothing wrong with thinking. The mind is not the enemy. It's a wonderfully creative instrument. But it can also do harm when we think we're not good enough, or we have low self-esteem and all that. But in the knowingness that's prior to the mind, everything is fresh and new in that instant. But when we go into the mind, we get a label for what we're seeing. In each instant, pure seeing is happening. We're seeing, just as it is. That means unaltered, unmodified, and uncorrected. As soon as we label it—"Oh, I like this, or I don't like this"—we're altering it, correcting it, or modifying it. We go into it from memory of the past. And that's when problems and suffering arise.

Pure knowingness is always what you are before the labeling. Look around the room right now. [*Pause*] What did you see?

V: I saw the wall, all the people, the clock, and the floor.

Bob: Actually, you saw much more than that. You saw the clothes everyone was wearing. You saw all the furniture. You saw the paintings on the wall. You saw all sorts of things. But you didn't label everything. As pure knowingness, you saw everything. The pure knowingness is always with you. There's never any problem when just the knowingness is there. It's when you start labeling and translating everything that problems can arise.

You Can't Imagine the Pyramids Without Consciousness (or, Time Only Appears to Exist)

V: If everything is oneness, then there is no judgment.

Bob: That's right. When our sense of separation began at a very young age, and we began trying to become whole, that's when the idea of God came to us. This was an imagined or conceptual image about some future time when we would sit next to someone on a throne in a place called heaven. And we imagine a resurrection. Or, if we're from the East, we believe in reincarnation. This is all projection of a future time. Well, the ancients have told us from way back that existence is omnipresent. It's timeless. There is no past or future. Ask yourself, "Is there a past or future if I don't think about it."

V: So, how about the pyramids and the Romans and Egyptians of five thousand years ago?

Bob: The only reality they have for you is right now when you're recalling them. Isn't that a fact?

V: But when I'm looking at them . . .

Bob: But you're not looking at them now. It's only a memory—an idea in your mind. You can talk about two billion light years away. But it's right now when you're talking about it. If it's not divided from some reference point, you can't have time or space.

V: So, when I look at the pyramids . . .

Bob: Looking in this room right now, what's everything contained in?

V: Space.

Bob: Yes. In awareness, or consciousness. Now, aren't the Egyptian pyramids contained in that consciousness, or awareness, also?

V: Yes.

Bob: They're appearing to you as thoughts. The *actuality's* not here. And does the consciousness that's with you have any beginning?

V: It's right now.

Bob: It has no beginning. It has no end. You can imagine a time when the pyramids were not or when they will not be. But that imagining couldn't take place without awareness right now. And that awareness has no substance. It's no thing that the mind can grasp. The pyramids are some form—they're some thing.

V: Historically, the pyramids existed five thousand years ago. But you say there is no five thousand years ago. There is only thought. When I think of what has happened within the last five thousand years . . .

Bob: It boggles the mind. Time needs a reference point, and there is no reference point for time. When did time start?

V: So, everything past is just in our mind? History tells us there was a past. You say that there is no time. So, everything is an illusion?

Bob: It's all appearance. Go outside and look at the sky. Can you tell today's sky from tomorrow's sky? Can you tell space right now from the space five minutes ago? There's no reference point there. Where are you going to measure it from? Our reference point is always invalid. Your reference point is simply the image you have for yourself. The concept of time will work in the appearance we live in. But that doesn't mean it's real.

The Psychological Suffering Goes Away

V: Isn't this just a play of semantics? In the end, what good is understanding all this? Am I going to be more at peace because of this information? Am I going to live a happier life?

Bob: Let me ask you this: *Who* wants to know? It's "me" that wants to know, and this "me" is only an idea or image you have about yourself. You have to investigate and see that that "me" is false. It's just a bunch of thoughts you have in your mind.

Now—without wanting to know—get on with the living of life and being, and see how the functioning goes on from there. You'll never find the answer in the mind. You're being lived. When did you begin? When the sperm met the ovum in your mother's body? When your mother ate the food that grew her body to make the ovum? You can't find a time when you began.

V: How has this made your life better? What good is this knowledge unless it makes a difference. Does it make you really happy?

Bob: The main thing is that the psychological suffering goes away.

V: You have no psychological suffering?

Bob: No. Years ago, I was full of anxiety, anger, fear, and so on.

V: And when you understood this, everything stopped?

Bob: Not immediately. A lot of the old habit patterns could be triggered for a while. Like a post-hypnotic suggestion, the emotions could come back sometimes. But after constantly seeing through them—when no energy or belief was going into these habits—they eventually fell off. Nothing can live without energy. And there was nothing "I" ever did. There was nothing "I" did to bring me to this. Years ago, I thought I was doing everything. But it all just happened as it did. There's no independent nature in this so-called "me." Only consciousness, or awareness, is real, and that is who I am and who we all are.

Anthony: Is there anything in Advaita that speaks to the heart? What I long for is something that will touch my heart. This discussion is necessarily intellectual, and that's wonderful. But part of me would like to *feel* my way to the truth. What speaks to me most is not the words and concepts, but the equanimity you seem to have. What is the heart of this path? What is the feminine part of non-duality?

Bob: When you relax into presence awareness and just be, then you'll find what you're looking for. When you're living without so much labeling, accepting life just as it is, without trying to change, alter, and modify, then your heart will be satisfied.

Everything we've talked about regarding what is real and what is appearance is in your dictionary. They call this the phenomenal universe—the manifest world. Look up the word "phenomenon." It's described as "that which appears to be." Look at the word "noumenon," which is the unmanifest world. It's described as "that which is." So the unmanifest world is reality. The manifest world is appearance. You can call it a dream if you like. Intelligence energy is vibrating into different patterns and displaying in different shapes and forms. Staying with that essence that you are, sitting with it for a while, you get the subtleties, and no matter what's happening in the outer, there will be a sense of well-being constantly with you. It doesn't stop all the dramas and happenings from occurring, but when you stop attributing the happenings to a "me," you'll have a constant sense that everything is okay. Nothing is ever wrong.

V: Do you teach this full-time in Australia?

Bob: Yes.

V: Are people very interested there?

Bob: Not particularly. Most want to hear stories. They want to hear about experiences.

*

Sunday

You Can't Split Up Consciousness Like a Thing

Visitor: Do we have any control of our lives?

Bob: As an entity, no.

V: Then we are not responsible for what we do?

Bob: No.

V: Then why punish criminals? They're just expressing energy.

Bob: The judge who sentences the criminals is also just expressing energy. The judge isn't responsible for sentencing the criminal. The pairs of opposites are always functioning in the world of duality. But this is all appearance only. The essence itself is never touched. Life is living on life. It can't know death.

V: If the manifest world is just an appearance, why are we here? What is the point of this? What is my purpose?

Audience Member: There's no sense. There's no point. We're not even here. This is just like a dream. It happens, and then after you wake up, you realize it never happened.

Bob: By asking what sense does existence make, and why are we here, and what is our purpose, you're trying try to split consciousness up like a thing. That's like a drop of water from the ocean trying to separate itself and ask what the ocean is doing. Ocean water appears as a wave or bit of spray, but it's still only ocean.

Audience Member: [*To visitor*] When you try to talk about consciousness, your brain gets in the way. To experience it is to know it.

Bob: You'll never find the answer in the mind. The mind is a thing. What we are, in essence, is no thing. We are the unmanifest. A thing can never grasp no thing. We look for the answer in the mind, where it can't be found. And there's no way out of the mind except full stop. In that full stop, your thought has stopped, but you're still aware. There's a difference between thought and pure intelligence. Whenever you're being without thinking—even if for only a brief moment—you're beyond thought. People spend years trying to go beyond thought. But it's actually simple.

V: If society understood non-duality, so many laws and cultures would change. Society says a man should love only one woman. If we are all one, then when a man loves a woman, he is loving all women. [*Group laughter*] And children would be told they belong to everyone. And my house would become your house.

Bob: Manifestation vibrates into pairs of opposites. But no matter what happens—predator and prey, wars or whatever—life isn't actually affected. Millions of life forms are carrying on. When they die, something else takes their place. More life develops from the ashes of those so-called dead life forms. Life never had any beginning. It never had any end. What you are in actuality is birthless, deathless, bodiless, timeless, mindless. Intelligence displays in all kinds of shapes and forms, but nothing actually ever happened. If the earth were blown up tonight, every particle would be in space. No particle would be lost. But you could never call it earth again.

V: Oneness is too easy.

Bob: It's so simple, we miss it. The ancients have been saying this for centuries.

*

The Final Weekend
The Sunday After the Hurricane

The Mind is Just a Translator

Visitor: I keep bringing past memories into present situations. How do I let go of the past?

Bob: What you have to look at is this: *Who* is hanging onto the past? The logical answer is, "It's happening to me." Have a look. Where is this "me" that I call myself? Isn't that word "me" just a label? Without that label, what's there? Drop that label right now. What's there with you?

V: Well, it's hard to drop the label.

Bob: Just pause for a minute and don't label.

V: There's nothing.

Bob: That's right. There's nothing. But you're still here. You're still seeing, hearing, and touching. You're still aware. In that instant, you're prior to the mind. The mind is so closely aligned with pure intelligence that it's come to believe it's the intelligence itself. In fact, the mind is just a translator. The knowing is still there without the translating.

Rita: If I were in a high level of consciousness, I would be able to live without any problem. I could let anything happen without any stress or fear.

Bob: What you're doing now is what everyone does. You're looking for the answer in the mind. You're trying to work everything out. But look at it another way. You're seeing right now? Does your eye say, "I see"? You're hearing now. Does your ear say, "I hear"?

Rita: No.

Bob: You're translating the seeing with a thought, "I see." And you translate the hearing with a thought, "I hear." Now, ask yourself: Does the thought "I see" actually do the seeing?

Rita: No.

Bob: Is the thought "I'm aware" the awareness?

Rita: No.

Bob: Is the thought "I choose" the choice maker?

Rita: No.

Bob: What I'm pointing out is that the thought has no power. When you're trying to work out what to do and what not to do, realize that choices will be made and activities will happen. You're being lived, and it's been that way since you were a child. Allow thoughts to do what they're supposed to do—just translate. The mind can be used properly.

Content Is Happening on Wakefulness

Rita: Well, if I would go within . . .

Bob: If *who* would go within? You're looking for a reference point. Any reference point you adopt is false.

Rita: If I could go within and be one with consciousness, I would be one with everything, and I wouldn't have to ask questions. And I wouldn't need any answers. I would be one with hurricanes and everything.

Bob: You are.

Rita: But how do I bring that to conscious awareness?

Bob: Have a look. You're awake right now. You woke up this morning, got dressed, and ate breakfast. You drove here and you're hearing this talk now. All sorts of activities have taken place. Has the wakefulness that has been with you all day changed?

Rita: No, that's always been the same.

Bob: That's right. So, everything that has happened has been the *content* of the wakefulness. It couldn't have happened without the wakefulness. So the content is appearance. This content is happening on the wakefulness. And the wakefulness has not in any way been contaminated by the happenings—by the appearance. But your focus has been in the content. Settle back right now, and realize that before any thought is happening, you're still seeing; you're aware of seeing, hearing, and thoughts happening. Instead of letting your focus go into them, just be aware that they're happening. Then you'll get the taste and realize that you've always been that awareness, but the focus has gone into the content. If I ask you what the first thing you're seeing right now is, what would you say?

Rita: Space.

Bob: That's right. But very few people realize that. They always say the first thing they see is the content. So, treat awareness the same way. Always remember that nothing can take place without that awareness that you are. Things are appearing in space, and in essence they can't be anything other than space. It's just that they're appearing different. So all these appearances and things will continue happening as before, but they won't be attributed to an entity. Because the "me" has been investigated and seen to be insubstantial and without any independent nature. Then you'll realize that you've been lived ever since the time the sperm and ovum that made you came together—or even before that!

Focus on the Experiencing, Not the Experience

Rita: I've heard that before, but I know it intellectually. I don't know it in my experience. I have had experiences of oneness, but then my focus fell out of it. So, how do I keep the focus on my oneness?

Bob: You're focusing on your experience now. Experiences, no matter how sublime or exotic, are not what you're looking for. Experience comes and goes. You are the experiencING. You are the essence in which everything appears and disappears. Just the same as you are the seeing. The seeing is split up into the seer and the seen—the subject and the object. We focus on this—rather than realizing that the seeing is happening *first*. It's happening first and foremost, and things are appearing on it. Instead of looking for a bigger and better experience, realize that not a single experience could take place without the experiencing essence. You subtly relax back into that. And you realize you never left it. Relaxing back into it, you'll see there's a subtle warmth or well-being in that. It's constantly with you.

Rita: So, there's an experience there?

Bob: If I like to translate it, yes. Innately, we already know this. The natural state has been covered over with reasoning and acquired mind. But it's always there, and you can always settle back into it. There's nowhere you can go to it or get to it—because you already are That. All that can happen is you can recognize that when you focus on the self center or reference point, there's a resistance to what is. "What is" means unaltered, unmodified, and uncorrected. The only thing to ever correct or modify anything is the mind. When the mind is altering and modifying life, there's a subtle resistance or a tenseness within you. Then, from the point of non-resistance, you'll notice a subtle relaxation, and in that instance you'll realize you're there. This will become a habit.

V: Recently my husband and I were buying a house. Suddenly, I had a great fear about it. It was just negative conditioning from the past. How do I break the spell?

Bob: You have to remember that there's nothing wrong with right now unless you think about it. Drop everything, and come back to the immediacy of the moment. Realize that resistance in the moment. You might need to remind yourself—with a thought—that the same old rubbish is coming up, full stop. If you struggle with the old thoughts, it just creates more resistance. It doesn't allow energy to flow. Thoughts, feelings, and emotions are always going to come. The idea is not to resist them.

James: Bob, when you talk about how we are all being lived, it conjures up an image in me that there's *someone* doing that. But you don't mean that. Right?

Bob: Right. I don't mean that. Life is living itself. Life is fulfilling itself in all its variety of patterns of energy. The patterns of energy appear, and we mistakenly take them to be real. Everything in creation can be broken down into pure intelligence energy. The livingness is happening in all its diversity, which is duality. The whole manifestation is dualism.

James: There's no how or why it's happening. It's just happening. And the mind cannot tolerate that fact.

Bob: The mind constantly looks for an answer. Instead of taking its true place as a translator of what's going on. We put labels on everything, and that's where our apparent bondage comes from.

Rita: The problem I have is that I want to be in activity and still be aware of who I really am. How can I be constantly aware?

Bob: Just know that everything is That. No matter how things are appearing, it's still that essence. Even when terrible things are happening, you see through the appearance and remember the essence. I know that all of you sitting here are pure intelligence energy, whether you know it or not. I know there is no center within you that has any substance or independent nature. That's quite simple to see, just like knowing two plus two equals four. Once you know that, nobody can convince you that two and two equals five or six. Investigate and know the truth about oneness. Then you will realize there is nothing whatsoever that is not That. Life is awareness constantly seeing awareness.

Rita: If I'm thinking negative thoughts, should I get involved in them or let them go?

Bob: Get rid of the idea that there's a you that can do anything. If thinking is happening, full stop. That's what's happening. If you're saying, "I think," you've split it up—you've divided it—and there will be resistance. In trying to stop it or trying to go along with it, there is resistance.

Rita: So you presume I am so aware?

Bob: You are totally aware! See, you've got this *concept* of awareness, and you think it's some sort of special state or some special way to be. Drop that. Drop your concept of awareness.

Have you dropped it right now?

Rita: Right now I'm fine because I'm focusing there.

Bob: Drop the focus off awareness and just be.

Rita: If I fear something, I'll dwell on it. I'll think about it over and over and over.

Bob: That's right. What I'm saying is start to look differently. Start asking yourself, "What's all this happening on? If I weren't aware, could all this be happening?" Doing that introduces you back to your natural state, which is awareness. Under no circumstances can you negate your awareness. Under no circumstances can you say, "I am not." You can't get away from presence awareness.

Rita: So, it's easier for the feelings to pass if I just feel something instead of saying, "*I'm* feeling?"

Bob: Yes, because you're not taking delivery of anything. There's no reference point to take delivery. You may still take action based on an emotion. If there's fear, you may need to do something to get out of danger. But you don't take delivery of the emotion.

Just Let Thoughts and Feelings Be

James: Fear is happening, but not to anybody. Rita said she feels like she's a thinker, and she doesn't want to be thinking. Well, *she's* not thinking. Thinking is happening, but it's not her doing the thinking.

Rita: I know the theory very well after being with a teacher for seven years. Intellectually, we all know it. But how do we actually always be aware of that, so we don't react so often?

Bob: [*To James*] Tell her what you realized about understanding intellectually. Now, listen carefully to what he's saying.

James: Either you know something or you don't. If Bob tells you to go get a cup of blue water from the ocean, you would say you can't because you know the water isn't blue even though it looks blue. You don't say, "Well, I know the water isn't blue intellectually."

Rita: Okay.

James: So, when you say, "Intellectually, I know I'm not the doer, or intellectually, I know it's not me thinking," it's not accurate.

Rita: I agree. But you're talking about concepts. I'm talking about practicality. How do we free ourselves from reactions and thoughts. How do we know *all the time* that oneness is all there is? And I'm not talking about thinking this. I'm talking about being it.

Bob: What you're doing is looking for a future event. What's wrong with right now? Anything wrong with right now?

Rita: No. Nothing. But what if someone comes up and pinches me hard?

Wouldn't there be a reaction?

Bob: A response would immediately come up. It would be happening *now*. You wouldn't have to hypothesize, "What will I do and how will I be?" You wouldn't have to hypothesize.

Rita: I understand that if I were totally aware, all answers would come automatically without thinking. But I live in this world.

Bob: If you understand that, live from that point of view, and you'll know that when you try to figure out "How should I live?" you'll never work it out. That will keep you in that mind pattern. I'm talking about practicality here. I'm talking about living from that point.

Rita: I'm asking how to stop the automatic behavior. That's my question.

Bob: That will drop off of its own accord. You'll be alert to it in the moment. That so-called automatic behavior might change altogether.

Rita: So, you're saying that until it happens on its own accord, we're going to suffer—until we learn differently?

Emmett: She wants a tip!

James: One tip is to stop saying, "I know this intellectually." The fact is, you actually know what Bob is saying, and you're injecting a "but." You're saying, "I know it *but* . . . I know it *intellectually*." If you stop that and start saying "I do understand," then when an upset happens, you'll learn how to accept life as it is. You'll see occurrences as happenings rather than something personal happening to *you*, which causes nothing but resistance.

Bob: The "but" takes you into time again. What conditioning is there if you don't think about it? You're still going to have a mind that thinks in the pairs of opposites. But when there's no entity (no center or reference point) taking delivery, thoughts and pairs of opposites just flow.

Rita: I have pictures in my mind that I can't stop. How can I stop the negative pictures in my mind, so I don't think about them?

Bob: Be with them, and watch them unfold without wanting to stop them. Focus on that which the thoughts are appearing on. Be with awareness, which is no thing. You woke up this morning. You've been awake all day. Has that wakefulness been touched by any thoughts or feelings that have come up? Just like the reflections in the mirror haven't affected the mirror at all. And you can't say the reflections aren't there, but when you try to grasp the reflections, you can't. That's the same as the thoughts and feelings that arise in you. In the same way you don't believe in the reality of reflections in a mirror, you don't believe in the reality of thoughts and feelings. So, if you just let thoughts and feelings be, without attributing belief or power to them, they aren't going to hurt you. What you are is the essence that everything is appearing on.

Emmett: It seems to me that there's so much religious conditioning that we have to let go of. The idea that there's a God who cares, and who is human-like. A God who wants us to be a certain way and cares that we have sad thoughts and wants us to be happy—all that stuff. Without giving that up, our tendency will always be to wonder about our thoughts and what bad things we did that have caused our current problems. That requires major investigation if we want to unravel that conditioning of why "I" as an individual am suffering. Our beliefs keep this problem alive.

Bob: That's exactly right. Our beliefs become the reference point. But the belief can never be the actuality. The actuality is factual. It's what's happening right now. This is a fact. It's not a belief.

CHAPTER SEVEN

I Am That, Thou Art That – Now What?

*

Eight months have passed, as these words are written, since Bob and Barbara left my home in Longboat Key. Aside from meeting my wife and the birth of my son, I consider the summer with Bob the most fortunate experience of my life. There was a period in my twenties when I taught meditation and went on many several-month-long meditation courses, during which I thought I had found the answer to life. But that was a function of belief. In fact, meditation and all the concepts connected to it are essentially no different from any other worldly experience. The seeming *experiences* of transcendental states come and go like everything else in relative existence. In fact, transcendence is who we are. We need not search for it. It is the very basis of our experience. Further, meditation as a spiritual path is based on the notion of a someday when the great enlightenment will result. A someday that of course does not exist because the present moment is the only reality possible.

Odd as this sounds, other than ultimate freedom, understanding nonduality provides no gain. In fact, there is loss. There is loss of intensity, loss of belief in a real world, loss of desire to become someone special, and loss of fears and worries in general. Concerns for the future, other than practicalities of life, such as, in my case, how I will teach nonduality and so on, rarely arise. The desire for enlightenment, or liberation, or wholeness, that cursed lifelong monkey on my back, has disappeared completely—and along with it, the nagging sense of separation I thought would never leave.

On the other hand, the false reference point exposed throughout this book—the "me"—often rears its head. No doubt about it. And this is to be expected. Contrary to what so many spiritual seekers have been taught, *as long as there is a body and an apparent worldly existence, there will be preferences and desires*. This is because the very nature of life is to go in the direction of greater happiness and charm. It is only when getting caught up in, or attached to, desires or the false reference point that a problem arises. Such episodes occur by sheer force of habit. But these are transitory experiences only. They happen against a backdrop of who I truly am (consciousness, or no thing) and are quickly seen through and dropped. Before Bob's visit, there was *never* a clear knowing of my true unbounded nature. I did not know, viscerally, who I was and had no idea how to find out. That "not knowing" was the basis of my sense of separation from Essence, or Source, for over fifty years.

During moments when I do get caught in the reference point and my sense of unboundedness is briefly hidden, a "contraction" of sorts occurs. Contractions are rare and short-lived, but they do occur. When they happen, Intelligence arises to meet the challenge, and a realization comes that who I truly am is consciousness, or awareness, or no thing. Contractions dissipate quickly because they are based on a false sense of identity that cannot stand up to investigation. At this point, investigation comes up on its own when necessary, just as Bob said it would. Contractions are not pleasant, but I have grasped non-dual understanding enough to know they are no more real or relevant than anything else. They do not mean understanding is lacking any more than positive experiences mean understanding is present. There is nothing to understand and no "one" to do the understanding. What happens, happens. Knowing this allows energies, so-called positive or negative ones, to come and go very quickly and to do so without sticking. For this I am eternally grateful.

As mentioned already, the experiences of those who grasp non-duality vary from person to person due to different nervous systems, different genetics, different backgrounds, and so on. In my case, the "flashiest" experience is the effortless living Bob talks about. Within a few weeks after Bob left, there was an ease and grace to life and a noticeable ability to fulfill desires effortlessly that has continued to this day. Solutions to problems often arise from out of nowhere, and they happen on their own with no particular rhyme or reason. These occurrences are so startling and so alien to my previous existence that when they happen, my first thought is that there is some god or force of nature bestowing them. How long this desire fulfillment will last, I have no clue. It could stay forever; it could vanish tomorrow. My ultimate conclusion, however, is that when these somewhat miraculous solutions occur, it is because the nature of existence is, as the Hindus call it, sat chit ananda, or eternal bliss consciousness. And the only thing hindering our experience of this is our "getting in the way."

How do we get in the way? By believing in a separate identity, or false reference point, and thinking we are the doers of our lives. This leads to a vicious circle of desire, frustration, and willfulness. Before non-duality, this behavior was positively my mode of operation. Now that there is greater acceptance of what is, it is no wonder that desires fulfill themselves much more easily. Of course, this explanation is completely conceptual. Further, it is critical to realize that different people have different experiences. Not everyone who embraces non-duality will experience the same desire fulfillment as me. Some may experience peacefulness or extended periods of silence. Some may find their intuition increasing. Some may experience nothing other than a sense of freedom and wholeness. Different nervous systems produce different experiences. Aside from the transitory enjoyment experiences bring, they are completely unimportant. As emphasized throughout this text, experience is not what is needed. Understanding, or knowingness, is all.

There is another point worth mentioning. During my years of study with Hindu philosophy and meditation, one so-called traditional teaching was that when a person has attained "the great enlightenment," confirmation from the guru is necessary. This concept did not likely originate with non-dualists, who consider bondage a fiction in the first place and therefore enlightenment a false distinction. Everyone is pure intelligence energy, or space, or no thing, whether they know it or not. It is the search itself that is the problem. What is fascinating is that from the moment Sailor Bob arrived on the scene, he began confirming that consciousness, or pure intelligence energy, is who we are, and we should therefore stop seeking! He did not confirm ultimate freedom on the basis of our apparent experience. He confirmed it on the basis of reality. Just like the gurus in the parable mentioned earlier in this book, Sailor Bob repeated, "You are That." But he said it in hundreds of different ways. Anyone who had ears to hear was never the same again.

But my purpose in writing this book was not to share my life. It was to share non-duality with you, dear reader. Before proceeding further, however, some preparation for this chapter is necessary. First, regarding this autobiographical account, the longer one lives this understanding, the harder it is to write about "oneself" in a non-dual context. By the time I reached Chapter Seven, the notion of writing "my" story began to feel more and more absurd. I can find no self center within, and I am more and more aware that James is simply an appearance being lived. And, from the non-dual viewpoint, the title of this Chapter, *I Am That, Thou Art That – Now What*, is ridiculous. The term "now" implies the possibility of a past, as if now was not always happening. Finally, addressing the hows and whys of "gaining" non-dual understanding is fallacious. There is, of course, nothing to "get." There is only a seeing that who you are is no thing, space, or emptiness. And that will either happen or not, regardless of anything in the world of appearance, including reading this book. There has never been any *real* cause and effect to anything that has happened in my life, or in anyone else's. There is only apparent cause and effect. Likewise, there is no *real* reason for me to share my findings in hopes that it will aid you in your path. As mentioned throughout, we are living in a dream world, a world of appearance, a world which is as real as a reflection in a mirror. The reflection is seen, but it has no independent nature. On the other hand, within our world things are happening that *appear* to have plenty of causes, effects, and consequences—which is *apparently* why non-dualists teach and why I have presented this book.

The rest of this chapter is a last-ditch attempt to fulfill my promise in the Introduction to take readers beyond the need for help—in case Bob's dialogues have not completed the task. The most difficult feature that non-duality seekers encounter is the massive contradiction between reality and appearance. How does one see and embrace reality when appearance shows up so starkly different? Most teachers I know of, particularly Sailor Bob, point as directly as they can toward reality. They do not, generally, focus much on the world of appearance, because people are already only too familiar with that world. Further, the world of appearance is a world of concepts. Upon entering that world, there are as many opinions and viewpoints as there are people. So, for the most part non-dualists do their best to point to reality, and to ignore appearance. This method is analogous to bringing light into a dark room rather than analyzing or addressing the darkness.

For many seekers, however, hearing about reality is simply not enough. In the end, in order to appreciate reality *all concepts must be dropped*. Reality—also known as space, or no thing, or consciousness, and also described as non-conceptual, ever-fresh, self-shining presence awareness, just this and nothing else—is beyond concepts. And, dropping all concepts can be quite hard for some. Additionally, those who have been "on the path" for quite some time are often filled with more concepts than beginners. Longtime seekers have generally been drenched in teachings that are now, ironically, in the way. The material ahead is an attempt to break up some firmly rooted concepts that may have accrued, particularly through the teachings of the many Eastern movements that have gained popularity during the last fifty years. What follows is written for those who may actually understand non-duality as it has been presented so far, but are still waiting for some miraculous experience, transcendental bliss, or some such extraordinary happening before stopping their search and accepting "what is." The material is also written for those who believe that their gurus are more special than everyone else—as if some people are more consciousness, or space, or no thing, than anyone else. As if someone being aware that they are consciousness is, *in reality*, meaningful.

Veteran non-dualists in particular, please bear in mind that I am now about to address issues and concepts that have no basis in reality but are nonetheless quite substantial for those who are still attached to appearance. Let me again state that the purpose of the following section is an attempt to shatter some false concepts that may be in the way for certain seekers. In the same way that the stopping of my search clearly *seemed* related to a kind of surrender to Sailor Bob, perhaps there are some *apparent* misconceptions which, when clarified, can make a difference for some readers. Let me also state here and now, unequivocally, that there is no such thing as liberation because no one is, in fact, in bondage. Bondage only ever appears real because of a bunch of thoughts and images in the mind. As has been said in many ways by many teachers, the only difference between a "realized" being and an unrealized being is that the unrealized one believes there is a difference! It is for those who still believe there is a difference that the next pages are written.

If you have truly understood the first six chapters of this book, you are now either beyond the need for help or very close to it. How do you know if you have understood the teaching? Simple. If it is clear that what you were seeking, you already are, you have understood. If it is obvious that trying to change or become better is pointless, you have understood. If judging or criticizing others—or their actions—now appears absurd, understanding has happened. This does not mean that preferences have ceased. But preferences do not alter the understanding that we are all being lived and that *all* reference points are false. If it is now obvious that meditation is unnecessary—and that life itself is meditation—understanding has occurred. If it is clear that who you truly are is space, or no thing, then understanding has happened. If it is clear that everything in creation is transitory, and only presence awareness, or the "right here, right now," is real, understanding has occurred. If death is no longer a concern because you realize all that really dies are the thoughts and images of an individual "me," you have understood. If you are beginning to accept experiences as they are rather than judging everything from the "like" or "dislike" perspective, and if your addiction to chasing pleasure and avoiding pain is dramatically subsiding, then you have understood. If you have realized that the answer to life is not in the mind, and this has generated longer periods of "being without labeling," you have understood.

If understanding has happened, life as you knew it is finished. Or, as Leo Hartong so beautifully puts it, "You have awakened to the dream." (You have not awakened *from* the dream, because you are still here, and the dream continues. You have awakened *to* the dream.) Werner Erhard used to say that life is a game where what is *not* is more important than what *is*. When understanding dawns, nothing is more important than anything else because life is seen as appearance only. The idea that one thing is more important than something else is illusion, pure and simple.

Non-dual understanding requires no effort whatsoever. What is helpful is earnestness, openness, and, most of all, being ripe. Being ripe, as mentioned in the Introduction, has to do with being ready to die to your individual identity. It has to do with being ready to see your game ending. In the short time I have been teaching, I have noticed that many say they want liberation, but their actions belie the fact. Clearly, they still enjoy the wonderful/terrible game of life within the pairs of opposites. They want it to be extremely important if their favored politician wins or loses (as if they can possibly know the full ramifications of such an event). They want it to be meaningful and significant when they or someone they know makes a seeming mistake. They want to indulge their feelings fully when some apparently good or bad thing happens. And they want to be able to know *something*—instead of knowing *nothing*. In other words, they do not want their game to end. It is too much fun. Others, when directly confronted, admit they want to have certain mystical or metaphysical experiences before ending their game. Which is perfectly fine. Life is to enjoy. Life is to fulfill apparent desires. Why else would consciousness have manifested in the first place? Furthermore, there are, in reality, no "people" wanting the game to continue or wanting it to end. Although there are apparent entities doing so, what is really happening is that consciousness is playing a game with itself. The game is called hide and seek. And within this game of hide and seek, some illusory individuals are apparently seeking while other illusory individuals are apparently finding. In the end, it is all irrelevant. It is just a game.

If you feel you have understood non-duality but believe that someone as ordinary as yourself couldn't have what saints and seers spent their lives seeking, remember that Nisargadatta Maharaj—one of the greatest gnanis ever—advised seekers they could get the understanding within one week if they were serious. Sailor Bob said virtually the same thing. Unless there are lingering doubts or questions, what is needed now is to simply live what you have learned. Investigation of the false "me" will likely come up on its own. It is helpful to remember that a lifetime of conditioning does not often fall away instantaneously. But bad habits can and do fall away. They do so if (in the world of appearance) you are earnest and if (in reality) they are meant to.

If you have read this far and deeply understood what was conveyed, your search is now over. But what exactly does that mean? Has the search ended because you are now enlightened . . . liberated . . . awakened? It is important to realize that these terms are nothing more than labels. They exist only in the world of duality and only for the purpose of dualistic thinking. They are useful for such delusional thoughts as *"I am enlightened, and he or she is not.* Or, *"He or she is enlightened, and I am not."* If you are committed to non-duality, drop the distinction now. It is a phantom, the belief of which causes untold apparent suffering. Before shouting from the rooftops that your search has ended and allowing your head to swell, which is possible if your understanding is inauthentic or superficial, remember that your search has not ended "successfully." It ended because the validity of seeking was seen for what it is—pure illusion or, pardon my French, pure crap. There never was any "one" to seek or get any thing. And, bondage never actually existed. It was merely a thought in the mind that arose the instant there was a belief in an individual "me."

Beware of succumbing to old habits of trying to make something special out of nothing. Otherwise, the belief that you have reached "the end" becomes yet another concept to get lost in. And then your game will not be over. It will begin again! Then you will start believing in a "me" who got enlightened. And then there will appear to be a "me" who can lose enlightenment and do all sorts of things. From there comes more getting lost, more becoming, and more misleading others. (This is one reason why "realized beings" are often advised to wait some time before teaching.) Remember that while you may have seen through the false "me" and your search may have ended, manifest creation functions in an apparently evolutionary way. Nothing in our lives is static. Your search may be over, but your fullness or emptiness (however you wish to verbalize it) continues its apparent growth. Do not kid yourself that Sailor Bob's or Nisargadatta's *experience* was the same when they learned of non-duality as it is or was twenty or thirty years after abiding in understanding. Nisargadatta said as much in the transcriptions of his final books. Sailor Bob, being the strict non-dualist that he is, avoids the question altogether because change or growth exists only in the world of appearance—a world he rarely acknowledges when teaching. When I pressed him on the issue privately, he said there was no possibility of a "deepening" because consciousness, or no thing, cannot be touched—ever. It is infinite and unbounded and is *who we are.* But, as apparent time goes by, there can be "fewer clouds and more sun." In other words, we can know our true nature with more and more clarity, something I have definitely noticed in the time since Bob left.

Your apparent search may have ended, or maybe it has not. In either case, do not conceptualize "an end" to anything. Your apparent life process—whatever it may be and whichever direction it may take—continues until the body dies. In the world of *appearance*, there will always be growth—even growth of consciousness. But, if you go searching for, or expecting, this growth, whatever apparent freedom non-dual understanding has brought may begin to dissipate, and you may again begin to enjoy the game of hide and seek with your Self. Remember, experience—or growth of consciousness—is not what anyone needs. We are the experiencING. Right here, right now is good enough. Period.

All this being the case, what are we to think of the spiritual paths, gurus, and mentors of the past several thousand years? Furthermore, if the search has ended, is this all there is? Where, exactly, is the euphoria? Is there a "deepening?" Does presence awareness get stronger or more prevalent with time? What about the persistent thought, "Sure, I now feel free, but I couldn't possibly have what Shankara or Nisargadatta or Ramana or Papaji had." And, what about the fact that so many "enlightened" gurus behave in such a scandalous way? These and many other issues are definitely worth confronting. Before doing so, however, let us discuss paradox.

Paradox is defined as "a situation involving apparently contradictory elements" and "a seemingly contradictory statement that may nonetheless be true." At the entrance of nearly all temples in India, stand two guarding lions. The lions represent the two elements that keep people from realizing God—doubt and paradox. If you have read this far, doubt (that God, or pure intelligence energy, or oneness, exists) has obviously been conquered. Paradox, on the other hand, can be quite beguiling and is in my view critical. Why? For many reasons. First, because our apparent existence is wholly paradoxical. If who we really are is consciousness, or space, or no thing, but we are only able to know that we are consciousness, or space, or no thing, by virtue of an *illusory* phenomenon called body and mind, then it is a good idea to become comfortable with paradox. Also, non-duality, liberation, awakening, or whatever name one wishes to give it, is a function of understanding—not

experience—despite how often it has been misrepresented. Yet, because
our apparent existence shows up in a world of experience, that is where
we look to evaluate ourselves and our standing. We look to our quality
of experience. And rightly so. If non-dual understanding, or awakening,
does not improve our lives, why bother with it in the first place?
Paradoxically, everyone who claims to have awakened to the dream says
the same thing: Their experiences are irrelevant. Understanding is all.
Paradox, paradox, and more paradox.

As if this is not enough, here comes a whopper. The desire to seek
enlightenment—to seek an end to our apparent individuality—most often
seems to occur when one has realized that life as an individual is a losing
proposition. The game of life, when you believe you are an individual,
simply cannot be won. (Have you noticed?) Suffering lurks behind every
corner. For every gain, there is a loss. Realizing this, many of us turn
inward in an attempt to find lasting peace, which of course only exists
within the real Self, which is eternal, unbounded, and infinite. We long
to lose apparent individuality and merge with our universal nature.
Unfortunately, despite what so many gurus have said or intimated over
the last several thousand years, it is impossible to completely lose this
apparent individuality while in human form. We can of course come
close. That is what enlightenment, or liberation, is all about. We can
understand that we are infinite, we can often feel infinite, and we can
behave from an unbounded perspective. But we can never completely
lose our seeming individuality while appearing in a human body. This,
for some, is one heck of a dilemma. Some believe that anyone who has
awakened to the dream is now *completely* free from apparent individuality. They believe that liberated people are aware that their reference point
is false and are completely unaffected by it forever and ever. But this is
simply impossible until the dream of existence is over. It is impossible
until the body and mind cease. Within the dream, some people are aware
of their true natures and some are not. But the dream continues until *it*
decides to end. The dream is the guiding force—it controls the strings,
not us.

It may seem to be only a slight problem that apparent individuality
cannot completely cease as long as one has a human body. After all,
sages and liberated beings are nonetheless remarkably aware of their

infinite being. But it is no small matter. It is this very phenomenon that causes apparent quagmires for the so-called awakened. What I mean by a quagmire is what happens when one who has "awakened" finds the dream taking him—or her—toward some enjoyment that breaks cultural rules, regulations, ethics, and morals. If the person has truly awakened, of course, the quagmire is not too big a deal. It is simply a predicament within a dream of which the person is aware. Seen through the eyes of seekers, however, the predicament (of a guru enjoying controversial preferences) is much more serious. To the follower, or seeker, the situation reeks of desire, indulgence in a reference point, and downright selfishness. This occurs because the seeker believes awakening to be perfection personified. He or she thinks awakening means no desires whatsoever and total freedom from "selfish" behavior. The seeker has not understood that the uncontrollable events and circumstances of illusory existence simply cannot end while one is in a body. There will always be an apparent reference point and apparent preferences and desires. In fact, the awakened person is no different from someone who is "unrealized" except that he or she is *aware* that his or her reference point—the "me"—is false. The sage has looked to find an independent entity within and has positively realized there is no one there.

Many teachers have stated that every single occurrence in a person's life is an invitation to realize one's divinity, one's true nature. True enough. But every *moment* is an invitation to indulge and enjoy one's apparent individual preferences. As mentioned earlier in this book, during my search I spent at least fifteen years contemplating the controversial behavior exhibited by so many twentieth-century gurus. For fifteen years I questioned whether liberation was worthwhile since it was clear that I did not want to behave like the so-called liberated gurus I saw. These were (and in some cases, still are) gurus who presented eloquent spiritual teachings that enriched and empowered thousands upon thousands of people, but whose own lives would eventually demonstrate an apparent disregard for ethics, morals, or simple concern for fellow human beings. I am speaking of teachers with huge followings who seemed to alter our world dramatically for the better but who lied when it suited them, professed celibacy while sleeping with their students, traumatized students under the guise of "ego busting" while allowing themselves to be worshiped and adored, admitted on their death beds to lying about spiritual knowledge for fear seekers would not buy what they were selling, slept with young children of their disciples, amassed billions (not millions) of dollars while their disciples worked for less than meager salaries, bragged about how many women they slept with, amassed fleets of expensive automobiles, told disciples they needed high-priced courses or products in order to attain liberation, and on and on. My concern, of course, was not about the teachers. My concern was what value there could be in awakening if this is how the so-called enlightened lived. My concern was about the real meaning of enlightenment, or "higher consciousness."

Most seekers and disciples who encounter this problem feel the need to choose between four options. The first one is to deny any problem exists by disbelieving disturbing stories about their teachers. Bad behaviors are dismissed as rumors, lies, and misunderstandings, and this allows the disciple to ignore any wrongdoing. The seeker accepts that other peoples' gurus may be faulty, but not his or hers. The second option is to assume that anything the guru does must be for the good of the student or the world. If the guru's actions are clearly selfish or harmful, they are deemed "unfathomable"—as if the disciple cannot understand the workings of such a perfect master. Everything the guru does is perfect. This includes lying if it succeeds in attracting more followers. It includes having sex with children, which is explained as actually good for the youngster or a valuable method of "opening the *chakras"* (bodily energy centers). It includes finding all possible ways to get hold of their disciples' money, explained as helping the seeker learn surrender and egolessness. It includes performing ordinary magic tricks and calling them miracles, explained as doing *anything* to inspire peoples' belief in miracles and God. And on and on it goes. The third option is to say that enlightened gurus are only human and should not be judged too harshly. Instead, they may be forgiven their sins, which should be balanced with all the positive effects they have created. The final option of course is to conclude one has been duped and go find another guru who hopefully will behave better.

The problem with all four options is that none of them addresses the real dilemma. What exactly was the "enlightenment" ancient seers and sages spoke about? What should seekers look for in the first place? How can it be that people who demonstrate tremendous spiritual understanding and experience occasionally behave so badly? Mind you, I am not talking about lifelong con artists. I am talking about talented and brilliant mystics and spiritualists who, for the vast majority of their lives, served others selflessly. Teachers who profoundly enriched the lives of most of their students, and who seem to have made the world a better place. The fact that so very many twentieth-century gurus have succumbed to fame, power, greed, and sexual abuse begs the questions: Were these people ever truly "awakened," and does liberation, or enlightenment, have any actual meaning? (Note: I am addressing the distinction called enlightenment within the world of *appearance* only. In reality, of course, bondage is an illusion, and therefore liberation cannot possibly exist.)

As far as I can tell, there are three possible *realistic* explanations. One: The spiritual teachings about enlightenment have been a lie from the beginning of time. Two: Liberation exists but no one (or very close to no one) in our day and age has achieved it. Three: Many modern-day gurus have become self-realized, but popular perception of enlightenment is seriously flawed. And, seekers have drastically underestimated nature's ability to keep the game of hide and seek (between consciousness and itself) going. If this third explanation is accurate, and I am convinced it is, the teachers themselves—both current and age-old—are largely (in the world of appearance) to blame. They have, unfortunately, publicized the "positive" features of liberation while ignoring or downplaying their "human" traits. They have emphasized their freedoms and downplayed or kept secret the fact that preferences and desires cannot possibly disappear entirely as long as the mind and body appear to exist. Such teachers also seem to have neglected to explain how perfectly—and I do mean *perfectly*—the game of hide and seek was designed. We are endowed with a seeming reference point that can be *understood* as false but can positively never disappear. How can a being that is illusory in the first place annihilate its own illusory experience? What a conundrum!

Saints and sages certainly may have experienced and understood their true unbounded natures and realized the illusion of apparent existence. They may even, *possibly,* have seen through the illusion to such an extent that ordinary laws of nature cease operating, thus allowing them to perform miracles. But, never forget that these same sages and seers *prefer* peace over war, and *prefer* well-being for themselves and their loved ones. They would be deranged or insane not to. (I am not saying they are strongly attached to their preferences, but preferences clearly are present.) Thus, they do have desires, preferences, and some semblance of a reference point. Again I say, the false reference point can be seen through, but *it cannot completely disappear*. Liberated beings do not lose their enjoyments and preferences just because they know their true natures. Does the controversial behavior of gurus now make *some* sense?

Neither well-behaved nor poorly behaved gurus have an independent self within, any more than the rest of us. In reality, teachers and gurus are not making their own choices and decisions any more than anyone else. *There is, truly, no difference between a Buddha and an ordinary person.* This point must be understood. When Sailor Bob and Nisargadatta and other non-dualists say we are being lived, they mean all of us. When they say we are illusory beings living illusory existences dictated by "cognizing emptiness," they mean everyone. Thus, in reality there are no teachers or gurus making proper or improper choices. No one deserves blame, any more than someone deserves credit. Of course, I am speaking about reality, not appearance. Within appearance, there is a vast amount of room for blame and credit (as well as apparent repercussions for apparent positive or negative actions)—*if the appearance is where you wish to live.*

So, what exactly should a seeker look for? What is the *apparent* difference between an ordinary person and a self-realized one? There are probably as many answers as there are paths and gurus. A good definition from the non-dual perspective is that a realized person knows, with firm conviction, that consciousness is all there is. A quote from Ramesh Balsekar, Nisargadatta's translator and author of over twenty non-duality books, may also help:

> What does self-realization mean to the sage? Self-realiza-
> tion, to the sage, simply means the realization—the
> absolute and total conviction—that in the words of the
> Buddha: *"Events happen, deeds are done, but there is no*

doer thereof." In day-to-day living, both the sage and the ordinary person respond to their respective names being called. Therefore, in both cases, there is identification with the body and the name as an individual entity separate from all others. Where then is the difference between a sage and an ordinary person? The answer lies in the fact that the sage knows that *"Events happen, deeds are done, but there is no individual doer thereof,"* whereas the ordinary person has the conviction that each individual performs his or her action and is responsible for it.

Regarding the confusion over today's gurus, incidentally, the fault is not caused simply by poor teachings. It is also caused by disciples wanting to have their cake and eat it too. We want to believe that someone else can have enlightenment, but we cannot. We want our gurus to be able to create ethereal bodies, levitate in the air, alter the laws of nature at will, while still maintaining human emotions and qualities. Not that we actually want gurus to have human qualities, but a plausible explanation is needed when our guru cries upon the death of loved one—or whenever the guru's reference point rears its head. We want to believe our gurus have no reference point whatsoever and then enjoy the "charm" of that sage's preferences and "idiosyncracies." We want to believe our guru is desireless and then create a contrived explanation for why he or she prefers more followers rather than fewer, and more money rather than poverty. We want to believe gurus have complete control over nature even while dying of strokes or heart attacks (and in one case, suicide by pills) in what we describe as "conscious" deaths. In short, there has been a remarkable naiveté among modern-day seekers and an unwillingness to think for ourselves. Too many of us want a model of enlightenment that fits our pictures rather than having our pictures fit reality. There is no way out of this dilemma, as far as I can tell, except to embrace a definition of liberation *that stands up to investigation.*

I write these words not for academic reasons, but to address students who seem to understand non-duality but refuse to stop their search and, as Advaitan Gregg Goode puts it, take a stand in consciousness. They refuse because they are still convinced, in their heart of hearts, that enlightenment makes a person superhuman and that liberation is an experience—not an understanding, or knowingness. They are still convinced that what is needed is a blissful experience of samadhi, even while admitting that one does not have to be enlightened to achieve that state. They are convinced awakening is characterized by ever-present bliss, even after teachers have bluntly stated that emotional and psychological ups and downs still occur but are simply not resisted or taken seriously. They are convinced that liberation is a remarkable "feeling" even though so many saints and sages have said that when they "awakened" they realized they had always been awake. They believe that awakened individuals are perfected beings of light who perform non-stop miracles, even though some of these same individuals have said there is no difference between a Buddha and an ordinary person. Worst of all perhaps, seekers are still chasing some "state" they believe they will enjoy, even after being told that liberation is the falling away of an individual "me" who can enjoy anything and even after being told that liberation is about losing everything and gaining nothing (no thing). They are actually committed to the concept that right now is *not* good enough. Which is fine, except for the fact that right now is all there is. The future clearly does not exist. It is merely an image in the mind.

Finally, of critical—actually monumental—importance, seekers must realize, once and for all, that as long as they believe there is an individual "me" to gain liberation, they will never find what they say they want. As long as seekers believe that enlightened individuals exist, delusion persists. Ultimate freedom is who we are, by virtue of our unbounded nature. The moment one believes in individuality, for oneself or for one's guru, apparent freedom vanishes. When seekers believe there is a person to gain something, their apparent bondage must remain intact. It cannot possibly dissolve.

As discussed earlier, if enlightenment is an understanding and not an experience, what good is it? Part of the answer was that when one understands reality, experience does change. How could it not? How could guilt or psychological suffering persist for long if one understands there is no doer? How can one continue to try to fill the apparent void that was created when the individual "me" was believed in if that separate "me" is now clearly seen to be false? Along with understanding comes a sense of wholeness and completion. But this does not occur until one has understood that the "me" is false and stopped seeking. That is when a person takes a true stand in consciousness. For those who have understood and are ready to take such a stand, congratulations. For those who have understood and are unwilling to stop their search and take a stand, congratulations. Either way, the dream continues. Isn't it great?

If you have understood that consciousness is all there is and seen that the "me" is nothing more than a collection of thoughts and images, it does not necessarily mean you will instantaneously stop getting lost or caught in the reference point. Habits being what they are, you probably will from time to time. Neither does having the understanding mean that contractions will be painless. They almost certainly will hurt. But if you are able to live what you now know, the pain will be remarkably short-lived. The reason for this is that psychological suffering cannot continue without energy. When contractions come, Intelligence arises to meet the challenge. When apparent pain or suffering happen, a thought soon arises: "Who is in pain? Who is this happening to?" When you look deeply, you will not be able to find any independent entity. And that will be the beginning of the end. Whatever psychological concern has arisen begins to die for lack of energy—for lack of attention— because it has been seen as a false or illusory problem. It has been seen as happening to no one.

As apparent time goes by and understanding apparently deepens, contractions occur less and less. You will begin to marvel at the fact that there was a time when so many of your thoughts and actions related to solving the problem of feeling separate. You will forget that so much of your life was about becoming this or becoming that. If, by the way, you think your contractions mean something when they occur—that your understanding is shallow or inauthentic or some such concept—at least remind yourself of the good company you are in. Remind yourself that "So-and-So Guru," who has thirty-five thousand disciples, and who awakened to the dream in a flash of blissful ecstasy and communed with Lord Shiva on the astral plane, blah blah blah, recently got lost in his desires and was caught having sex with his secretary. Remember that "So-and-So Guru," who has been spreading peace and joy around the world and transmitting kundalini by tapping people on the forehead for sixteen years, was recently exposed for having stashed forty million dollars to avoid taxes. And on and on. You get the point? Everyone has apparent desires, and they sometimes result in apparent contractions. In case it is not yet clear, let me state one more time: There is not now, nor has there ever been, any *true* difference between a Buddha and an ordinary person.

If you have seen that the "me" is false and that who you truly are is consciousness, or no thing, then you have gone as far as any saint, sage, or seer. As Bob so eloquently puts it, no one has ever gone beyond no thing. The sages' dramatic experiences are just what happened. In the same way that some people have more artistic or mechanical abilities than others, some people have flashier mystical occurrences. If you desire such experiences, they can probably be developed, and there is nothing wrong with doing so. But they are not what the sages and seers were pointing to when they spoke about liberation and ultimate freedom. Despite how it may appear, those with flashy experiences are not one iota more oneness, or consciousness, than you. And if anyone asks for help, you may say confidently and truthfully, "You are That, and that is what you truly need to know." Whether they understand is not your business. Whether they understand is a function of the ongoing dream apparently taking place.

If you wish to continue seeking, enjoy the game. If you wish to take a stand in consciousness, by all means do so. What does it mean to take a stand in consciousness? It means remembering what you have learned and maintaining the conviction of what you know. It means living non-dual understanding even when old habits take you places you positively don't like. How do you live non-dual understanding when you suddenly find yourself lost in the false reference point? Simply by accepting such happenings gracefully as part of the dream of your so-called life. Accepting gracefully means not resisting and not conceptualizing or giving undue meaning to what has happened in the world of appearance. More than anything, taking a stand in consciousness means remembering that consciousness is all there is and that who you truly are cannot be cut by the sword, burned by fire, dried by wind, or drowned by water.

If your experience is anything like mine, you will be thrilled beyond words to no longer feel separate from your source. You will also be thrilled to no longer be concerned about gaining enlightenment or "becoming" someone special. But you may in the beginning days be constantly judging and evaluating your experience. You may be looking to see if your mind is empty or still. You may wonder whether you will someday perform "miracles." And you may contemplate what your experience will be after many years of abiding in oneness. For my part, I can say that in the time it has taken to write this book these mental gymnastics have disappeared. They are gone. Right here, right now is fine. The longer time passes, the clearer it becomes that Bob taught me nothing instead of something! And I marvel at this newfound freedom that was, paradoxically, always present.

If you do find yourself judging your experience, expect to be fooled. I learned this a few months after Bob left when visiting the dentist to fix a broken crown. The crown had been poorly inserted and had bothered me for more than a year. I had not returned to have it fixed because of how stressful my last several visits had been. Aside from the fact that dental work has always been difficult due to my sensitive nature, in the last twenty years I had been a major "gagger." Whenever dentists put a large plastic x-ray part or a gooey substance in my mouth (to take an "impression") and told me to sit still, my mind would race and a "gag war" would begin between my self-control and my reflexes. This occurred even if I listened to loud music through a headset to divert my attention. In short, I hated dentistry. During this episode, as I drove to the dentist I was fairly relaxed. As I neared the office, however, my heart began pounding. The more it pounded, the more I recalled the anxiety of my last few dental appointments. Then came the judging: "I thought I was free. Here I am, scared of a future that doesn't exist. Oh God, how could I have deceived myself again? Blah, blah,blah." But something had changed—dramatically. I knew it the moment the dentist stuck a large plastic, goo-filled object in the back of my mouth and told me to sit still for five minutes. This time my mind did not race. In fact, it said nothing. Shortly after that, the dentist repeated the five-minute process, and again my mind was quiet. Finally it spoke: "This is unbelievable. How many years has it been since I haven't gagged for a dentist?" The more time passes, the less I draw conclusions. And the less I care what comes. Fear, anger, upset, "negative" emotions, and so on—they all arise from time to time. And they leave almost as fast as they came. They mean nothing. Why give them energy?

There is one important facet of the teaching that does not appear in this text, even within all the recorded dialogues. And that is that once a person has grasped non-duality, insights continually occur. I do not mean the "cognitions" that spiritual scriptures often relate, which are generally characterized as psychic impressions coming from the ethers. Insights are simply realizations about life and spiritual issues that naturally occur when one realizes that consciousness is all there is and when one has stopped searching. After Bob returned to Australia, both Kerry and I have called him every week or two. We often discuss whatever insights we have noticed. Some insights are simple; some are profound. Do not be surprised if you begin having them. And, after digesting non-duality, by all means re-read your favorite spiritual authors to see if their teachings now have deeper meaning than before. Certain teachings will appear far more profound, while others may seem downright fraudulent.

Some of you who enjoy meditation may wish to continue, while others may not. When non-dual understanding takes hold, all of life feels like meditation. Spiritually speaking, there is nothing necessarily positive or negative about meditating. In the early days of one's search, it can certainly open the mind and provide flexibility. And, for those who wish to enjoy mystical, blissful, and peaceful experiences, meditation is excellent. For getting rid of one's sense of separation and seeing clearly that individuality is false, however, meditation is just about useless. In rare cases, there are those who begin meditation and immediately understand their true natures. But for meditators who do not self-realize right away, it is foolhardy to believe that more of the same experience will produce different results. Of course one may, after years and years and years of meditation, finally give up in frustration (like Buddha) and thus awaken. If this is how your dream unfolds, enjoy the film. No path, Advaita or otherwise, is intrinsically better than another. As they say, what is medicine to one is poison to another.

For those of you who still consider that you cannot have ultimate freedom because Ramana had such and such experience, and Yogananda had such and such experience, and Papaji had such and such experience, and you have had *none* of these, please be consistent. If you must make comparisons, be fair. Make a list of all the famous gurus you know, and judge their experiences against each another. Decide who had the best experiences, whose were good, and whose were borderline. See if you can tell who made the cut and who did not. If one guru lived five hundred years, while another lived on the scent of roses, while another could read minds, while another could heal snake bites, while another could raise people from the dead, while another could create ethereal bodies, while another could cognize the Vedas, and so on, try to decipher which experiences are most significant and which are least, and why everyone's experiences vary so wildly. Try to determine exactly which experiences prove someone is liberated and which do not. Oh, and try not to forget that for thousands of years sages and seers have emphatically stated that there is no experience that proves enlightenment, and that any experience that takes place in space and time can be learned by one who is not self-realized.

Finally, since most of us have heard about the miracles performed by yogis and gurus who "alter the laws of nature," but so few have actually seen one, it is definitely worth contemplating why they are so fascinating. Of course, nearly everyone has seen or experienced psychic phenomenon and perhaps even mental telepathy. But these are natural abilities that creatures in the animal kingdom probably use regularly for daily survival. As for gurus who can transmit temporary energies or cast brief "spells" of unity, or oneness, to others, this may be comparable to snakes who hypnotize birds. Or to other animals who mentally affect other creatures. Regarding levitation, making oneself invisible, creating ethereal bodies, creating objects out of thin air, and so on, neither I nor any of my friends have actually seen these phenomenon firsthand. (Satya Sai Baba in India is famous for materializing objects, but there are so many people on Web sites devoted to proving he is an ordinary magician that I am not including him.) This does not, of course, prove anything. Such miracles may indeed exist and simply be very rare. Or, maybe they are exaggerations. Unless one has seen or experienced such things firsthand, who really knows?

What is critical to see, however, is the reason such miracles are so captivating. They are captivating because performing them makes us special. And being special keeps our illusion of individuality intact—the same way that our belief in reincarnation keeps the hope of our individuality alive. The same way that believing our guru is special keeps our concept of individuality intact, because if he or she is special then someday we can be special. Special means distinctive, or separate, or individual. The desire to become special perfectly exemplifies the sentiment that life is a game where what is *not* is more important than what *is*. As long as we keep the hope of miracles alive, we can keep our game—our illusion of individuality—alive. Living the understanding that consciousness is all there is, is the end of that game. What is so good about "Game Over"? It is the end of psychological suffering. It is the end of a game that could not be won. Now—any takers?

*

As usual in the world of appearance, all good things come to an end. Five weeks with Bob and Barbara passed in a flash, and it was time to send them to Kerry's house in Connecticut for the last legs of their journey. The night before leaving, we enjoyed a celebration dinner at the Columbia Restaurant, a fancy Cuban eatery that had become one of their favorites. Dell and Emmett came along, and Bob ordered the giant "1905 Salad" for which the restaurant is famous. As always, we teased him about his love of food and how much he could eat. He complained about the ten or twelve pounds he had gained, which convinced us that he had enjoyed all the wonderful tourist restaurants we had taken them to. Dell presented Bob and Barb with some beautiful prints of paintings he had made. Vashti and I gave them a few rolls of United States silver dollars. We thanked Bob profusely for the wonderful knowledge and wisdom he had shared and promised to keep the teaching alive. Aside from all Vashti and I had learned, Bob had restored our faith that spiritual teachers with strictly pure motives still exist. Here was a man who had found the answer to life and whose peace and contentment are palpable. He is a rarity who wants nothing from others and whose greatest enjoyment is spreading non-duality. He is a gem if ever there was one, and I marvel daily at my good fortune in having him at my house for five weeks.

Throughout this text, Sailor Bob has stated over and over that there is no difference between a Buddha and an ordinary person. He has also said that anyone who has seen that he or she is "no thing" has gone as far as any saint, sage, or seer. When, within my commentary and story, I have glorified Sailor Bob or made him out to be something special, I have done so only to express my heartfelt feelings and appreciation. Within the world of appearance, of course Bob is special. He has been living non-duality and teaching it for over thirty years. As a result, he rarely gets caught in the reference point. But he is truly no different from any of us. He has the normal range of emotions and reactions and has even had ups and downs in his married life after realizing his true nature. To the extent that we consider him different, we do Bob, ourselves, and anyone with whom we share the knowledge a serious disservice. While Bob does not throw people out of his talks for being overly devotional as Nisargadatta did, he is unimpressed by such expression. It is one thing to be humbled by, and grateful to, a spiritual teacher. But to consider him or her to be different is a mistake. That is why centuries ago one guru told his students, "If you see the Buddha on the road, kill him." He meant that if you happen to see an "awakened" soul, do not make him or her out to be special. See an ordinary soul who simply knows his or her true nature. As mentioned already, the difference between a realized soul and one who is unrealized is that the unrealized person believes there is a difference.

If you have understood the teachings in this book, you now know what sages and seers know, no matter how often you get caught in your reference point. If you have this understanding and still feel the need to travel to Australia to see Bob in person, by all means do so. Bob has the most charming Australian belly laugh. And when I tell him that someone has gotten the understanding and wants to see him, I get to hear that laugh. Why does he laugh? For one thing, he is pleased. Very pleased. For another, he knows there is no *actual* need to see him. If you have looked within to find a self and have found nothing there and know that that nothing is who you are, then you have realized. If you wish to speak with Bob, details are in the back of this book. If you wish to speak with

Kerry or myself, or hear our talks, feel free.

The day after our celebration dinner, Vashti, Julian, and I drove Bob and Barbara to the airport and sent them up to Kerry's house in Connecticut. The scene was as heartfelt as any I have known. As we hugged goodbye, there were four grownups in tears. Barb was particularly upset because we had all grown so close, and she was sure we would never see each other again—something I doubt, since I am now considering a trip to Australia. I told Bob that in a few weeks, after he returned home, we would mail the birthday present Vashti and I had given him on July twenty-first. It was a large, fancy clock that plays a pretty tune each and every hour. Some time after doing so, we received the following e-mail.

Hi James,

Just received the clock and photos. So now there is a constant hourly reminder of you all, just in case I should happen to forget. Am getting some beautiful e-mails from different people who resonated with the talks. Some intend to come to Oz [Australia] to have a few days of one to one, to clear any lingering doubts. So in you and Kerry getting me over there, you have started a tidal wave that will surge around the world. And, as I won't be around forever, my "sons" will have to carry on the apparent lineage. Keep up the good work, write the book, hold meetings, and talk to those who are waiting to hear it from you. And though this is a conceptual story (in essence, it is true), all the teachers in the lineage are behind you. Have confidence in that.

Love to you, Vashti, and Julian.

Sailor Bob

Although all dualities come from the One, do not be attached even to this One.

—Seng T'san, *Hsin Hsin Ming*